WORKING AUSTRALIA

THE AUSTRALIAN EXPERIENCE

Also in the series

Aboriginal Australians: Black Response to White Dominance 1788-1980
Richard Broome

Australia's Immigrants: 1788-1978
Geoffrey Sherington

Dispossession: Black Australians and White Invaders
Compiled by Henry Reynolds

Inventing Australia: Images and Identity 1688-1980
Richard White

Out of Luck: Poor Australians and Social Welfare 1788-1988
Stephen Garton

Spoils and Spoilers: Australians make their environment 1788-1980
Geoffrey Bolton

THE AUSTRALIAN EXPERIENCE
Editor: Ann Curthoys

WORKING AUSTRALIA

CHARLIE FOX

ALLEN & UNWIN

To Mum and Dad, Jan and Katie

© Charlie Fox, 1991
This book is copyright under the Berne Convention.
No reproduction without permission. All rights
reserved.

First published in 1991
Allen & Unwin Pty Ltd
8 Napier Street, North Sydney, NSW 2059

National Library of Australia
Cataloguing-in-Publication entry:

Fox, Charlie.
  Working Australia.
  Bibliography.
  Includes index.
  ISBN 0 04 442351 9.
    1. Work — Social aspects — Australia. 2. Work — History. 3. Labor supply — Australia — History. 4. Working class — Australia — History. I. Title. (Series: Australian experience).
306.360994

Set in 10/11pt Times Roman by Excel Imaging, Sydney
Printed by Kin Keong Printing Co. Pte Ltd, Singapore

Contents

Abbreviations vii

Acknowledgements viii

Introduction ix

1 Before and after the invasion 1
    Happier than we 1
    God, work and the Aborigines 12

2 The felonry and the free 17
    The suffering convict 18
    We must have labour 24

3 Working in the country 32
    Strong masculine labour 33
    Love of freehold 38
    A Chinaman will stand for hours 44

4 Working in the city 54
    The factory system 54
    'Gentlemen Jims' and the casual poor 60
    Do servant girls earn their wages? 66

5 Work and the middle class 73
    Sufficient classical proficiency 73
    A perfect substitute for pen and ink 79
    When you manage a man 86

6	Control and protection	92
	We have come 16 000 miles to better our conditions	92
	A fair and reasonable wage	96
	Born to cook	105
7	Managing the paid and unpaid workforce	110
	Hiking in the factory	111
	The cuddling hour	119
8	Unemployment and full employment	125
	We want work!	125
	Take a war job!	133
	A high and stable level of employment	138
9	The changing workforce 1945–1974	143
	Reshaping the office worker	144
	Doing the dirty jobs	149
	The unions and the un-unionised	158
10	Management, technology and the future	165
	An active animal	166
	The replacement of body and mind by a machine	169
	The electronic cottage	175

Endnotes   181

Bibliography   206

Index   215

Abbreviations

ACTU	Australian Council of Trade Unions
AEU	Amalgamated Engineering Union
ALP	Australian Labor Party
ATEA	Australian Telecommunications Employees' Association
AWU	Australian Workers' Union
CAGEO	Council of Australian Government Employee Organisations
CTU	Clothing Trades Union
WEB	Women's Employment Board

Acknowledgements

For their help in various ways I would like to thank Jan Gothard, Raelene Frances, Marilyn Lake, Joan and Pat Fox, Bruce Scates, Jane Kenway, Lenore Layman, Michael Hess, Tom Stannage and Joanna Sassoon. For financial assistance I thank the History Department of the University of Western Australia, and Cheryl MacFarlane, Barbara Williamson, Joyce Barkley, Judy Bolton and Marlene Hall for typing the manuscript.

For permission to use illustrations I am grateful to the *Bulletin* (no.1), *New Idea* (no.3), Battye Library, Perth (no.'s 4, 10, 19, 20, 21, 22), West Australian Newspapers (no.13), University of Melbourne Archives (no.'s 5, 12, 23), Tooth's Brewery (no.'s 7, 11), Archives Office of Tasmania (no.'s 6, 16), Riddell Publishing Pty Ltd (no.18), Museum of Victoria (no.9), *Business Review Weekly* (no.'s 14, 17), *Modern Office* (no.15) and La Trobe Collection, State Library of Victoria (no.8).

Introduction

Work has no intrinsic meaning. Its meaning is produced by the culture in which it is performed. In some cultures there is no such thing as work and no such person as a worker. In others the same word describes those who work with their heads and those who work with their hands. In some cultures people's work is given meaning by its place in systems of religion or of magic. In others there is a positive hostility to innovation of technique. In yet others the same values inform both work and leisure such that the two categories merge into one, which is life. In every culture, at one time or another, the home was the centre of work, and people worked at home where family and kinship determined who worked on what, with whom and who shared the work's benefits.

Australia today is like none of these. It is a capitalist society in which most people have to sell their labour to survive. Employers purchase it, appropriate the value it produces above the wages they pay and deploy it with land, buildings and equipment to produce their profit. Yet there are workplaces where this does not happen. Many Australians work for governments which have quite different purposes from capitalists and there are many more who escape wage labour altogether by becoming self-employed. Conventionally the workplace defines what work is; it is paid work done in a workplace other than the home. But the home is also a workplace. Work in the home occupies a nether world. It is both obvious and unseen. 'Mum is a housewife. She doesn't work.' Over the last 200 years work has come to mean paid employment.

Our lives are shaped by our need to work. If once there was no work and no leisure, as if they were one and the same, then the history of the last 200 years has seen them rigidly separated, and although we might work hard at our leisure we are not permitted to 'leisure' at our work. Work, rest and recreation are the divisions of our daily life. For those in paid work our days are structured around the eight-hour day, our week is structured by the forty-hour week and we look forward to our annual four-week holiday. Across our divided lives we bcome adults when we go to work and become senior citizens when we retire from work and get our gold watch. These are the physical and mental structures created by the dominant place of paid work in our ideas of what work is. The workplace rhythms of a housewife and mother are created by the needs of husbands and children. A housewife does not work from nine to five.

We derive our identity from our work. It defines our sense of ourselves. Our first question to a new acquaintance is 'What do you do?' We ask children what they want to be when they grow up. Our new friends never answer 'When?' Children never answer 'I want to be tall'. This is very convenient, of course, because we think that we can read character, interest and political opinions from a person's occupation. But these are simply occupations. There are other ways in which work defines our sense of self. At its most fundamental level it is whether we work or not. Housewives have a lowly status in the minds of paid workers and in their own minds, yet only the unemployed have no status at all. Thomas Carlysle once wrote: 'A man perfects himself by working... Consider how even in the meanest sort of labour the whole soul of a man is composed into a real kind of harmony the instant he sets himself to work'. To have no work is to be reviled. Many people like their work, most probably hate it, yet like it or loathe it we are all conditioned to think that it is necessary for our sense of worth. Few people nowadays hold to the idea that in our work lies our salvation, yet an ethic of work still dominates our way of thinking about people.

In Australia our job fits into two hierarchies, one on the job, the other outside it. People are unequal at their work. There are divisions of power and authority based, in the final analysis, on the power of the boss to hire and fire. Outside the workplace, society values some jobs more than others. A job's value is usually, but not always, measured in the pay it earns. However, there are more important divisions. Where we stand in these relationships influences our sense of our collective selves; whether we are 'workers' or 'working class', whether we are 'employed', 'salary earners' or 'middle class'. Usually our workplace position makes us an adversary of someone else; sometimes it makes us outright enemies. Then we are told not to think like that, but to think of ourselves as part of a family or a team.

Our sex also defines our work. Depending on our sex there are myriad kinds of work we can and cannot do. Even in the 1990s the odds are that men will work with men and women with women. For some men this is fine because they affirm their sexual identity in their work, especially if it is dangerous, needs muscular strength or if they have to use big or complex machines. The gendered makeup of many workplaces means, too, that some women have to conform to notions of femininity to please their usually male bosses. Other images are based on national and racial stereotypes. The capacity for hard work or laziness is frequently ascribed to particular ethnic groups, as is a preparedness to make a fuss about

INTRODUCTION

working conditions or to placidly accept them. Some employers will employ only people from a particular country. Others will employ people from different countries but put them next to each other so they cannot talk. The logic which links both strategies is higher productivity and profit.

These are ways in which work defines our sense of ourselves, but it also determines a wide range of social practices too because our pay depends on what work we do. So what we earn largely determines whether we live in the stink of a factory suburb or whether we have a home with a view of the water. It allows us to buy a certain kind of car or it condemns us to a life of waiting for buses. With our savings we can holiday either in a caravan or in Paris or New York. Our earnings determine whether we send our children to a selective private school or to the local state school. Each of these makes up our 'cultural capital' and is the outward expression of our social class, while in turn this directs us and our children into certain kinds of work. Working-class children get working-class jobs. Middle-class children get middle-class jobs. The dictum is as applicable in the 1990s as it was in the 1890s. The workplace is structured on equality and it has always generated inequality in the wider society.

Till recently the workplace has been foreign territory to students of Australian society. We often see photographs or television pictures of people smiling happily or skylarking as they leave a factory gate or trudging down a city street on their way to the station. Yet only those workers know what goes on inside those gates and those offices, the rest of us live in profound ignorance, if we even want to know. What is involved in producing a product or a service, the skills and techniques needed to produce them, who in these workplaces does what, and the internal relationships, are all mysteries. And they are mysteries because there are two public images of work. The first is subsumed in the outcomes of wages and conditions cases that are heard in our arbitration system. The second is in the product that is produced, the concrete, seeable manifestation of the work that produces it. Yet the real work, what actually happens, is always kept hidden.

The workplace is also the 'foreign country' of history. Even social history, which has supposedly opened up the whole of human experience to us, has rarely attempted to enter the gates of that factory to see what happens inside. The neglect has been remedied to an extent in the 1980s, yet it is still remarkable when we consider how much of people's lives is spent at work how little has been revealed. If there is one aspect of Australia's history which needs a little light and air, then it is surely the workplace. We shall then begin to understand a little better the vast range of experiences of the Australian people, and we may not like all that we see.

1 Before and after the invasion

Is it possible to speak of work in a culture which is so different to our own, a culture which does not segregate time into work time and leisure time or label its members as workers or non-workers? Aborigines, in their traditional culture, did not divide their days into work and not-work, as we do. Neither did they work as workers. Rather they 'worked' as members of a family, a band, a tribe, a self-regulated community. They collected or hunted as wife and husband, as mother and father, in their place in a continuum of kinship relationships. As we approach the twenty-first century, the way we label work, the meanings we give to work, have a status settled long ago, in the cultural baggage brought to Australia by the British invaders. Different peoples regard work very differently. The Aboriginal way of working reminds us that the term does not have a universal meaning. Instead, it must be considered in its place in specific cultures and specific periods.

Happier than we

When Europeans came to the place later named Australia, they confronted a people who had occupied the continent for over 40 000 years. Archaeologists argue that they had ventured out probably on rafts or canoes from the islands of South-east Asia, arriving at a land mass very different from that of today. It was bigger and there was a land link between New Guinea, today's mainland and Tasmania. It was so close to the South-east Asian islands, that it might have been but a day or two's journey for the first human settlers to arrive on the north-western or northern coasts. It was another 30 000 years before the polar ice caps melted, the oceanic level rose and the continent took the shape it has today. Over subsequent thousands of years, the descendants of the first settlers spread right across the continent, living in relative harmony with their land, constructing complex religious beliefs to explain their arrival and their existence, and building intricate social relationships which defined where each person stood in relation to every other.

There were between 750 000 and 1 million Aboriginal people in

Australia when the British came.[1] They were divided into nearly 900 different tribes, each of which had a common genealogy, a special relationship to a particular area of country, its own dialect or language and its own name. Sometimes they lived in a state of war with each other, but most times they lived in peace. Tribes did not have any political connections with each other, so they did not have national chiefs or inter-tribal governments. The anthropologist A.P. Elkin, searching for a metaphor to describe exactly what their relationship to each other was, described neighbouring tribes when they had common cultural elements as communities of tribes. In the wider sense he called the entire tribal system 'a constellation', each tribe individual in itself but inhabiting the same universe.[2]

Within the tribes were smaller social groups which anthropologists call 'bands'. These were made up of between 20 and 50 people, and were members of related families tied together by kinship and friendship. They stayed together most but not all of the time, and sometimes they might have split into smaller groups of one, two or more families. At other times they mixed in bigger tribal gatherings and in the great trans-tribal feasts and ceremonies. They were economic units too. The members lived as a group, hunted or gathered food for the group and distributed what they caught and gathered within the group. They moved over closely defined areas—their country—which varied according to the abundance of food and the density of the population.

Every Aborigine was part of a tight knit and complex system of kinship. Every member of a kinship group considered the other members as part of a large family and used close family terms to describe and embrace both close and distant relatives. For example, those who in the western family came to be called aunts or uncles were classified with mothers and fathers and called mothers and fathers. Similarly those who in the western family are called cousins were classified as brothers and sisters and called brother or sister. However, a distinction was made between the children of brothers and sisters. The children of brothers were thought of as sons and daughters but the children of sisters were thought of as nieces and nephews. And in marriage relationships, spouses and relatives joined by marriage were classed with blood relatives, as mothers, cousins and so on.[3]

Kinship patterns had many effects, an important one being that they defined a person's relationship to a particular piece of land or territory. The male line of a family had an attachment to one piece of country. The female line all belonged to another piece of country. This is very important in considering the ways Aborigines related to their prime resource, the land. Aborigines regarded the land they occupied through their father's clan as land which they owned. Their conception of ownership was different from the western sense of property, in which owners enjoy exclusive rights to use and dispose of land. In traditional Aboriginal culture ownership was more a religious matter, the owners maintaining their relationship through religious ritual. Land with which they were connected through their mother's side was regarded differently and the difference is very difficult to explain. Anthropologists seem to agree that the term manager best describes the relationship, so managers organised the ritual dances and ritual decorative designs, which reinforced a person's attachment to a place. The purpose of this arrangement seems to have been to prevent the father's clan assuming complete control over a place. Sharing control and sharing ritual expressed the mutuality which governed Aboriginal society.[4]

These kinship relations were the grid on which Aborigines placed and knew every person they came into contact with. Everyone knew everyone else because everyone was in close or distant ways related to everyone else in their social world. But kin relations were also flexible. By working out people's religious affiliations even strangers could be incorporated into a network. And if that didn't work, then strangers were adopted as brothers or sisters.

Kinship made Aborigines familiar with each other, but it also prescribed rules of behaviour because for each kind of relationship there was an appropriate behaviour. Often these were restrictive, defining the limits of possible marriage, specifying who could or could not talk to or look at whom, determining who did what in conversation, camping, visiting, childbirth, and initiations. And so it was in work. A person worked as a part of a kinship group, gathering or hunting food to fulfil kinship obligations, receiving food for the same reason. A young man might give an old man the pick of a day's hunting, so the kinship bonds were strengthened, while kinship networks were renewed as each child learned her or his obligations in the mutuality of the family and kin group.

Students of Aboriginal culture call it a hunter-gatherer culture, in which men hunted the big game and caught the big fish while women gathered the vegetables and fruit and caught small game. Work was strictly defined by sex. Men did not gather and women did not hunt, men made and carried their own weapons—spears, clubs, boomerangs and shields. Women made and carried their own implements—the digging sticks, the wooden carrying trays and reed baskets.

The women produced most of the Aboriginal diet, so much so that in places like Arnhem Land men worked rarely and spent most of their time engaged in other pursuits.[5] The supply of vegetables was more regular than the supply of game and, of course, it didn't run away. Aboriginal women had to know their country intimately; where to find the roots that ran beneath the soil surface, how to recognise which fruits were edible and which were poisonous, how to prepare the poisonous ones to make them safe. They had to know intimately the habits of fish, goannas and lizards and where birds' eggs could be found. They learned these skills as girls from their mothers, and fellow wives and female relations. Gathering was done as a group, not for efficiency's sake but rather so that the women could share the burden of looking after infants and children. This made gathering a very sociable exercise. Digging and carrying, finding and giving were interspersed with rest, conversation and eating. In fertile parts of the country, when women went out from the camps to forage, they might spend only one or two hours a day in their labours, so bountiful were the resources. In the deserts where plant life was sparse they gathered for longer, often spending six or seven hours away from their camps, but once again work was interspersed with rest.[6]

Men's work was rather different, for they worked in pairs or singly. Whereas women might range across a wide area, men's work depended on where their quarry led them. Hunters needed the same skills as women; knowledge of their country, the best place to seek and follow game, the habits and reactions of each hunted species. They also needed stealth and cunning, for the paramount skill in hunting lies less in throwing the spear than in stalking the quarry and getting close enough to throw a spear swiftly and accurately. The best hunters could get to within about twenty metres of kangaroos or wallabies, without being seen, heard or smelt.[7] In the tribes which inhabited the coast or the river banks, men did most of the fishing. Fish were caught with lines and hooks in some parts of the continent. In others they were speared from canoes or logs or by swimmers. In others they were netted, and in yet others they were driven into fish traps and speared.

However, hunting was not always like this. Sometimes it was a tribal matter, where large numbers of people working together killed large numbers of quarry. Peter Beveridge, a nineteenth-century observer of Aborigines, described the way ducks were caught on the Murray River. A net, sometimes 100 metres long, was suspended between trees across the river. Young men then went up river to disturb the ducks which flew off along the river's course. When the ducks became inclined to leave the river's course other men, strategically placed in trees, threw bark rings in the air, and made hawk calls. The frightened ducks returned to the river until, in their hundreds, they flew into the nets.[8]

There was a second division of labour in traditional Aboriginal society, based not on sex but on age. Younger men did most of the hunting, frequently with uninitiated youths. These youths were taken in hand by their elders and prepared for initiation into adulthood, and their part of the bargain was to provide food for their teachers and their families. Ritual and religious requirements sometimes made this necessary, and young men were forbidden to eat food that they caught.[9] As for the relationship between women, women of all ages did much the same kind of work. However, the nature of the Aboriginal family meant that older women and girls worked together in ways similar to men. When a man had more than one wife, the younger wife or wives were often children, in this case the older women taught the younger girls the skills and the local knowledge necessary for gathering.[10]

If women gathered most of the food and if young men gathered food for elder males, then elder males would seem to have had the easier life. The early European settlers thought so. They thought Aboriginal society was a gerentocracy, a male one at that, and one in which the women were the chattels of their men.[11] Many of the early male anthropologists thought the same.[12] However, anthropologists have argued that the work of men and women actually complemented each other, that because the distribution of food was tied to kinship obligations, then each side made an interlocking investment in food supplies. Men, for example, were obliged to share their food with their mothers and mothers-in-law. In any case women, whilst foraging, ate much of what they produced and gave the rest to the men. There was also much more reciprocity between younger and older men than the first anthropologists realised. The younger gave their catch to their elders in exchange for initiation and education into the ritual secrets and the secret knowledge of the tribe.[13]

Aboriginal life and labour was tied very closely to the seasons, for the Aborigines needed to know which vegetables grew where and when, and where and when game was most prolific. A.P. Elkin recalled the pattern of food production of the Karadjeri tribe of the north-west:

> They named five seasons: (i) *Wilburu*, around our September, when hot, equinoctial south-east winds blow from the deserts; kangaroo, goanna and honey are main foods; there are no fruits. (ii) *Ladja*, the very hot season, which is a good time for hunting kangaroos, because they do not 'run' as fast or far as in the cold season. (iii) *Manggala*, the wet season when various fruits and a nut called nalgo are available; kangaroos, wallabies, goannas and fish are plentiful. (iv) *Marul* is the period, about March to April, when the rains are ending; the tree-fruits are finished, but nalgo and the mangrove pod can be obtained, and also fish and other game. (v) *Pargana*, when the south-east winds blow again, but now they are cold; fish

is caught up the salt creeks and honey collected; hibernating goannas are dug out of their winter resorts; and parties hunt the kangaroo. And so the Karadjeri cycle ends.[14]

In some instances the seasonal variations in food supply meant that the tribes might rove far and often over their range. Geoffrey Blainey describes this nicely as 'the logic of unending travel' and he shows how the Wik Monkan tribe of Cape York moved many times across its range taking advantage of local resource and climatic variations. Ferguson shows how the smaller bands from the Albany region in Western Australia journeyed over their range not only to search for food but also to visit relatives.[15] The tribes of Lake Condah in south-west Victoria did not have to move at all because their fish and eel traps and a plentiful supply of game and birds provided them with a steady supply of food.[16]

One implication of this cycle of travel was that food was produced for immediate use, not for storage. In fact Aborigines lacked the technical means for storage, although whether this was a cause or effect of travel is open to argument. Aborigines did not salt, freeze or boil food because they did not make containers in which they could cook, but constant travel made carrying food from place to place difficult and the ready availability of food probably made it unnecessary anyway. Why did each band move so often? The answer is that after a band had left a particular area, that area would regenerate, ready for the next visit in the cycle.

The production of food depended on the manufacture of weapons and tools. Spears, clubs, boomerangs, and throwing sticks were used in one kind of hunting and nets, lines and hooks, snares, decoys, harpoons and traps in another. Digging sticks of great variety were used for gathering and trays, baskets and bags were used to transport food. Aborigines built temporary bush dwellings in the north and mud huts in the south. River and sea dwellers built canoes, and those Aborigines living in the south manufactured massive coats out of animal skins. Other Aborigines engaged in quite massive feats of engineering. The eel and fish traps at Lake Bolac run over hundreds of yards and there are still the remains of permanent wooden fish traps of impressive size on many parts of the coast.[17]

These were the finished products that were made by tools, and these tools changed over the 40 000 years in which Aborigines had inhabited the continent. The Aboriginal tool kit included cutting tools like axes and adzes, scraping tools, needles for sewing, knives for cutting, and tools for grinding. At first these were made of stone; for example, axes were simply sharpened stones held in the hand. They were often large and awkward to use, but the tendency in tool making was for tools to become smaller, easier to handle and more efficient. They were made of different materials too; stone adzes became hafted axes with wooden handles, knives and needles were made with bone and shell. And after the visits of the Macassan trepang fishermen to the northern coast, in the eighteenth and early nineteenth century, Aborigines began to use glass, iron, and nails from the rubbish the Macassans left behind. Archaeologists who have studied the artifacts of Aboriginal civilisations say that the tool kit in the fossil record developed from large to small, from the inefficient to the efficient and from the simple to the varied. The hafted axe is a good example. The sharpened stone is an inefficient cutting instrument; it can only be used with the force in a person's arm. The hafted axe (or the woomera thrown spear) is more efficient because it amplifies the body's strength. It lengthens the arm and makes use of the wrist and so permits more leverage and force.[18]

The settled tribes and complex engineering work of the Lake Condah tribes alert us to the question of agriculture. It has long been assumed that Aborigines did not farm the land, living off its bounty without altering it in any way, other than in the very short-term use of resources. It is true that Aborigines did not cultivate the land and neither did they domesticate animals for food, nevertheless they did practise a kind of agriculture. For instance, north-eastern tribes dug tubers from the ground but left the top attached to the root so it would regrow while Aborigines along the Darling River were observed by the explorer, Thomas Mitchell, to harvest, and stack grass:

> the grass had been pulled, to a great extent, and piled in hayricks, so that the aspect of the desert was softened into the agreeable semblance of a hayfield . . . we found the ricks, or hay-cocks, extending for miles . . . the grass was of one kind, a species of *Panicum* . . . and not a spike of it was left in the soil, over the whole of the ground . . . The grass was beautifully green beneath the heaps and full of seed.[19]

And then there is fire. The early European settlers were very impressed (and worried) by the number of bush fires in Australia. At first they ascribed it to the dryness of the country but they soon found that many were deliberately lit by Aborigines, for whom firing the landcover was a form of 'firestick' farming.[20] Plainly, burning a piece of land distracted and drove out animals and birds and made them easier to kill, however, the regeneration of plant life was more important. After a fire, new grass grew more quickly because the ashes mixed with rain and made an excellent fertiliser, and animals flocked to these new, sweet, young pastures, so hunting was made easier. In principle, then, firestick farming was a form of long-term planning, not much different from any other kind of farming.[21]

Aborigines produced food for immediate consumption. However, much production was not for consumption but for exchange. Artifacts, tools, raw materials, even songs, dances and stories were produced and exchanged with neighbouring bands and tribes. Great exchange routes developed and so grand were they that articles natural only to one side of the continent were traded along exchange routes right across to the other. Archaeologists have found pearl shell from the north-west coast near the Great Australian Bight and baler shell from the far north on the south-east coast.[22] Men from the Diyari, Arabana and Tirora tribes of the Lake Eyre region travelled up to 500 kilometres to the Flinders Ranges to trade goods for red ochre, which they used in their sacred rituals.[23]

Frequently these exchanges were made in big ceremonies when members of several tribes congregated together. Perhaps the best known, and certainly the biggest of these in the south-east were the annual gatherings on the Bogong high plains, when exchange accompanied ritual and feasting on the bogong moths.[24] James Dawson, a Victorian observer, described another great meeting place, near the present town of Terang, 100 miles north of Melbourne:

> At the periodical great meetings trading is carried on by the exchange of articles peculiar to distant parts of the country. A favourite place of meeting for the purpose of barter is a hill called Noorat, near Terang. In that locality the forest kangaroos are plentiful, and the skins of the young ones found there are considered superior to all others for making rugs. The Aborigines from the Geelong district bring the best stones for making axes, and a kind of wattle gum celebrated for its adhesiveness. This Geelong gum is useful in fixing the handles of stone axes and the splinters of flint in spears, and for cementing the joints of bark buckets, that it is carried in large lumps all over the Western District. Greenstone for axes is obtained also from a quarry on Spring Creek, near Goodwood; and sandstone for grinding them is got from the salt creek near Lake Boloke. Obsidian or volcanic glass, for scraping and polishing weapons, is found near Dunkeld. The Wimmera country supplies the maleen saplings, found in the mallee scrub, for making spears. The Cape Otway forest supplies the wood for the bundit spears, and the grass-tree stalk for forming the butt piece of the light spear, and for producing fire; also a red clay, found on the sea coast, which is used as a paint.[25]

Meetings of this sort were held for a combination of exchange, ritual and ceremonial reasons. Certainly trade then, as now, was a way of distributing something useful to people who didn't have it and it was also a way of conferring prestige on honoured but distant relatives by giving them exotic artifacts. But exchange is also giving, and, as the American anthropologist Marshall Sahlins pointed out, exchanging of gifts was one way of tying tribes together in friendship.[26]

One of the long but observable processes in western countries is the progressive divorce of work and religion. To be sure, all work, even when we think it is meaningless, is invested with meanings, but few of these now relate wholly to religion. This was not the case with Aborigines and work, for their work was made religious and ritualised in many different ways. However, to fully understand these connections we need to detour through that marvellously complex metaphysics of Aboriginal religion.

Common to all Aboriginal religions was (and is) the Dreaming. In the Dreaming creative beings appeared on an empty earth or from the sea and gave the earth its colour, its shape, its distinctive topography. They did this both deliberately and unconsciously, leaving parts of themselves behind as mountains or rocks and leaving rivers, valleys and waterholes in their wake. They created life and gave it its forms and habits, its laws, rituals and institutions. The Arabana people of central Australia, for example, accounted for the making of Lake Eyre in this way:

> An old woman who was looking for food at Maluna saw a big kangaroo (*kungara*) which she desired to kill, but a boy Wilkuda, sprang out of her inside ... and chased the kangaroo in a westerly direction across what is now Lake Eyre. He camped near the site of Peake station homestead. Next morning he managed to kill the kangaroo and put it on the fire at Ngurupana; this is the place of the tail; it is near Keckwick's Pile. Wilkuda then went to sleep, but when he woke up, instead of finding a cooked kangaroo, he discovered that the kangaroo had got off the fire and run away. He chased it into a mob of kangaroos near Kununa, but managed to cut it out of the mob, for he *had* to catch this particular kangaroo.
>
> Continuing the chase, he grew very weary. At this stage, an old man who was hunting with a dog came along, and seeing the big kangaroo, and thinking it was just an ordinary kangaroo, caught it with the help of his dog, and killed and skinned it. Wilkuda at length came up to the old man and told him it was his kangaroo, adding 'you can eat the flesh, but give me the skin'.
>
> Wilkuda then went off with the skin, making back east. Arriving at a spot near Guduna, he contemplated making a lake there with the skin, but a little bird told him *not* to do so, as people had to walk about there. So he rolled up the skin and walked down the Nulkuna (Nilkinna Creek). The bird again stopped him from making a lake, telling him not

to put the skin down Anna Creek way. Passing to a spot east of Anna Creek he threw down the skin, which became Lake Eyre, while he himself turned into stone; his knife and bag in which he carried the skin can also be seen there in stone, and, strangely enough, the kangaroo is likewise there in stone.[27]

To Aborigines the Dreaming was both past and present, past in the sense that it was 'the beginning' and present because the landscape, names, and the social organisation the ancestors left are all permanent evidence of their existence. The Dreaming gave certain places their sacred character, but in one sense all the earth was sacred. In the Dreaming the creative beings frequently had animal and plant as well as human qualities, they were the 'prototypes of natural species'. Aborigines considered themselves contemporary manifestations of their ancestral heroes through these species. Anthropologists label this kind of religion totemism or species filiation, to signify the close identification of humans to other species or parts of the land. Each Aborigine, Aboriginal clan, the two sexes in each clan and the several categories of kinship were affiliated to a species. At the basic level each individual had his or her *conception filiation*. There was a belief amongst observers that Aborigines did not understand that childbirth was related to sexual intercourse. They did, of course, otherwise they would not have had intricate marriage laws to prohibit incest. However, the ritual aspect was more significant. In this, conception came about when a spirit entered a woman's body. Which spirit was a question of interpreting signs that were contiguous to the appearance of pregnancy or birth. The point of these affiliations was to associate each person or group with the natural non-human world and to associate them with the sacred sites, the homes of their ancestors. Aborigines did not separate themselves from the natural world or the Dreaming. They considered themselves part of it, it part of them, and it was their species affiliation which linked them.[28]

Every culture has to plan for its material future. Firestick farming is one way in which Aborigines did this but they planned it in religious terms as well. Increase ceremonies were rituals in which Aborigines recreated a part or all of a founding drama and so tried to increase the number of a particular species or of themselves. That is, increase ceremonies renewed life. It was a way to encourage or coerce nature into increasing its bounty.[29]

Religion structured work in other ways too. Food taboos restricted what people could kill for food and eat. People could not kill and eat their own species affiliation, because that would be killing or eating their link to the Dreaming and, spiritually, themselves. Nor could a person enter a place of ritual significance to hunt food or take food. The anthropologist T.G.H. Strehlow described waterholes and rivers in central Australia teer water birds, kangaroos and emus, but the Aranda people, to they were sacred places, could not enter them, even in pursuit animals they had wounded outside.[30] Ritual taboos also prohibited young women from eating certain kinds of food. Young men, too, had to give food they had caught before and during initiation to the old men of the tribe. And food from particular places was available only to those old men who had relationships with the land. Taboos also structured the production of goods for exchange. For example, only the old men of the Georgiana River tribe, those who knew the sacred and ritual life of their people, were allowed to pick and cook the narcotic pituri bush.[31]

From the first day of the European invasion of the Antipodes there has been a controversy about the standard of living of the Australian Aborigines, and the associated questions have often been asked: Why did the Aborigines not develop a settled agriculture? Why did they not cultivate the land and domesticate animals? They had the opportunity to, because of their contacts with the agriculturalists of New Guinea across Torres Strait and the trepang fishermen from Malacca.[32]

Captain James Cook had a strong view about the first question:

> From what I have said of the Natives of New-Holland they may appear to some to be the most wretched people upon Earth, but in reality they are far more happier than we Europeans. They live in a Tranquillity which is not disturb'd by the Inequality of Condition: The Earth and sea of their own accord furnishes them with all things necessary for life, they covet not Magnificent Houses, Household-stuff &c, they live in a warm and fine Climate and enjoy a very wholesome Air, so that they have very little need of Clothing and this they seem to be fully sensible of, for many to whom we gave Cloth &c to, left it carelessly upon the Sea beach and in the woods as a thing they had no manner of use for. In short they seem'd to set no Value upon any thing we gave them, nor would they ever part with any thing of their own for any one article we could offer them; this in my opinion argues that they think themselves provided with all the necessarys of Life and that they have no superfluities.[33]

Later, historians put Cook into his eighteenth-century context and showed how his views were made through the prism of the popular stereotype of the 'noble savage', happy, healthy, free and pagan but uninfected by the vices of so-called civilised Europe.[34] However, anthropologists and archaeologists have since turned this argument on its head. Cook may have been expressing a stereotype but in effect he was right. Aborigines, they now argue, produced as much food as they needed and produced it quickly and easily, even in the harshest country hunting or gathering for no more than six or seven hours a day. The reason they did not resort to agriculture was not because they were incapable of it but because they did not need it.[35]

God, work and the Aborigines

When mid-eighteenth-century Europeans thought about the Aboriginal inhabitants of 'New Holland', they thought of them not as occupiers of a continent but as little more than beasts living in a state of nature, human only in their possession of language and family. Land was land in this period of European expansion, and it might be seized for imperial aggrandisement, or capitalist profit. A set of conventions developed in Europe in the eighteenth century which governed the relationship between colonial powers and the 'new world' and which set rules for the colonisation of new territory. Thus an indigenous population might be 'persuaded' to accept a European overlordship, new territories might be purchased from the indigenous population or, finally, lands might be seized unilaterally if they seemed to be uninhabited. If there were people on 'uninhabited' land, how could it be legally taken? Christianity and eighteenth-century philosophy provided the answers. After Adam and Eve fell from grace, so the doctrine said, God gave 'the world in common' to humanity for industrious purposes. But humankind might have left the land in a state of nature, in which case a person's property lodged only in the labour of his or her body or the results of that body's work. Hence the 'savage' possessed his kill because he had expended labour on it, he had mixed his labour with it, but he was still a 'savage' living in a state of nature.[36]

Civilisation, so the argument continued, only began when people removed themselves from the state of nature and mixed their labour with the soil so that the object of their labour, the soil, became their property. If a people over whom Europeans wanted sovereignity had reached this exalted state and advanced beyond the state of nature, and had cultivated the land, if they had made roads and towns, had developed customs, commerce and religions, if they had made laws and governments, then they had sovereignty over the land. And if they had that, then colonialisers had to persuade them to lease it or accept the Europeans' overlordship of it.

Otherwise the land was 'empty'. It could be seized and permanently possessed by the simple expedient of claiming it in symbolic ways (raising a flag, or shooting a volley of shots from rifles), by leaving proof of occupation or by occupying it.[37] The British

Colonial Office gave its instructions to James Cook thus:

> ... with the Consent of the Natives take possession of Convenient Situations in the [Southern Continent] in the Name of the King of Great Britain; or, if you find the Country uninhabited take Possession for His Majesty by setting up Proper Marks and Inscriptions, as first discoverers and possessors.[38]

Cook, although he respected the 'natives of New Holland', thought they lived in this state of nature, and that the land was *terra nullius*, an empty land, ripe for the taking. So he took it, or at least its eastern half, for the British Crown by doing nothing more than firing three volleys from small arms on an island near Cape York. He aptly named this island Possession Island. Somewhere between there and England Cook named this new colony New South Wales.[39] His fleeting glimpses of the Aborigines were enough for the British Crown to seize the 'unoccupied' land of the Antipodes.

The ideology of work underpinned the seizure of the continent. Later colonists agreed with Cook that the Aborigines did not mix their labour with the soil so they had no legal or moral right to it. As the *Sydney Herald* put it in 1838:

> ... this vast country was to them a common—they bestowed no labor upon the land—their ownership, their right, was nothing more than that of the Emu or the Kangaroo. They bestowed no labor upon the land and that—and that only—it is which gives a right of property to it. Where, we ask, is the man endowed with even a modicum of reasoning powers, who will assert that this great continent was ever intended by the Creator to remain an unproductive wilderness? ... The British people ... took possession ... ; and they had a perfect right to do so, under the Divine authority, by which man was commanded to go forth and people, and *till* the land. Herein we find the right to the dominion which the British Crown, or, more properly speaking, the British people, exercise over the continent of New Holland.[40]

'Their right was nothing more than the emu or kangaroo'. Peter Cunningham, the surgeon, extended the bestial metaphors:

> How is it that the abject animal state in which the [Aborigines] live should place them at the very zero of civilisation, constituting in a measure the connecting link between man and the monkey tribe—for really some of the old women only seem to require a tail to complete the identity.[41]

What rights had this 'barely human race', a race which did not mix its labour with the soil, a race without government, religion, laws, restraint, culture or civilisation? The common answer was 'none'.

From 1788 to the 1850s there were three economies at work in the British colonies in Australia. One was the Aboriginal hunter-gatherer society of amazing longevity but in the south of the continent, in rapid decline. The second economy was the convict system which mixed punishment with work. The third was a peculiar version of capitalism complete with waged and un-free labour. Aborigines played no part in the second economy but they were crucial to the third. They had nothing the Europeans wanted to trade, they had nothing the Europeans wanted to buy—but they did have labour to be exploited, and skills which might be put to some use.

After many years of ignoring the fact, historians are now beginning to see just how important the labour of Aborigines was in the early growing colonies. On the pastoral properties and farms Aboriginal men were shepherds, stockmen and sheep washers. They gathered potatoes, picked vegetables and carted bark. Aboriginal women and girls worked as domestic servants.[42] The settlers did not use them as much as they could have. They preferred to use assigned convicts in New South Wales and Van Dieman's Land, but were prepared to use Aborigines if all else failed. After all, they were cheap. They were never paid in cash, only in rations—flour, sugar, blankets, grog and tobacco.[43]

The Europeans were ambivalent about the Aborigines' potential as workers, although not about their status. No less a person than Governor Macquarie said of them in 1814:

> Scarcely Emerged from the remotest State of rude and Uncivilized Nature, these People appear to possess some Qualities, which, if properly Cultivated and Encouraged, Might render them not only less wretched and destitute by Reason of their Wild wandering and Unsettled Habits, but progressively Useful to the Country. According to their Capabilities either as Labourers in Agricultural Employ or among the lower Class of Mechanics.[44]

Pastoralists were less optimistic. The propensity of Aborigines to leave their jobs and wander made them 'irresponsible and feckless', their aversion to regular work made them unemployable.[45] Others observed the fatal impact of European diseases and thought few Aborigines were sufficiently robust to work anyway.[46]

Aborigines, though, were unambivalent about European patterns of work. They had no desire to join the labour force. They despised the sedentary life of the shepherds and so they incorporated life on the stations into their existing cycle of movement, working, consuming the white man's comestibles which they found attractive, like tea, tobacco, sugar, flour and liquor, and then moving on.[47] What the squatters regarded as 'their indomitable propensity to wander' was to the Aborigines their cultural imperative, their traditional movement in search of food.

Their wandering was broken, however, by the imperative of settlement, the creation of pastoralism itself. As the sheep spread down the eastern colonies and inland so the tribal economies were destroyed. Cattle and sheep are no respecters of land. They competed with the native game for feed, they trampled and muddied water courses, they rooted out the vegetables that Aboriginal women foraged for. White men shot the native game or poisoned it for skins, for sport or because it was a nuisance. In response Aborigines could do one of three things; they could retaliate, spear the sheep, kill the shepherds and try to drive the pastoralists from their country; they could retreat from the frontier and encroach on to their neighbours' territory; or they could turn to the pastoralists for protection and rations. In fact they did all three. The first two choices meant an inevitably escalating violence as the frontier became a battleground. The third gave Aborigines some protection as friendly pastoralists gave them refuge from their fellow whites.

We have seen the way Aborigines used their intimate knowledge of their environment to make their lives comfortable. It might have been expected that the Europeans would make use of these skills in ways to make their own lives easier. They did not, of course. Generally they remained wilfully ignorant of Aboriginal skills, an ignorance produced by the ethnocentric notion that only European knowledge was real knowledge and that Aboriginal knowledge was animal instinct. Some explorers, however, thought differently, especially those like Strezlecki and Eyre, whose lives were saved by their Aboriginal guides, and those who used Aboriginal knowledge to find food and water in the desolate environments they passed through.[48] The British also used Aboriginal men as police in native police forces in Port Phillip in the 1840s and Queensland in the 1860s. Why would Aborigines join police forces which by all accounts were used mainly against other Aborigines? The historian, Marie Fels, shows how the members of these forces wanted to share power and authority with the European invaders who were plainly in Australia to stay. She also shows how they used the prestige and the material benefits like uniforms, rifles and houses derived from membership of these forces to extend their influence within their own tribes, and how, in the areas where tribal hostilities were still strong, the native police added new dimensions and new technologies too, to their traditional techniques of warfare.[49]

While some Europeans exploited Aboriginal labour, and others predicted and welcomed the prospect of the extinction of the Aboriginal race, humanitarians and philanthropists sought to help the indigenous population. The humanitarians' solutions were, in effect, to turn Aborigines into Europeans through Christianity and work. These sentiments were a development from the late eighteenth and early nineteenth-century anti-slavery movements in Britain, and grew out of fear that the inevitable result of colonialism in the new world would be the destruction of the newly subject populations. Australian colonial administrations came under pressure from Britain and from Antipodean Christian and philanthropic groups to adopt humanitarian policies. The Aboriginal protectorates were one effect of this, the mission stations of various Christian denominations another. Their aims were fundamentally similar, to protect the Aborigines from cruelty and oppression, to promote their moral and religious improvement, to induce them to build houses and adopt more settled habits, to teach them farming skills, in fact to do anything which would 'civilise' them.[50]

Macquarie wanted to turn Aborigines into a rural proletariat. The protectors and missionaries hoped they would become small cultivators, perhaps even peasant farmers. 'Social improvement and civilisation' meant the adoption of Christian religion and morality. Building houses and farms was the solution to their 'propensity to wander'. We can almost hear that classical nineteenth-century refrain 'God and Work. God and Work'. Physical survival obviously meant cultural extinction.

2 The felonry and the free

If Australia began as a jail, how did it develop so quickly into a capitalist economy? Where did the owners of capital, the sellers of labour and the market for their produce come from? And how did this system develop into the post-industrial condition it is now in, when few other than convicts and soldiers arrived with the first fleet? Capital was not brought to the colony. The embryo capitalists, the officers and officials of the administration, made their money from monopolising the cargoes of visiting trading ships and selling these to the Government store or to a group of small retailers for large profits. It was nothing less than a racket which was broken only by growing competition from merchant capitalists like Robert Campbell, and by the officers' increasing interest in that most desirable and available of property, the land. Land grants and free convict labour (until 1804, when Governor Hunter made landowners support their own convicts) meant easy pickings for men anxious to invest their commercial profits in the capital which could give them social status. The produce they grew they also sold to the Commissariat so the state as consumer underwrote their profits and their pretensions and they invested both of these in more and more land, buying it, being granted it, or squatting on it. It was cheap land for the capitalists. The false doctrine of *terra nullius* underwrote the huge expansion in the pastoral industry in Australia.

Capital was accumulated locally too, by embryo merchants investing in transport and finance, banks and insurance. The most interesting of these were sharp emancipist capitalists like Simeon Lord, Henry Kable, Joseph Underwood and Samuel Terry. Terry began with a shop and a liquor license, retailing the goods monopolised by the officers. He ended up in milling, brewing, shipping and holding shares. Investing in whaling, sealing, sandalwood, salt, shipbuilding, each of these men made fortunes in the small and insignificant New South Wales economy.[1] They were not appreciated for it though. Governor Hunter said of them in 1802: 'Some of the very dregs of those who have been sent here as convicts, are now in possession of their horses, chaise, servants and other symbols of wealth.'[2]

Capital was also imported from merchants in Calcutta and

London and invested both in the trading and the new pastoral sectors. Most of it was family or individual's capital but several big public companies were floated in England to invest in land and sheep. The Van Diemen's Land Company, the Clyde Company, which took up land near Geelong in Port Phillip, and the Australian Agricultural Company (given 1 million acres as a grant by the administration in Sydney) were the biggest.

In the 1820s the surgeon Peter Cunningham described Sydney, where

> thirty-eight years ago, not a human hut was to be counted, nor the slightest hum of commerce heard, we have now a city occupying a mile square, crowded with industrious citizens, and teeming with vehicles wheeling along the varied productions of the soil—the market-dues for this traffic renting, the present year, at 840£., and the toll-gate dues at 1000£., the town containing twenty-two agents for the management of shipping affairs; eleven auctioneers for expeditiously disposing of colonial and foreign wares; a chamber of commerce to push forward and watch over colonial enterprise, effect insurances, and arbitrate in matters relating to shipping; two flourishing banks, dividing forty percent on their advances; and three newspapers (one weekly, and two printed twice a week) in one of which I counted one day 124 advertisements ... [3]

Elizabeth Macarthur, who told her mother that she and her husband had 'every reasonable expectation of reaping the most material advantages', was right.[4]

The suffering convict

The first convicts began their journey to Botany Bay in 1787; 568 males and 191 females were sent together with 13 children and a military establishment of 211 men, 27 wives and 14 children. Between then and 1852, when transportation to Australia's eastern seaboard was abolished, 122 620 male and 24 960 female convicts were sent to endure their penance on the other side of the world from their homes. Overall 80 000 were sent to New South Wales and 67 000 to Van Diemen's Land, although the number that arrived was less because many (2834) died en route.[5]

Most of these convicts were transported for larceny; for petty offences which today would be given a suspended sentence and not much more. Most were repeating offenders, that is they were transported for a second or third offence. They were mostly from the cities of England, although most women were Irish. A large proportion were country people from England and Ireland transported for stealing animals. There were also political prisoners, machine breakers, forgers, embezzlers, military offenders, arsonists and vagrants and many more.[6] Were they, though, actually criminals or were they members of a criminal sub-culture, where work was despised and honesty unknown? A generation of historians has agreed that they were, plainly and simply, thieves, an unprepossessing lot of incorrigible rogues, an unlucky part (in that they were caught) of that lumpen-proletariat spewed up by the rapid industrialisation and urbanisation of the industrial revolution.[7]

Were they just this? Were they not also workers who stole to get by, or who did as workers had always done—pilfered from their employers, or stolen to survive unemployment and poverty? The details of convicts' crimes, punishments and occupations were recorded on what were known as the convict indents, the government's record of its convict charges. Earlier historians looked at convicts' criminal records and defined them as criminals. Later historians instead looked at their former occupations and defined them as workers who strayed into crime from over 1000 separate occupations.[8] The names of some of these occupations give an indication of just how wide the range of men's jobs was in Britain. There were sword polishers, fishhook makers, cricket ball stitchers, watch chain gilders, ironfounders, book binders, bargemen, sweeps, wool carders, nail makers, stocking makers and many, many more.[9] Generally the range of convicts' occupations tended to replicate the occupational range in Britain. A great number were skilled or semi-skilled workers—indeed, between 6 percent and 14 percent were highly skilled artisans—only about 28 percent were labourers and under 50 percent might be defined as unskilled. About half of all the convicts could read and write (the figure was 75 percent for English convicts).[10]

What convicts actually ended up doing in the colony depended very largely on their former occupations. Cricket-ball stitchers, watch-chain gilders and bargemen had no chance of doing their kind of work in New South Wales but gentlemen convicts were often pardoned immediately on their arrival in Sydney and given appropriate jobs, and convict clerks found their skills useful to the colonial administrations.[11] George Howe, for example, a printer transported for shoplifting in 1803, was given the job of running Governor King's printing press, and convict printers working on colonial newspapers were indistinguishable from ordinary employees.[12] Skilled tradesmen, too, were in high demand and often went into their trades. Construction workers were also; carpenters, coopers, ironmongers, masons, plasterers, sailmakers, tailors and tanners were highly sought after as colonial administrators struggled to build the colony. Indeed Governor Macquarie lifted them from the convict transports as soon as they anchored in Sydney harbour.[13]

Unskilled urban workers were less useful than skilled workers, so unskilled urban workers remained unskilled urban workers or became rural workers, although, here too, experienced rural labourers were more valuable to the colony. Generally, convicts were more likely to be given work in their usual occupations if they were on assignment than if they stayed in the city on government work. In city or country, though, they tended to return to their previous jobs when they got their tickets of leave, or when they had done their time.

Women convicts were vilified as prostitutes by contemporaries and historians.[14] Some were. Perhaps between 13 percent and 20 percent of convict women described themselves as prostitutes or used the current slang and described themselves on their original arrest as being 'on the town'. However, prostitution was not a transportable crime. Rather, the label 'prostitute' was affixed by the British middle-class to women whose moral code was different from their own. Robert Hughes shows how 'In the mouths of Authority, the word prostitute was less a job description than a general term of abuse'.[15] Overwhelmingly, convict women were transported for petty theft, most being repeat offenders. Most recidivists were sent to Van Diemen's Land, and first offenders to New South Wales. According to the indents, their crimes were minor—stealing small amounts of money, cloth, clothing, jewellery and so on. They were mainly domestic servants; housemaids, kitchen maids, nursemaids, cooks and servants of all work. Some worked in the clothing industry using skills like seamstressing, millinery and dressmaking, while the others were unskilled urban and rural workers. The limited range of occupations compared to men's is not surprising. The occupational make up of convict women was broadly similar to the occupational structure of women's employment in Britain, and the sexual division of labour in Britain restricted women to a very narrow range of jobs.[16] From the standpoint of the 1990s, what is most impressive is the number of women in domestic service. The growth in domestic service in the late eighteenth and nineteenth centuries was the product of the growth of the servant-employing middle-class. In the 1850s nearly 27 percent of employed women in Britain were domestic servants.[17]

Most historians divide the convict system on the eastern seaboard into two distinct periods, separated in 1840 by the abolition of assignment, the end of transportation to New South Wales and the beginning of the probation system in Van Diemen's Land. In the first period there were differences in the experiences of work, differences between those on assignment to private employers (a scheme begun by Governor Phillip in his search for the most efficient kind of work organisation), those working in government gangs and those in the secondary punishment gangs, on places like Norfolk Island, Port Macquarie or Port Arthur. In the second system, the probation system, all the convicts began work in probation gangs. If they behaved themselves they were given a probation pass which allowed them to work more or less freely for wages from approved employers. Then they might get a ticket of leave, with which they could work for whoever they chose, then, ultimately, on condition of good behaviour, they were given an absolute pardon.

In terms of convicts' work, Governor Phillip established the primary feature of the convict system in New South Wales, that is, he provided for task work and free time in which convicts might work when, where and for whom they pleased, for wages. It was a way of getting convicts to work and to get them off the government store, for Phillip believed that convicts who had 'passed their lives in habits of vice and indolence' would not work. Free time was given, though, only after the governor's time had been spent, and the convicts had completed their set tasks. If they did these quickly they could have afternoons off. Observers noted convicts around Sydney working hard in the mornings for the government, then working for themselves or idling about Sydney in the afternoon. In this way they could earn the money to buy lodgings or build the huts they would live in. Later Governor Macquarie tried hard to abolish free work on weekdays but he left it alone on weekends.[18]

The work done in the government gangs was a major source of employment for convicts right through the period. It reached its peak under Macquarie and his massive building programme. Gangs of varying sorts were formed, largely of skilled men; lumber and dockyard gangs, building gangs, agricultural gangs, road and mining gangs, water carrying gangs and more. The outdoor road gangs were composed of the unskilled convicts.[19] Life on the road gangs was regarded as extremely harsh, but it was not as harsh as the life on the ironed punishment gangs or in the places of secondary punishment. Working for the gangs, too, under Macquarie, often meant the end of task and free time, for he wanted convicts to work hard and by working hard to save their souls.[20]

Women convicts, once in the Antipodes, suffered more than men because of the sexual division of labour and the vast preponderance of men. On arrival, many women were whisked off the convict ships by soldiers, officers and free settlers desperate for wives, concubines, domestic servants or prostitutes. The rest had to buy private lodgings, but if they could not they were sent to the female factories. A Lieutenant in the Rum Corps described their situation in 1816:

> The Women, bad as they are, are really to be pitied; the principal place for their reception is at Parramatta; there such as are not sent to Service go to the Factory to work, and after they have done what is required of them by Government, with the exception of such as are punished by Fine, are let loose upon the Inhabitants to find a lodging where they can, there not being any Public Building to lodge them in ... [21]

They often paid for this, in the current slang, by 'buttock and twang'. That is to say, moneyless and friendless, they were forced into prostitution.[22]

Generally there was a much greater emphasis on women's reproductive labour than their productive labour in the colonies, hence the great emphasis on the marriage of convict women and the supposed civilising effect of marriage itself. Be this as it may, the marriage rate amongst convict women was low. Cohabitation and prostitution were other and often better options.[23]

Other than marriage convict women could work really only as domestic servants. Male settlers did not want female convicts as servants, much preferring free female labour, so from the 1820s an increasing number of women convicts were packed into the overcrowded factories, where a few worked but most did not. Governor Gipps observed:

> With the exception of a few employed in cooking, washing, or other such necessary employment, they were all in absolute idleness ... they all pass their time from morning to night without any sort of occupation, except when it may come to their turn to cook, to wash, or to draw water for the establishment.[24]

On assignment things were different. Convict women with husbands already in the colony were assigned to them, propertied women were given tickets of leave and others were picked off the ships and assigned as domestic servants to officers and settlers. About half of the female convicts were assigned to private settlers, although settlers' choices were based less on skill and more on looks. As always, the work they did was defined by the sexual division of labour. Treated as objects for the gratification of the settlers' sexual proclivities, their skills were vastly under utilised.

In fact most convicts were assigned to private employers. Assigned convicts were not slaves, as many critics of the system claimed, because they were controlled by the government, could be taken away from their masters and, of course, made free on the completion of their sentence. And they could still work in their own time because the logic of the assignment system was task work, just as it was on government work.[25] When the task was done the convict could work for wages for her or his master or anyone else. The rates of pay for most jobs were set by the state, but payment was not necessarily in cash, sometimes it was in kind, sometimes it was in rum. Most assignment was in the country. The rapidly expanding pastoral economy was constantly and chronically short of labour and the squatters clamoured long and loud for cheap convict workers. The country was also thought to be more pure and wholesome than the towns, more likely to reform the convicts into habits of regular and disciplined labour. However, not all convicts were sent to the bush. Many went to workshops in Sydney and Parramatta, many more went to building sites, and many women to private homes as domestics. In the country they worked at a variety of farm and station work. Again skilled workers were in most demand for the multitude of building and repairing jobs that new properties required and so too were experienced farm labourers. What most employers got, though, was not to their liking; city boys with no experience of bush life and old 'lags' unsuited for anything but the mindless routine of shepherding.

Masters of assigned convicts were really an arm of the convict system, hence of the colonial state, so their power in the relationship with their convicts was backed by the authority of the state. State regulations demanded that the convicts be obedient, deferential, hard working and careful, and these were enforced by a disciplinary system based on local magistrates courts, where the local magistrates were invariably 'respectable' landowners. The threat of a flogging, banishment to an iron gang or to the living hell of Norfolk Island and ultimately execution itself were the controls masters could, and did, frequently make use of. Flogging was the most common of punishments. It was treated more as an everyday occurrence, a response to local refractions of the system of deference, obedience and power. However, punishments were often much harder. James Mudie, a large landowner in New South Wales, had four of his convicts executed for a 'rebellion' in which they shot at his son-in-law and overseer, flogged a master at another farm, and robbed some houses.[26]

Work relations on assignment depended first on that division between what Mudie later called the 'felonry' and the 'free', between convicts and free settlers. But there was, too, a difference in the social class of each. In the eighteenth and nineteenth centuries, the gulf between the poor and unrespectable and the better off and respectable was unbridgeable. Nevertheless, it was not a relationship where the convicts were utterly impotent. In the first place the law enshrined certain rights for convicts. They could, in theory, take action against masters for ill usage or insufficient rations, but when the local magistrates were also convict masters, their applications were often fruitless. In fact, Hirst refers to convicts and masters actually racing each other to local magistrates to get their complaints in first.[27] A charge of absconding, a flogging or a spell in an ironed gang was at stake if the convict lost the race or the case.

Because convicts on assignment could work for themselves after their tasks had been completed, they had some small measure of power to control their lives. Depending on their skills and their scarcity, skilled workers could bargain for higher wages and better conditions. This freedom was relative, of course. What the skilled could bargain for, the unskilled could not, and those whose talents were limited and hence more easily dominated felt the sting of the lash more often than their skilled counterparts.

There is another matter—the question of resistance and solidarity. We have seen the case of James Mudie's servants and their fate, but there were many other ways in which convicts could resist. Refusing to work, working slowly, malingering, being insolent and absconding were all forms of resistance. Taking masters to court expressed a belief in convicts' rights and the belief that the law protected them. However, as the historian Alan Atkinson points out, each of these implicitly accepted the rules of the convict system and the power relationships which underpinned it. Only rebellion or physical violence really threatened the system, yet a multitude of actions and words indicate that there was a sense of solidarity between some convicts, in opposition to respectable society.[28] How else can the actions of the women convicts in Hobart's female factory be interpreted? Greeting a visit by the Lieutenant Governor and chaplain, they turned around, lifted their skirts and then 'smacked their posteriors with loud report'.[29] Nevertheless it is possible to make too much of this kind of solidarity, for prisons the world over have seen this sort of freemasonry. There is a view, among some historians, that the origins of working-class radicalism in Australia derives in part from convict solidarity, but it would be unwise to overemphasise this.[30] There are just too many examples of convict policemen, informers, brawls and murders to argue for a uniform sense of convict consciousness.

We must have labour

The social relations of free labour in the colonies were transplanted from Britain. Convictism was peculiarly Australian but, except in the sense that industry in Australia was both rural and primitive, the character of work was much the same as that which the settlers had left behind. The sexual division of labour remained much the same. The divisions between the unskilled workers and the skilled workers were similar. The protestant work ethic migrated with the protestants and the very different attitudes to work held by the working class migrated with them. However, that dialectic between insubordination and deference, which characterised work relations in Britain, seems to have developed differently in the colonies and there were major differences in the exploitation of the Aborigines and in the distinction which grew between the bond and the free.

The labour market in the early years of white settlement was a very peculiar one, an uneasy relationship between a nominally free market of nominally free workers and the unfree convicts fettered by the legal restrictions on their labour. What happened in one affected what happened in the other. The free market began quickly in New South Wales, peopled by convicts working in their free time, ticket of leave, pardoned and expired sentence convicts and free emigrant workers, and it increased as children born in the colony began work. Of course some took themselves out of the market by taking up farming, but because their incomes were so low, most had to supplement them by doing paid work for wealthier neighbours.

For much of the time these early labour markets worked to the advantage of male workers, especially those with skills who bargained vigorously with employers for high wages, much higher than they could get in Britain. However, these wages were more likely to be found around the towns. Few free workers wanted to work in the bush, fearing attacks by Aborigines or more stringent work rules imposed by masters whose sense of workplace discipline was honed on convicts. The towns, too, for all their smallness, were very lively places, with pubs, eating houses and plenty of other places in which to have a good time. This reluctance to 'go bush' affected the rural labour market. Pastoral workers were able to take advantage of their scarcity and they too demanded high wages, especially in Port Phillip and South Australia, where there were no convicts.

High wages was the major cost masters had to bear and they tried to avoid this in several ways. They indentured workers brought from Britain (and other places) on wages well below the colonial rates; they paid workers in the debased local currency; they forced workers to accept payment in kind at heavily inflated prices; but mostly they tried to flood the labour market with convicts or free immigrants.

Nineteenth-century political economy regarded the labour market as it did any other market. It thought that supply and demand regulated the cost of labour, and that wages rose and fell according to whether there was an over- or under-supply of workers. If there was unemployment, so the argument went, all workers had to do was accept a lower wage and then there would be jobs for everyone. Employers, particularly the pastoralists, knew that the answer to their problem of high wages lay in increasing the number of workers. As the *Sydney Herald* declared:

> We must either retard the progress of colonial improvement and prosperity, or we must go ahead to every region for cheap labour ... the settlers must endeavour to obtain at moderate rates some accessible source and fountain of labour, unless we give up the struggle and ruin the colony.[31]

At its most systematic, this was done by manipulating the price of land and using the funds from land sales to finance the migration of free workers. So in New South Wales the sale of land replaced the old system of land grants, while in the new colony of South Australia land was sold at a 'sufficient price' to pay for emigrant workers and to keep it out of the reach of these workers when they arrived. In this way, land would be the basis of a new capitalist class and a supply of labour would be assured and in constant supply.

Some New South Wales and Van Diemen's Land employers preferred convicts to free workers, after all, they were cheap and easy to discipline. Some pastoralists preferred what they called 'coolie' labour, that is workers from China or India, or Pacific Islanders and Maoris. They worked hard, it was assumed, ate little and could be paid much lower wages than those demanded by British workers.[32] Other pastoralists imported northern European labour (the Macarthurs imported six families of vine-dressers from Germany) on contracts.[33] However, most workers were not indentured and it was to deal with these that the colonial legislatures passed the Masters' and Servants' Acts.

The origins of these acts go right back to medieval England, but the colonial acts had more recent connections with the English Masters' and Servants' Acts of the eighteenth and nineteenth centuries. These were passed in the context of the increasing urbanism of the industrial revolution, the breakdown of those bonds of deference which were passing with the old Britain, and the beginning of the idea that all work relations could be seen in forms of domestic service—hence the language of the Acts' titles.[34]

In Australia the first Masters' and Servants' Act was passed in New South Wales in 1828 (it was the 1823 British Act applied to the colony), and in the 1830s and 1840s all the other Australian colonies passed similar acts and amended them to extend their coverage. The Acts enforced verbal or written contracts between employers and employees in practically every field, except for seamen and clerks, who signed specific contracts. Contracts were of three types; the indentures; those which dealt with a certain job (such as sowing a field of wheat), and those which tied a worker to a master for a period of time (such as six months or a year). Most were of the first and second kinds, but what made these contracts different from any signed today was the criminal sanctions which underpinned them. Employees could be charged by their masters with many things—absconding from work; refusing or neglecting to work; wilfully or negligently spoiling, destroying or losing property; insolence and insubordination; failing to obey instructions. For breaches of the acts, they could be sent to jail for up to six months, or fined and ordered to forfeit all wages and, to add insult to injury, they could then be sent back to work for their original masters. Employers could be taken to court by workers for refusing to pay wages; not providing proper rations; ill-usage; detention of property. But they could only be fined and ordered to pay damages. The inequalities in the acts make more sense when we see that their longer titles were 'an Act for the Better Regulation of servants, labourers and workpeople'.[35]

The Acts were obviously designed to permit employers to make the free labour relationship resemble the assigned servant one, it was no coincidence that two amendments which tightened the existing Acts in New South Wales and Tasmania accompanied the end of transportation. However, many of the charges brought against employees were for insubordination, so the Acts must be seen as an attempt to enshrine in law the patterns of deference that employers, especially those of some status, thought they were owed by the workforce.[36] Masters wanted the law to force their workers to work hard, loyally and soberly. Manning Clark shows something of what the workers wanted:

> In December 1839 Learmonth, a squatter near Ballarat in the western district of Victoria, lost nine hundred lambs from his fold during a severe storm. He sent two shepherds, Mooney and Gabb, to search for them, but they procured rum from a dray that arrived at the run and became as drunk as fiddlers. The two of them and all the men who had come for the shearing spent the next day in bed recovering from the debauch. Two weeks later Learmonth discharged all the shearers for repeated drunkenness, whereupon they celebrated their departure with such gusto that his cook-housekeeper, Ben Good, did nothing for two days, being, as his master put it, 'unwell from the effects of drink brought up by the dray'. On one beautiful bright day in April 1840 Learmonth went up to see the fence-splitters on his run, and when he returned, he found all the men raving drunk from the wine that had been brought up from Melbourne the previous day. For days the men remained drunken and unruly and threatened to bolt till Learmonth appeased them, at least for the moment, by handing out more bottles of wine.[37]

It is not wise to overemphasise the importance of the alcohol, although, in the colonies it assumed an importance unknown today. However, the quotation does show that these workers were an independent lot. In the final analysis, this independence is based on the workers' ideas about their rights and privileges as 'free-born Englishmen'. Workers had often come to Australia to escape the social structure in Britain. Currency lads and lasses were universally known as free-thinking types and ex-convicts could hardly be expected to give deference to a class of people to whom they had been assigned. Nevertheless, although thousands of cases were brought by masters against insubordinate servants, thousands more were over wages.[38] Servants on time contracts, particularly those bought out under indenture, continually 'bolted' in search of higher wages, which, given the chronic labour shortage, was easy to find. There is, though, a further implication of this. Despite the fact that the Acts were plainly directed at servants, despite the fact that the magistrates, especially in the bush, were pastoralists themselves and did not treat servants favourably, servants nevertheless used the Acts themselves whenever they could. Obviously, the courts and the acts had a kind of legitimacy to workers. This was a shock to some employers. *The Port Phillip Gazette*, in the midst of the 1843 depression, peevishly complained that

> ... men who would be respectable members of society if they could—and who ought to be respectable members of society, [were] sneaking about the Police office like so many thieves and vagabonds, and afraid to meet the eye of an acquaintance—far less of a friend—simply because they are unable to meet the demands of their laborers.[39]

It seemed that the world had been turned upside down, the natural order had been inverted. Yet there is yet another point that needs to be considered. Most rural workers were either isolated or itinerant and so were impossible to organise, yet knowledge of pay rates and conditions of work circulated freely amongst them, as did the knowledge of what was a fair rate. Russell Ward has argued that it was in the independent nature of the outback shearers that we find the forerunner of an Australian working-class consciousness, but it seems more sensible to look for it amongst all rural employees.[40]

Independence and deference are states of mind, but states of mind are partly the products of the way work is organised, and the level of organisation of the workers. Most male free workers worked on jobs that were seasonal. Steady work with one employer might only have been done by the respectable clerk in an office or the highly sought after artisan, the possessor of a skilled trade. Even within the peak period of demand work was intermittent.

Seamen, for example, signed on for one voyage at a time. Sealers signed on to sealing gangs for a specified time, were dropped at isolated islands to make their kills and then were picked up at the expiration of their contract. Whalers, like seamen, signed on for a voyage. Shearers shore a flock of sheep and moved on. Harvesters harvested a crop and moved on. Sawyers and timber cutters cut their timber on contracts and stockmen drove a herd of cattle to its destination, then went onto another.[41] There were peaks and troughs in the demand for labour, for example, when crops were ripe there was plenty of demand for rural workers, but it dried up when the harvesting was done.

Nevertheless, country workers seemed to be able to switch jobs fairly easily. Benjamin Boyce, for example, a seaman by trade, jumped ship in Adelaide in 1842 and took up a job on a dairy. Then in quick succession he went cutting hay, splitting trees and putting up rough houses and fences, working for a publican, shearing sheep, mowing wheat, and ploughing and driving bullocks before he went back to shearing and harvesting.[42]

Shepherds were the exception to the rule. They acquired a reputation for listlessness and dullness (and to many observers mental deficiency), but their work was hard, demanding, dangerous and highly responsible. They looked after flocks of hundreds of sheep, watching over them by day, rounding them up and enclosing them by night. It was an isolated, lonely job, made even less pleasant by the ubiquitous dingo, the hostile Aborigines and squatter-masters who took advantage of their isolation to exploit them.[43]

Work was more stable in the towns, many workers found regular jobs with single employers for one, or two, or several years. Most jobs were related to urban growth although, by 1850, only 25 percent of the population lived in towns. Builders were in great demand, especially skilled tradesmen such as carpenters, bricklayers, stonemasons and blacksmiths. In Sydney at least, there was a growing manufacturing sector. Some factories like Simeon Lord's woollen mill and the Gas Light Company works employed between 20 and 40 regular workers, but these were small compared with the big convict works. Several hundred convicts in over 40 different trades worked in the Sydney lumber yard and between 100 and 250 women worked in the Parramatta Female Factory.

By 1850 there were 390 factories in New South Wales, although to call them factories is a misnomer because most were tiny workshops where a master-craftsman employed a labourer and a few apprentices. In these artisanal trades were wheelrights, shoemakers, blacksmiths, tanners, and iron-founders. There were millers, salt makers, harness and saddle makers, brewers, rope makers and those who made tallow, the industries necessary for the survival of the tiny colonies. In 1850 there were about 1000 workers in

Sydney's factories and about 2000 more in other jobs and trades.[44] This was men's work! From the first 'free' job given to the first 'free' worker in Australia, the paid workforce has been divided on grounds of gender. Whilst men could, and did, do practically any kind of paid work, with the notable exception of domestic work, women could do little except that domestic work. There was no clothing industry to speak of, that big employer of women's labour in Britain. What seamstresses and laundresses there were worked from their homes and were constantly undercut by the manufacture of clothing and laundrying in the female factories. Some women went into business as publicans, schoolteachers, small retailers and the like, but really the only two options open to women were domestic service or marriage.[45]

Work for domestic servants in Australia was easy to find but hard to do. There were few of the grand houses of England in the Antipodes, therefore little of that highly developed specialisation of tasks found below stairs. This, and the seemingly permanent shortage of domestics, turned the typical servant into a maid-of-all-work, one who could cook, clean, wash, sew, care for children, and so on. Bigger households could divide the work. There, kitchen maids worked with ladies' maids and the maids-of-all-work.[46] Older women were more likely to be housekeepers, a job with much higher status than maid, and much greater responsibility. Most housekeepers tended to be ex-convict women. Free settlers much preferred their maids to be free rather than ex-convicts, although they complained constantly about both. Caroline Chisholm once remarked that middle-class colonial women, used to dealing with assigned servants, treated their free domestics very badly.[47]

Faced with the hard and heavy work in service, women grasped the alternative—marriage—with both hands, only to find that the work was much the same, albeit done without the supervision of a mistress. In the towns the domestic division of labour was just as strict as the division of labour in the paid workplace. There was men's work and there was women's work. Men did heavy and handy work, women cooked, sewed, cleaned, washed and raised children. But they did more than that. Frequently they washed and cooked for neighbours, grew and sold produce and took in lodgers. In fact they did a range of tasks that would bring some extra income to the family.

On the small farms in the country, the division of labour was a little more flexible. Certainly women did the same work as their sisters in the towns, but they would also raise livestock, do general farm tasks and help in the fields come harvest time.[48] The pastoralists, though, employed few married women. Pastoralists regarded families as drains on profits, and much preferred to employ single men. This practice reduced the number of female immigrants but it also had the effect of improving the position of the domestic servants already in the colonies. The scarcity of domestic servants had one other effect too. In Australia, and particularly in the isolated areas of the various colonies, the work done by wealthy and poor women was in some ways quite similar. Not that middle-class women worked in the fields or on the farm, but they had to do household tasks which they would not have done in Britain, and they even seemed to enjoy doing them. Penelope Selby, a Port Phillip settler, wrote home to England in 1841 how she had become a 'first rate dairy woman and [I] can cure meat, make butter, cheese, fatten calves or pigs . . . [Additionally], I have all the baking, washing and in fact everything to do and that I am now within a month of my confinement you will allow that I have no time for dress or play . . .'[49] But this was the work which working-class women and women on poor farms had always done.

3 Working in the country

When Tom Roberts was painting 'Shearing the Rams', he remarked

> So, lying on piled wool bales, and hearing and seeing the troops come pattering into their pens, the quick running of the wool-carriers, the screwing of the presses, the subdued hum of hard fast working, and the rhythmic click of the shearers, the whole lit warm with the reflection of Australian sunlight, it seemed that I had there the best expression of my subject, a subject noble enough and worthy enough if I could express the meaning and spirit—of strong masculine labour, the patience of animals whose year's growth is being stripped from them for man's use, and the great human interest of the whole scene.[1]

The key idea is his identification of 'strong masculine labour' with the shearers. Of course Roberts was part of that late nineteenth-century nationalism which presented the bushman as the character on which a new nation might be built. But the icon that he, as well as Furphy, Lawson and Paterson chose, was a man at work. They were presenting an image of 'men's work', of strong masculine labour. There is no natural underpinning to men's work or women's work; both are cultural constructions, albeit extraordinarily powerful ones. 'Masculine' work in the nineteenth century was constructed against the image of women's work and defined in the exclusion of the non-European worker. Then it was built in opposition to the settled and constricted life of the small 'cocky' farmer so it expressed that sense of independence and solidarity that has become known as Australian mateship.

The Australian economy in the second half of the nineteenth century was driven by wool, gold and construction. Between 1860 and 1900 the quantity of wool exports rose from 100 million pounds to 500 million pounds weight and wheat production rose from 2.6 million bushels in 1855 to 48.3 million in 1901. Gold production jumped from 9.9 tonnes in 1857 to 106.4 tonnes in 1899. Between 1856 and 1901 the number of people employed in rural industries rose from 99 000 to 340 000, about 25 percent of the total workforce. By the early 1890s about half the population lived in the rural areas, and, crucially for this chapter, men there outnumbered women by about two to one.[2]

Strong masculine labour

What is striking about the bushman was his mobility in a rural economy that made independence necessary and in a rural labour market that was overwhelmingly masculine. Gold-diggers, drovers, shearers, shed hands, farm labourers, railway navvies, bullockies, splitters, fencers, sawyers and many others made up this itinerant workforce. Gold prospectors' horizons were bounded only by the continent or even other continents. By contrast farm labourers worked their way around their local district. The shearers fell in between. It was no coincidence that Roberts chose to lionise shearers because in the brave new world of late nineteenth-century nationalism it was the shearers who best filled the requirement for a new, genuinely 'Australian' symbol.

Gold mining in the nineteenth century travelled in a great arc from the south-east corner of the continent north through the eastern colonies, west across the top, and south through Western Australia to Kalgoorlie. Gold miners rushed from one field to the next, magnetised by fantastic rumours of new El Dorados, swarming like ants in the nooks and crannies of creeks or over the granite outcrops, forming booming and bustling gold towns which frequently faded away when disappointed diggers moved on. Ballarat and Bendigo, Ararat and Castlemaine in Victoria; Kiandra, Young and Gulgong in New South Wales; Port Curtis, Gympie, Cloncurry, Palmer River and Charters Towers in Queensland; Pine Creek and Yam Creek in the Northern Territory; Halls Creek, Yilgarn, Southern Cross, Coolgardie and Kalgoorlie in Western Australia—these are the golden names. Most of them are now solid and respectable towns, centres for their districts, riding resurgent mineral booms or waves of nostalgia catering to tourists. But most of these fields no longer exist, except as apparently random piles of bricks and cemeteries with headstones which testify to the fact that miners died young, for whether they worked in the settled districts of Victoria, the jungles of Queensland or the deserts of Western Australia, mining was a hard and dangerous job.

Although the itinerant gold seekers were individualists, they were not necessarily capitalists. Their preferred way of organising their work was not as bosses or as employees, but as partners or members of a group who could share the work, the risks, the capital, the profits and the losses of their mines. Most were alluvial miners, who in a pinch could afford some machinery to get beneath the surface, but who could not afford the heavy costs of really deep mining. Their shares might have been equal or they might not. One person out of ten might hold eight shares and the other nine two shares between them. Goldfield towns took on different characters depending on the nature of these arrangements and how easy it was to dig the gold out of the ground. Tent towns became mortar and brick towns only if there was gold far beneath the surface and there was capital to employ the machinery and the miners to dig it out. In some towns a big proportion of miners were 'tributers', men who leased a portion of an existing mine and paid a share of what they won from it to the owner as a 'tribute'. In one sense, in a town where capital and labour faced each other across the mine site, tributers retained their highly prized independence. However, in another, the tribute system was anything but rosy. The kind of labour force mine owners wanted was tied to the ease with which gold was being extracted. When there was plenty of gold and dividends to shareholders were high they employed workers as wage labour. When they were finding too much stone and not enough gold they were more inclined to put the workers on contract as tributers, let them do the work but take a share of what they found. It was a system that worked in gold mines, in the South Australian copper mines and others, but it was a system that was more to the benefit of the owners than to the workers.[3]

One pronounced result of the lust for gold was its effect on the local and inter-colonial labour markets. When gold was discovered at Ballarat 'the whole town of Geelong [was] in hysteria, gentlemen foaming at the mouth, ladies fainting, children turning somersaults'. Latrobe wrote that in Melbourne 'cottages are deserted, houses to let, business is at a standstill and even the schools are closed . . . the ships in the harbour are to a great extent deserted'.[4] When men swamped the eastern goldfields in Victoria they left labour shortages not only in Melbourne, but in all the eastern colonies. When they rushed to the Palmer River they abandoned pastoral and agricultural work not only in North Queensland but also in New South Wales and Victoria. And such was the rush to Coolgardie and Kalgoorlie in the 1890s that Victoria, by then in the depths of the 1890s depression, actually suffered a net loss of population.

The effects of this on an unregulated labour market can well be imagined. When thousands of men left Sydney for Port Curtis in 1858, those who decided not to go demanded and won higher wages, while in the 1850s in Victoria wages doubled. However, there was another side to the story. Very few diggers struck it rich, and most returned to their homes broke and hungry to flood the labour market they had just left, and to work for what they could get. Squatters and politicians paid rewards to prospectors who found gold because they knew it meant not only extra sales of meat but the extra labour of disappointed diggers.[5] Squatters also used the labour of part-time diggers, who worked during the seasonal peaks then disappeared to a new or old goldfield. As the historian of Victoria's western district, Margaret Kiddle, observed, squatters were both irritated and pleased. They had their workers but 'actually, as always, they found that labour was maddeningly independent and forever on the march from one job to another'.[6] Where gold diggings were a clear alternative, workers could afford to be independent.

When the English novelist Anthony Trollope visited Australia in 1871 and 1875, he was most impressed with the structure and character of the pastoral workforce. Observing their itinerant lives and independent character he called them 'the nomad tribe' of pastoral workers.[7] The 'nomad tribe' was a product of the structure of rural industry in Australia. Closer settlement in Victoria, South Australia, Tasmania and the areas closer to the New South Wales coast meant that it was largely an outback New South Wales and Queensland phenomenon, because pastoralism still dominated there. Climate, costs, distance and the system of land tenure encouraged big, sometimes huge, pastoral holdings, owned often by one man, a family, a company or, increasingly as the century passed, the banks and pastoral companies. Heavy requirement for capital put a share in the industry out of the reach of the bulk of the wage-earning population, who were hence forced to remain as a wage-earning, rural proletariat.[8] At least, they were until closer settlement spread to the outback and farmers began to break up the big estates and populate the countryside with small-holding 'yeoman' farmers.

These big stations were sometimes more like small towns than farms. In the 1860s Jondaryan station in the Darling Downs employed a permanent workforce of about 135, comprising shepherds, lambers and 'generally usefuls'.[9] On Mt Sturgeon in Victoria in the 1860s, apart from the household staff of gardeners, milkmen, coachmen, grooms and the like, there was a 'superintendent, a head overseer, three working overseers, six boundary riders, fifteen shepherds, a saddler, bullock drivers and stockriders, besides several hut cooks, a thistle cutter's cook, a stonemason, a ploughman and a number of boys'.[10]

There are three points to make about these permanent hands. Permanence was always relative. Shepherds, long thought by historians to be immobile, went regularly from job to job in search of higher pay. Advancing technology in the form of fencing drastically reduced the number of shepherds and hutkeepers from the 1860s on and threw them onto the rural labour market. Boundary or stock riders replaced them—young men, fond of horses and inclined to wear 'cabbage tree hats, red crimean shirts, Bedford cord breeches and long boots'.[11] These stable employees were outnumbered by as much as two to one by the itinerant workers who worked on contracts, day or piece rates. So at Mt Sturgeon, in addition to the permanent hands were 'eighty two labourers, forty seven thistle cutters, eight hut cooks, thirteen boys, four bullock drivers, six boundary riders, fifty eight carriers and forty two fencers engaged in contract work'.[12] Shearers are absent from this list, but shearing was only one of three peak work periods on the stations; the other two were lambing and wool washing. Other visitors included rabbit trappers and 'roo shooters, well sinkers and dam makers, drovers, splitters and fencers, and of course the shearing workforce, which was divided into many different occupations. In the sheds were shed hands, washers, picker uppers, rollers, dumpers, sweepers, classers, dossers and cooks, who all served those masters of the bush, the shearers.[13]

Shearers' work was archetypically itinerant. They ranged across the colonies and some even travelled to New Zealand to work. For most shearers the season lasted between a few weeks and several months. John Merritt estimates that about 20 000 shearers worked in New South Wales during the shearing season and about 33 000 all up shore in the eastern colonies.[14] That famous war historian C.E.W. Bean described the shearing season as a wave: 'The wave started in the four corners and along the innermost borders of Queensland. Some part of Australia is always in motion with it for by the time it dies on the outermost edge, it is beginning again in the centre'.[15]

When they weren't shearing shearers took up other occupations like clearing, fencing, rabbiting, building or mining. However, as the century passed and the number of small farms rose, shearing became the other job which kept farmers solvent. These shearers were not the wanderers that early generations were, or that were to be found in the backblocks of New South Wales and Queensland. The professional shearers still ranged across colonial borders, but the local shearers were less inclined to travel far from farm, home and family.[16]

Sheep and cattle production threw up the archetypal nomad tribesman. However, the unmechanised state of agriculture and its seasonal nature also threw up its own itinerant workforce, which moved around a much more restricted area. Wherever there was a crop to be picked this casual labour force was there to pick it. And the range of jobs it did was amazing—potato picking, pea picking, hop picking, onion picking, cutting lucerne, fruit picking and hoeing and manuring orchards, ploughing, harrowing, sewing, reaping, binding and threshing wheat, oats and barley, sewing rape seed, sewing bags, thatching roofs, felling trees, chopping wood, building walls, tending gardens, slaughtering and curing meat, draining swamps and grubbing roots, grooming and feeding horses, and carting manure.[17] From the 1880s, however, mechanisation began to kill off this kind of work. A good number of the seasonal wheat growing jobs declined, and so did the population of the country, as farmers began to buy combine harvesters and do the work themselves. Their former workers had little option but to take up their own farms if they could or move to the cities. According to the 'swaggie' Joseph Jenkins, this workforce could find work for only three months of the year, in December, January and February, when the crops were ready to harvest. Then there would be hundreds of weary feet shuffling from farm to farm trying to find a job. If they were lucky they might pick up work here and there or find employment on public works set up by governments to mop up winter unemployment. In bad seasons farmers could not afford to hire hands, then farmers found their itinerant workforce a pest and often drove applicants for work away with dogs. Jenkins did not like Victorian farmers. He thought they had three characteristics; 'exhausting the land, abusing horses and exploiting their workers'.[18]

We began this section with Tom Roberts' portrait of strong masculine labour and we should now explore this a little further. In the nineteenth century there were men's jobs and women's jobs, masculine and feminine work, which expressed and were reinforced by ideas about masculinity and femininity. In one sense the development of masculine work was a necessity in the bush because of this preponderance of single men, although this should not blind us to the numbers of women in the gold rush towns, the navvies' camps, and on the pastoral stations. Men, keeping company at work and at play, in the shearing shed or in the pub, created that masculine culture which valued competition and mateship. Women were the moss these male rolling stones could not gather.

However, there is more than this to consider. Working-class writers and radicals in the nineteenth century assiduously promoted a concept of manliness that related directly to the workplace and the relationship between 'master and man'. In the work of the Queensland socialist William Lane, manliness meant socialism, independence from the unmanly domination of the worker by his boss.[19] To the unionist W.G. Spence, manliness meant an engaging egalitarianism: 'Though forced to earn his living by working for another man, the Australian worker never lost his independence of spirit. He would not cringe to anyone. The employer was to him nothing more than a man—certainly no better than himself.'[20]

Tom Roberts might not have been thinking of this, though his place in the strongly nationalist Hiedelberg school of painting might lead us to conclude that he was. Roberts was describing the spectacle of shearers at work, their hard physical labour, the depths of their stamina, their roughly confident skill. Heavy manual labour has always been central to constructions of men's work and, hence, to constructions of masculinity. In the final analysis this boils down to men's bodies, and the valuation which is put on what men's bodies can do (and by extension what women's bodies supposedly cannot do). Work and manliness in the nineteenth century, then, were tied to independence and hard physical labour, and these were found in the bush workers. Yet both of these ideas are complex and contradictory because they were expressed in another context which sharply contrasted with the independent life of the 'nomad tribe', the small selector on the family farm.

Love of freehold

Although between 10 and 13 percent of bush workers were women, the 'bush' was mainly a masculine world, and our images of the inhabitants of the 'bush' are mostly masculine images.[21] The process by which the country as opposed to the 'bush' achieved a gender balance began after the Victorian gold rushes, when millions of acres were opened up for small-scale agriculture. Agriculture was a family business, where most rural women lived and worked. Independence to these women and their children was a world away from the world of William Lane or W.G. Spence.

From the 1860s, when the fourteen-year leases granted to the New South Wales squatters in 1847 were due to run out, each of the colonial parliaments passed laws which opened up the pastoral holdings to selection and purchase. Previously no more than 4000 land barons ran their sheep across empires of over 160 million acres, on rents of little more than the metaphorical peppercorn. Henceforth blocks of up to 640 acres could be selected by anyone with the capital, on condition that they reside on and improve the land. At first the blocks were small—ten acres around the outskirts of country towns—but later most were 320 acres, large enough, so legislators thought, to produce a new model citizen and a new model society.[22]

The stout yeoman farmer was the model and the myth. He was, as any dictionary might say, brave, doughty, vigorous, staunch and sturdy. Australians have a long history of wishing upon themselves a society based on the yeoman farmer. He underpinned the ideology behind selection, he was the basis of the closer settlement schemes of the late nineteenth and early twentieth century, and the returned diggers were to be turned into yeoman farmers in the soldier settlement schemes after World War I. It was an environmental vision in a way, almost as though those 'manly' virtues would spring from the soil itself. It was also a social vision, for the yeoman farmer was three things. He was independent (not for him wage labour and class conflict); he was conservative, a conservativism deriving from the possession of property; and he was a family man, the head of a happy and contented family living in a rural arcadia.

Ideologically, this independence linked the selector to both the gold digger and to the pastoral proletariat. Each escaped the relations of capitalism in one sense or another. Digger and selector both escaped them altogether. William Lane's mythical proletariat escaped them by overturning capitalism itself. W.G. Spence's proletariat escaped them by asserting that a man was as good as, if not better than, his master. The yeoman myth had a second personification too, a countryman, a refugee from the blight of the emerging industrial city.

These images illustrate the point that the yeoman ideal represented different things to different people. The first personification was a bourgeois myth and its appearance fits into a particular conjuncture of Australian history. The Melbourne *Argus* coined the phrase 'unlock the lands' and it was adopted as a slogan by the urban middle class, which wanted to smash the political power of the squattocracy by breaking its monopoly of the land. Selection, then, was a political weapon to the city politicians and they seized the leadership of the selection campaigns. Certainly they had other motives. An hereditary class of monopolists offended the principles of equality of opportunity. A prosperous farming community would be a consuming community, opening business to the urban manufacturers and merchants; governments, too, needed the funds which land sales would bring them.[23] But the vision must be taken seriously. As H.J. Wrixon, a Victorian country parliamentarian once observed, 'This love of freehold, of having a good home of his own to live in and leave to his children was inextricably and deeply connected with all the qualities which went to make good citizenship.'[24] Good citizenship underpinned the bourgeois vision, a vision made all the more desirable by the threat of thousands of unlucky and discontented diggers and thousands of hungry and angry city labourers. The prospect of land has always been a safety valve used to draw the steam away from urban working-class discontent, and selection was no different.

The other vision was the vision of the poor, the urban workers and the frustrated diggers, who yearned to return to that golden age before the agricultural and the industrial revolutions, when everyone had land. Historians now regard this as a myth, but the idea that the factory system had uprooted a prosperous and contented peasantry from its lands was cemented in the minds of the British workers who came to Australia. The land policies of the British Chartists, the Homestead Acts of the North American parliaments, the land hunger of the Irish labouring class all found an imagined home in the Australian countryside. And the urban masses, the ex-diggers, even the rural proletariat, formed that mass rank and file of radical politics in the 1860s to the 1880s which organised, demonstrated and sometimes rioted at the instigation of its bourgeois leadership in the struggle to 'unlock the lands' and break the power of the squatters.[25]

Historians agree that ultimately selection was a failure. The pastoralists began buying properties they squatted on while their political representatives delayed the first selection acts from their sanctuaries, the Legislative Councils. They were already favoured by the forms of the early acts and then they ruthlessly dummied, peacocked and bribed their way into freehold possession of vast tracts of Australia. In New South Wales in 1886, there were 552 holdings bigger than 10 000 acres, which was one half of all alienated land. Squatters took five-sixths of all the land opened by the first Victorian Act in 1861 and in the 1880s ten families between them owned two million acres. Even in South Australia, where selection was most successful, one-third of alienated land was owned by just 131 men. But their success was short lived. So many went into debt to purchase their runs that it would be more accurate to describe the city banks and pastoral finance companies as the real beneficiaries of selection.[26]

On the other hand, the success of the acts in installing a yeomanry on the land was also mixed. It was most successful in South Australia and least in New South Wales. In Victoria and Queensland perhaps 50 percent of those who selected land and settled on it became prosperous. In practically every case these were farmers with skill and capital, with kin networks to help with the work, who settled on rich soils in places like the Eastern Riverina in New South Wales and the Darling Downs in Queensland. The sign of their prosperity was the increased size of their holdings, for selectors quickly found that a 640-acre farm was too small.[27] They increased their holdings, though, at the expense of the selectors who did not succeed, who abandoned their farms and whose flight back to the cities or towns was the sign of their failure. Their struggle was against overwhelming odds. Lack of capital, skill and experience, holdings that were too small, governments unwilling to do more than provide the infrastructure for selection, meant that they slipped into a downward spiral of debt, poverty and squalor.

The domestic economy of the selector household began with selection itself. The yeoman farmer in the ideal was a family man so although single men and single women could select, the acts themselves were structured to settle a patriarchal family on each selection. Dependent wives and children could not select so, from the beginning, a type of family was implied. When it became apparent that an individual selector could not acquire enough land for a successful farm, families often selected together. Parents selected land next to selections made by adult sons. Brothers selected land alongside brothers and sisters. It was these combinations, essentially expressions of kinship relations, which combined land, capital and labour, that won the battle for survival. As Grimshaw et al. suggest, it was often the young couple without kin, without that extra land, capital and especially labour, that failed.[28] Kin was sometimes replaced by neighbours, especially in those areas where one ethnic group tended to concentrate. The clannish German Lutherans illustrate the point. Buxton described one entire community—eight families, two single men, 56 in all, who travelled from South Australia to Jindera near Albury in carts and wagons to farms of 320 acres on the Walla Walla station. Irish families, too, concentrated at Warnambool and Koroit in Southern Victoria where they grew potatoes and formed close-knit and well-off communities.[29]

Once having selected and settled on the farm, everybody in the family worked it. The head of the household, the male, was regarded as the most important. The men usually selected the farm and went on ahead of their families to build shelters and start work. They were the major source of labour for the farms' major source of income, and the direction the farm took was their decision. They brought other income to the family too, because many had to combine farming with paid work elsewhere; working the plough for neighbours, shearing for local squatters, working on government jobs such as road and rail building or share farming. A big proportion of ongoing capital was supplied in this way.

Men did not do work in the home, but on the small selections women certainly did men's work in the paddocks, for the exigencies of building a farm meant that the ideal of separate spheres for men and women had to be abandoned. The extent of women's work depended largely on the kind of farm it was, on its size, its health and the nature of the family, but certain kinds of work were common to all selector women. Women milked cows, fed chooks, gathered eggs, made butter and cheese, baked bread, preserved fruit and grew vegetables. Their domain was the near regions of the farm and what they produced was bartered or sold to neighbours or to shopkeepers in nearby towns. This kind of work did not replace their cooking, cleaning and mending. It was added to it. And women's work did not end there. On uncleared farms daughters worked alongside fathers and sons in the fields. Wives of dairy farmers worked alongside their men in the constant round of milking. Wives harvested wheat and maize crops and planted and pulled potatoes. And when husbands and sons went away to work, women ran their farms, often for months at a time.[30]

However, women worked hardest at bearing and raising children. Selectors' families were always large. Eight children seems to have been the norm but there were plenty of families of up to sixteen. This meant that, on average, selectors' wives might spend over twenty years in the worriesome and exhausting tasks of bearing and raising children. Isolation, problems of hygiene and ignorance made this a hazardous business and child mortality was high.[31] If there was one saving grace for women in big families, it was the fact that older children could look after the younger and so relieve the mother of some of her work.

What was a problem for the mother, though, was often a bonus for the farm. One South Australian family in the 1850s, the Herbigs, had sixteen children and they were all working:

> Gathering in the sheaves at harvest time saw all hands at the wheel. The day began at 4.00am and finished 10.00pm. Armed with scythes, and under Papa's spirited urgings and example, the seven eldest sons cut one behind the other, with the fastest at back and front to ensure a steady pace. Behind them, Caroline and the smaller children tied the sheaves with 'twine' made from corn stalks.[32]

Children were valued for their labour, and labour they did from the age of four or five. Buxton tells of Emily Krause who, at eight years of age, drove horses pulling harrows while her father broadcast wheat by hand from the back of a cart.[33] More commonly children helped with clearing, moved stock, gathered firewood, dug gardens, hunted game, helped in harvesting and in a range of other peripheral tasks.[34] The work daughters did depended largely on the number of sons in the family. Many sons meant that daughters were more likely to work in the mother's domain. Few sons meant that daughters like Kate Currie, from a Gippsland selector's family, cut scrub, felled trees, cut thistles, cut corn, dug drains and chopped logs, just as her father did.[35]

Children were not paid for their work, any more than wives were. Their rewards were the distant promises of inheritance if they were sons and dowries if they were daughters. If children were to earn a cash income they had to go off the farm to do it. Kate Currie's brother Tom went to Melbourne to work on the railways, but most joined shearing teams or ploughed, sowed and reaped for neighbouring farmers. Tom Currie sent part of his wages home.[36] Others, like Ned Kelly and his friends, spent the money they made from horse and cattle stealing 'hell raising'. Others saved it to put towards the cost of their own farm.

The amount of labour needed on farms declined as the century passed. Steam power replaced horse and bullock power and machines replaced hand labour. Abandoned blocks were snapped up by bigger farmers with more capital who could afford the new machinery. New technology also lightened women's work. A simple butter churn, for example, cut by half the amount of labour in making butter.[37] A longer-term trend, though, had a greater impact. Many of the things women produced were taken up and produced by rural capitalists. Butter factories replaced the home-churned butter. Canning factories produced canned fruit. Cheese factories replaced home-made cheese. Cheap clothing produced in city factories reduced the amount of clothing produced in the home. Improved transport and distribution did not help the selector's wife to find better markets. Instead they turned her into a consumer. To be sure this was a long and uneven process, but its ultimate result was the establishment of those separate spheres which the institution of selection had largely made redundant.[38]

Independence was achieved by successful selectors. They had avoided wage labour, often they became employers themselves, and generally they became that rural bourgeoisie, the bastion of conservatism that the middle-class city politicians wanted. But their independence was tempered by several factors. Farming is seasonal, so in the most basic sense farmers are dependent on the climate. Floods and droughts, mice and grasshopper plagues, wheat rust and other diseases will always remind farmers just how fragile their hold on the land is. Farming produced goods for international and inter- and intra-colonial markets. When the railways came to Monaro, wheat and dairy farmers envisaged a new world of markets, but they were swamped by better and cheaper wheat and cheese from elsewhere in New South Wales so they lost their own local market.[39] And unstable world commodity prices were a constant threat to all producers, as the terrible crash in wheat and wool prices in the 1920s showed. Then came debt and in some cases chronic indebtedness. This hit the poor selector hardest for the well-off farmer could at least enjoy the good seasons. There was no independence for the former. Theirs was a life of backbreaking toil, endless drudgery and hopeless poverty. Independence was a sham, not only for husbands but also for wives and children, whose unpaid work was more like slavery than a life of freedom. Henry Lawson, himself raised on a selection, once described the selectors he saw:

> [He] saw selectors slaving their lives away in dusty holes amongst the barren ridges: saw one or two carried home, in the end, on a sheet of bark; the old men worked till they died. Saw how the gaunt selectors' wives lived and toiled. Saw elder sons stoop-shouldered old men at 30. Noted, in dusty patches in the scrubs, the pile of chimney-stones, a blue-gum slab or two, and the remains of the fence—the ultimate result of 10 years', 15 years', and 20 years' hard, hopeless graft by strong men who died like broken-down bullocks further out.[40]

A Chinaman will stand for hours

As European settlement spread across the continent Aborigines were gradually incorporated into the European economy. Nowhere were they regarded as useful in anything but their labour. Europeans ignored their production and their medicines but used their capacity for work. This was most obvious in the north. Aborigines were the pastoral industries' labour force. They were the shepherds who looked after the flocks in the Gascoyne region of Western Australia, they were the stock workers who mustered and drove the cattle in the Kimberlies, the Northern Territory and Queensland. Aboriginal women served in the houses of pastoralists, and were used as prostitutes by white workers. They were rarely, if ever, paid for their skills. Instead they were given rations and clothing, housed in squalid camps and kept in order by a mixture of paternalism, beatings and murder. The Queensland historian Ray Evans defines their world as the 'omnipresence of sudden death', but wretched as it was, was it any worse than on the limits of the pastoral frontier?[41]

Frontier warfare followed a depressingly similar pattern. Pastoralists moved their stock into new pastures, and the stock, no respecter of water holes, grasses or sacred Aboriginal sites, muddied, trampled and ate their way through Aboriginal culture, religion, game and land. So Aborigines, often with little other recourse, began to kill the pastoralists' stock either for food or as a conscious strategy to drive the invaders away. Then came reprisals. Aborigines were shot. They responded in kind, attacking and killing stockmen. A guerilla warfare ensued until the Aborigines were either massacred, driven to seek the protection of missions, or, recognising their vulnerability, 'came in' peacefully to labour on the stations of the pastoralists who had dispossessed them. However, violence was not the only way in which Aborigines were transformed into a pastoral workforce. Many 'came in' to stations of their own accord, attracted by European goods such as tea, tobacco, sugar, flour and alcohol hoping, perhaps, to weld together this new world with their old culture.[42]

On most of the northern pastoral stations Aboriginal workers were subjected to a regime of strict discipline, imposed by the rifle, the stockwhip and the chain. Children and adults were kidnapped and taken to stations far from their homes to work. If they ran away they were chased, brought back, stockwhipped and, on occasions, beaten to death to serve as a warning to their fellows.[43] Yet ironically, on other stations, Aborigines were able to live some of their traditional life. Pastoralists had no interest in their beliefs or their culture, only in their labour. Often Aborigines lived as clans on stations which were on part of their tribal territory so they were able to maintain both their kin networks and their links with their land. They could also tie their traditional patterns of movement into the station's rhythms, engaging in secret rituals at times when there was not much station work to do. And they could supplement their rations with their traditional food.[44] They had to, of course, because their rations were so meagre.

Pastoralism dominated the north, but Aborigines were also affected by, and worked in other European industries. Mining was one example. Gold miners frequently prospected in front of the pastoral frontier, wreaking havoc on local environments and pushing Aborigines off their lands with frightening rapidity. Being transients, gold miners had little interest in Aborigines' labour, and made use of them only for sexual services or odd jobs.[45] Aborigines used gold miners for the European goods they wanted but few permanent relationships were established like those in the North Queensland tin mines, where local Aboriginal men worked both in the mines and in ancilliary jobs and Aboriginal women worked as domestics. In some circumstances they worked for wages, sometimes on contracts and sometimes just for food and tobacco. The relationships between them and the tin miners were much better than in gold mining, probably because they were able to establish long-term links with miners who were frequently of northern European rather than British origins.[46]

Another industry in which Aborigines were employed, pearling, resembles pastoralism at its worst. Hundreds of coastal Aborigines worked on the pearling boats in the north-west and north-east of Australia in the 1870s and 1880s and hundreds more were kidnapped from inland tribes when labour was short on the coast. And many of these were dumped on offshore islands to be there when needed. Their work was truly appalling, they dived ten hours a day, seven day weeks for the eight months of the pearling season, often given no more than two rests on their boats each day. Women were driven to work 'beachcombing' the reefs by stockwhip wielding overseers. One young woman in the north-west, discovered concealing pearlshell with her foot, was flogged until (as the perpertrator put it) 'she pissed and shit herself'.[47] It is little wonder that the pearling industry was the first in which Aboriginal employment was regulated by law in Western Australia.

If the brutality characteristic of work in the north was not so apparent in the south, it was only because the frontier wars had already been won and lost and the patterns of work had been established. Just as in the north, pastoralism was a big employer in the south and Aborigines did much the same kind of work— mustering, droving, casual labouring, boundary riding and shearing. Women, as usual, did domestic work on homesteads. The circumstances were rather different though, as large kin groups lived less often on the stations as permanent residents and more often in 'black camps' on the outskirts of town, from where they joined the rural, seasonal white workforce. Still, this did not mean that they were paid cash, those living on stations were more likely to be paid in the usual way, with rations and blankets. Nevertheless, Aborigines were able still to rely largely on their traditional resources, also putting these to commercial use by selling fish, and particularly kangaroo and possum skins, to white entrepreneurs.[48]

Closer settlement eventually killed off pastoralism in much of the south and with it the Aboriginal work in the pastoral industry. At first closer settlement, especially in new lands, provided Aborigines with a different kind of work—clearing, root picking, rabbit poisoning, bark stripping and later fencing. But in the long term it broke their remaining physical links with their land, reduced their ability to hunt and gather and so reinforced the process by which they became itinerant rural labourers. Some Aborigines became farmers themselves, but scarce capital, loose tenure of their land and drought meant that few lasted for long.[49]

Whilst most Aborigines were incorporated into the capitalist economy, a significant number were to be found in a quite different circumstance, on Christian missions and government stations. Missions dotted both northern and southern Australia. In their different ways Lutherans, Catholics, Anglicans and others sought out Aborigines both beyond and behind the frontier, protecting them from the onslaught of pastoralists and the depredations of the white settlers and townspeople who followed. As was the case before the gold rushes, their aim was to reclaim 'pagan souls', to teach them the virtues of European culture and instruct in the regular and disciplined performance of work. The government stations, such as those in Victoria, were much the same. Both found children more congenial to work with, young minds were easier to mould than old, so often children were taken from their parents and locked away, there to be trained in manual work if they were boys, or the skills needed to be wives and mothers if they were girls. Ironically it was the labour of adult Aborigines which enabled these places to survive because they grew the food, maintained the buildings, cleaned the houses and in some cases instructed the children in Christianity themselves. Often the men were paid a small wage to familiarise them with the connection between work and reward, but only men were paid because missionaries and station managers tried to construct the men as breadwinners and their women as dependents.[50]

The aim of this training in the white way was to provide the Aborigines with the capacity to make their way in the white world. In reality this was only open to part-Aborigines because social Darwinism, the dominant way of thinking about Aborigines, prescribed that full-blood Aborigines were doomed to destruction in the competition for racial survival. Part-Aborigines, so this doctrine said, would, having learned white skills, be ultimately absorbed both socially and racially into white society. The disappearance of the Aboriginal people was the ultimate solution to the European's Aboriginal problem.

The situation was quite different regarding the other non-European workers, the labourers imported to the colonies from Asia and the Pacific. If Europeans were fatalistic about the disappearance of the Aborigines they were paranoid about the appearance of these very different people from the north. Nevertheless, these workers formed the other half of that non-European workforce and whilst they were also vilified, exploited, abused, terrorised and ultimately excluded from white Australia, they were not killed, at least not in the numbers that Aborigines were.

There were two kinds of imported non-European workers in the nineteenth century. In the first group were those who were indentured to local employers to do work for which the employers could not find suitable labour in Australia. In the nineteenth century the great migrant workers were the Chinese, who went to work in places like Canada, the USA, South Africa, South America and Australia. Indian workers went in huge numbers to labour in places as far afield as East Africa, the West Indies, Fiji and South America. New Hebrideans and Solomon Islanders were seduced away to Peru, to Cuba, Fiji, New Caledonia, Samoa and Queensland. They went to the new world, the colonised world, where European investment in plantation agriculture and mining demanded labour which could not be supplied locally. They were not quite slaves, although the 'coolie trade' replaced the slave trade in places like the Caribbean and South America, and it replaced the convict system in Australia.

Migrants leave their homes for many reasons. They are pushed by unhappy circumstances to try their luck somewhere else. They are pulled by their imagination to a better life elsewhere. They wish ultimately to return to their homes richer and wiser people. Much of the Pacific island labour trade was nothing less than kidnapping. However most migrating labourers went at least half voluntarily, even if they were tricked into a new life that they found even worse than the old. For the Chinese 'coolie', life around Amoy and Macao, whence most of them came, was made hopeless by intense competition for land caused by a booming population. Floods, famines, financial crises and political turmoil drove many rural peasants into overcrowded cities, where they were easy prey for the silken lies of coolie agents. The attraction of a wage acquired by a period of work overseas was the vision of a return to their all-embracing and all-important families with wealth, power and prestige as their reward.[51] In Pacific islands such as the Solomons, young men, who were the major recruits of the labour trade, had little productive role and so little social importance. Little work was needed to survive in island economies and their importance was further diminished by the gradual introduction of new technologies. Young men, therefore, were obvious targets for recruiters. Returning home with material goods meant prestige and currency for reciprocity and exchange, as were the gifts the traders gave their families on signing up. There was the adventure, too, of travel and new experiences.[52]

The trade in indentured Chinese labour was dominated by British firms like Messrs Tait and Co. and Syme, Muir and Co., who employed 'coolie brokers' or 'kheh tons' at the Chinese end, and it was these 'crimps' who enticed, seduced or kidnapped their recruits away to the ships.[53] Pacific islanders were taken to Australia and Fiji for the sugar plantations, so plantation owners organised much of that trade. However, big companies like Burns Philp, the Pacific shipper, and the Colonial Sugar Refinery joined them and smaller companies in the local trade. On the islands, chiefs and 'passage masters' induced the recruits to sign up for their new occupations. Often these passage masters were returned indentured labourers themselves; usually, too, they were men of rank.[54]

The first indentured workers in the colonies were neither Chinese nor Pacific islanders but 'dhangars', some 300 Indian labourers imported to New South Wales in 1837 to work on pastoral stations and in distilleries. In 1844 another 100 became domestic servants. According to employers they were 'tractable and harmless' but slow and inefficient workers.[55] Chinese coolies were imported and indentured from 1848 to 1852. About 3000 worked on some of the big pastoral properties in New South Wales and South Australia as shepherds, farm workers and cooks. Afghans were imported to South Australia in the 1860s to work teams of camels in the centre and north of the colony. And later in the century, as the pearling industry opened up, thousands of Malays, Javanese, Cinghalese, Manilamen and Japanese divers were indentured to the owners of the pearling fleets which operated out of the northern ports.

Indentured migrant workers were supposed to return home after their contracts expired. Many did but many did not, preferring to stay and work in the colonies. Many Afghans stayed, with their camels, and eventually came to dominate the outback carrying business. Japanese pearlers sometimes became their own masters in the pearling waters of the north, and others became cooks in city and town hotels across the continent. Indians, long renowned for their sharp commercial skills, became hawkers of goods around city streets and country towns. Chinese indentured labourers and former miners turned their peasant horticultural skills to market gardening, their woodworking skills to cabinet making in the cities, and their culinary skills to cooking in hotels, or they opened laundries. Others continued to work or went to work on pastoral properties, or on wharves, or fished, made clothes or cut hair for a living. Chinese merchants, who had made profits from supplying goods to the Chinese diggers, became big employers of labour, working large gangs of Chinese clearing scrub and sinking dams in the country, even building a railway line in the Northern Territory.[56] Invariably these were men, for few women were indentured to work and few came to Australia with their men. However, one small group of women did come to Australia on a kind of indenture. Japanese prostitutes plied their trade in mining towns as far apart as Charters Towers and Kalgoorlie.[57] By 1901 there were probably 50 000 non-European workers in Australia, 30 000 of them Chinese. There were perhaps 4500 Indians, between 3000 and 4000 Japanese, about 7500 Pacific islanders and perhaps some hundreds of Afghans, Malays and others.[58]

By far the single biggest group of indentured workers was the Pacific islanders, brought to Queensland to work in the sugar plantations. By the time the trade was wound up in 1904, 62 475 Pacific islanders had come to Queensland, 11 443 in the peak year of 1883. They came, or were taken, from the Solomons, the New Hebrides, New Guinea, Bougainville and the multitudes of islands that make up Melanesia. Why Pacific islanders? Sugar planters believed that Europeans would or could not work in the tropics and Indian indentured labour was made difficult in this period by the restrictions placed on it by the British government and the Indian colonial administration. The Chinese 'coolie' trade was declining and, in fact, ended in the 1870s. Besides, the Pacific islands had certain advantages for the planters; there were no interfering governments to impose their humanitarian principles on the logistics of the trade, the islands were not too far distant, the islanders were known to be easily duped due to their inexperience of the trade and language, and they were thought to be cheap and docile to boot.[59]

The sugar industry began in the early 1860s around Brisbane, but spread quickly up the northern coast. Planters were attracted to the north by the climate, cheap land and the prospect of cheap, indentured labour. Especially around Mackay, the industry began as a plantation economy. A planter aristocracy, modelling itself on its Caribbean and southern USA equivalents, organised an almost feudal society, with themselves at its peak. They lived in grand mansions set amidst lush grounds and gardens, with managers and foremen mediating between the planters at the top and the mass of black, cheap labour at the bottom. But the plantations did not last too long. High costs, poor returns, depression and a liberal government intent on promoting small holdings led to their decline. By the late 1880s, sugar cultivation was dominated by small growers. However, the Colonial Sugar Refinery really monopolised the industry, setting quality controls and prices until the Queensland Government intervened to build cooperative central mills for the 'little man'.[60]

Historians of the labour trade divide the Pacific islanders into two groups, those on their first indentures and those who re-signed for a second or third period of work. The first group signed up for a three-year period at £6 a year, but those who re-signed were much more valued. If they re-signed while still in Queensland, they bargained for higher wages, sometimes up to £25 per year, and shorter contracts, sometimes as short as six months.[61]

The work they did depended largely on what the Queensland government let them do. At first they could be employed to work anywhere in Queensland on any kind of work, but from the 1880s they were segregated into tropical and sub-tropical agriculture and then into unskilled field work. In the 1890s they were excluded from the mills except for handling the cane. In the fields they were forbidden to do work such as ploughing, as the government, under pressure from the white working class, tried to open up occupations to white workers. Generally their work was hard, hot and tiring. They worked long hours, clearing land for cultivation, then ploughing and planting. While the cane grew they cleared the weeds from between the rows, ratooned it then later cut it with big cane knives, loaded it onto carts, trucks or railways and carted it to the mills. They did not necessarily stay on the one property. Sugar cutting is seasonal work. Skilful employers hired workers when they needed them and transferred them when they did not, to those who did. Those who did not work in the fields or mills (and they were the very young, the incapacitated and the few women that arrived), worked as domestic servants.[62]

Queensland government regulations set out their diet but not their hours of work or standards of accommodation. Their food consisted of meat, bread and potatoes, which they supplemented from their own gardens and from fish and game they caught themselves. The plantations housed them in barracks but they preferred to build their own grass huts. While historians disagree about the adequacy of their food and accommodation there is a wide agreement that their mortality rate was astoundingly high. Over the 40 years of the trade an average of 50 per 1000 workers died and in 1884 this reached an astonishing 147 per 1000. Clive Moore provides the most likely reasons why—inefficient and primitive health care, poor sanitation, a different climate combined with hard and alien work, and their culture which saw sickness as untreatable.[63]

The first Chinese to come to Australia were indentured labourers, brought out in the 1840s and early 1850s to work on the pastoral stations. Their numbers were small and in the mid-1850s they were swamped by the mass migration of the Chinese gold miners. By 1855 there were 10 000 Chinese in Victoria, most in Bendigo and Ballarat; by 1857 there were 25 000. Like their European counterparts, the Chinese rushed to new finds wherever they were, so in 1861 there were over 13 000 Chinese in New South Wales, most camped on the diggings there. In 1876, 8000 rushed to the Palmer River find in North Queensland. There were 7000 Chinese on diggings in the Northern Territory in 1888. They were absent from the Kalgoorlie and other Western Australian goldfields in the 1890s only because the government passed legislation excluding them.[64]

Most Chinese miners came from the Sze Yep or Four Districts, in Kwangtung province. They came to Australia in two ways—as individuals or groups financed by speculators or merchant brokers on the 'credit-ticket' system; or as labourers in groups of 25 or 30, hired by syndicates of Chinese merchants. At the Victorian gold fields they lived in camps designated by the Victorian government, an arrangement which suited them because it tied the diggers from the same locality together. Headmen in the camps were usually nominated by the merchant brokers and they supervised repayment of loans and exercised a close watch and control over the Chinese under their sway. From the end of the 1850s they tended to become independent, perhaps when their contracts had been fulfilled and their loans repaid.[65]

As they lived so they worked. Theirs was a highly organised and systematic form of labour, quite unlike the capricious enthusiasms of the white miners. Whereas white miners rushed from find to find, following rumour upon rumour, the Chinese tended to stay and work out a field, fine-combing abandoned mines and diggings, going over tailings and mullock dumps, stripping bare whole areas till not an inch of ground was left unturned. They worked hard, very hard, because they were expected to repay their debts and to repatriate their gold to their families. Their loans were usually given on the guarantee of their families, so sending their winnings home took on an added importance.[66] When the Europeans were not abusing them they sometimes might agree that the Chinese were good miners, especially on alluvial claims. As one official observed: 'They are good miners in the shallow ground. A Chinaman will stand for hours up to the middle in water, scooping gravel from the beds of streams while his partners wash the stuff in cradles or boxes on the bank.'[67] When their contracts expired, when they had made enough gold, or most often when the alluvial gold ran out, thousands of the Chinese diggers went home, but thousands also stayed on to become independent diggers or to do other kinds of work.

Their clannishness, their collective culture, their strong village bonds and their segregated living areas gave the Chinese diggers emotional and physical security, but they also provided an easy target for white diggers, who hated them as a race, despised their capacity for hard work and envied what they thought was their success. European and Chinese diggers did not usually compete for the same ground, but the hostility which permeated the goldfields shaped the social relationships of the fields, especially where the Chinese were able to work a good lead. The 'Canton lead' discovered at Ararat in 1857 by Chinese walking from Robe to Ballarat illustrates this very well. After working the lead to good effect for a short time, the Chinese who discovered it were evicted from it by a gang of white miners.[68] The range of incidents between the two groups ran from casual abuse and violence instigated by roughs or drunken white miners, to the full-scale organised campaigns of violence such as those at Buckland in Victoria and Lambing Flat in New South Wales, where the Chinese were driven from their camps, beaten, humiliated and some killed, their tents torn down and their camps looted and burned. The *Bathurst Star*, its attitude typical of the time, editorialised in 1861:

> Are we, then, tamely to submit to an invasion which, although at present peaceful, will at some future time become troublesome, if not bloody and turbulent, and which certainly seeks to possess itself of our wealth and the good things which ought to be reserved for our own kith and kindred whenever they choose to settle amongst us.[69]

This expresses the right which the white miners felt they had to the gold and it is this which caused each of the colonies with large Chinese populations to begin the process of excluding them. It began in Victoria in 1855, when a poll tax was imposed on the entry of Chinese and a limit placed on the number of arrivals. These Acts were easily evaded in the early years as the ship's captains unloaded their cargoes in South Australia and New South Wales and the Chinese trekked overland to the diggings. However, South Australia passed a similar act in 1857 and New South Wales in 1861. These had the desired effect—Chinese immigration was greatly reduced and the Acts were repealed. Queensland passed its own Act in 1877 after the Palmer River rush and so the first major round of exclusionary legislation was complete. The second round began in the 1880s when, in Charles Prices' term, 'the Great White Walls' were being built around the colonies. Victoria, New South Wales and South Australia re-imposed their laws. Queensland already had its Act. Tasmania joined in in 1887, South Australia applied its Act to the Northern Territory in 1888 and Western Australia passed a Chinese Immigration Act in 1889. The Chinese 'threat' had really dissipated by the 1880s, but racism became moulded into the growing understanding that the colonies might federate. A new, white, brave nation in the Pacific had no place for 'alien races'. The first major piece of legislation to pass through the New Commonwealth Parliament was the Immigration Restriction Bill of 1901, the aim of which, albeit concealed by a language test, was the continued exclusion of non-Europeans from Australia.[70]

4 Working in the city

The golden dreams of independence which had sucked the cities and towns dry of men in the 1850s had evaporated by the 1860s. Most returned, disappointed and despondent, to the prospect of a life of wage slavery, the sort of life they hoped they had left behind. With the digging out of alluvial gold only the slogans of the land reformers offered them any hope. But for most that, too, was chimerical. What did confront them was work in booming but erratic urban economies. The colonies urbanised in the second half of the nineteenth century; as we have seen, about half the population lived in cities and towns. The population of Melbourne and Sydney, though, increased spectacularly; from 123 000 to 474 000 in Melbourne in the three decades after 1861 and from 135 000 to 383 000 in Sydney between 1871 and 1891. In 1891 four out of every ten Victorians lived in the capital and Sydney was not far behind with 34 percent.[1] It is small wonder then that the industrialisation of Australia took off. In just one decade, the 1870s, manufacturing employment jumped from 3.1 percent to 10.7 percent of the total Australian workforce.[2] Housing, factories and other buildings were constructed to house the growing population, and to accommodate manufacturing and trade. Generations of economists have called this period 'the long boom'. We now question that label, as two historians have done in an aptly named article 'A Boom for Whom?'[3] It is impossible, though, to ignore the growth in the economy, the expansion of the big cities and the factors which combined to turn Sydney and Melbourne, at least, into modern cities, because they all shaped city work.

The factory system

The factory system began in Australia in the 1860s, growing slowly and very unevenly. Most manufactured goods were still made in a honeycomb of small workshops and jobbing factories where a single employer bought the labour of just a few tradesmen and their assistants. In Melbourne in the 1880s only half the industrial workforce worked in factories and of these only half employed more than 50 workers. In Sydney there were big factories with more than 100 hands, just as there were in Melbourne, but again most were small. Sydney's flour mills employed an average of ten to sixteen workers. There were only two bootmakers with more than 100 workers in the 1870s and a great deal of manufacturing of bread, confectionery and food was done by shopkeepers who retailed their own products. There were few factories in Perth, Adelaide, Brisbane and Hobart, where for instance clothing and boots were made,[4] but again most work was done in workshops. The ambitious manufacturer well knew the advantages of factory production. After all the factory had been operating for 100 years in Britain, so Australian manufacturing was based on ideas brought from Britain. Adam Smith, the Scottish political economist, had long before told the story of the wonderful wealth produced by factories and how the almost extravagant increases in productivity derived from the sub-division of each job. He used the making of a pin to illustrate the point. One pin maker, he said, working alone making pins could not make more than twenty pins a day. But in a divided process, ten men, each making one small part of a pin, could make thousands:

> One man draws out the wire, another straights it, a third cuts it, a fourth points it, a fifth grinds it at the top for receiving the head; to make the head requires two or three distinct operations; to put it on is a peculiar business, to whiten the pins is another; it is even a trade by itself to put them into the paper; and the important business of making a pin is, in this manner, divided into about eighteen distinct operations, which, in some manufactories, are all performed by distinct hands, though in others the same man will sometimes perform two or three of them. I have seen a small manufactory of this kind where ten men only were employed ... they could, when they exerted themselves, make among them about twelve pounds of pins in a day. There are in a pound upwards of four thousand pins of a middling size. Those ten persons, therefore, could make among them upwards of forty-eight thousand pins in a day. Each person, therefore, making a tenth part of forty-eight thousand pins, might be considered as making four thousand eight hundred pins in a day.[5]

The sub-divided work process fascinated Smith. He thought it increased the dexterity of the worker, endlessly performing the one task. It ended the need for him or her to walk about the factory in search of tools and materials and such a concentrated specialisation, he concluded, could not help but encourage the invention of specialised machinery.[6]

Smith described all of this in *The Wealth of Nations* in 1776, and there were plenty of factories in nineteenth-century Australia which looked remarkably like Smith's hypothetical pin factory. The pin actually provided another British political economist and engineer, Charles Babbage, with a model to expand further what was becoming a science of technique. He agreed with Smith's account of the advantages of sub-dividing the work, but he took it one step further by applying a formula which could replace most skilled workers in a productive process with unskilled workers. He recognised that no manufacturer could work with a completely unskilled workforce, but a combination of skill and unskill could be purchased in exactly the quantity needed if the unskilled parts of a job were peeled off from the skilled. So while a skilled man drew the wire, pointed it, made the head and whitened the finished product, unskilled women and children could straighten it, cut it, head it and paper it, and be given less pay.[7]

Neither of these principles needed to use machinery to subdivide the work and neither did most of the early factories here. Yet the machine came to symbolise the factory system in Australia. When the machine arrived in Australia, Britain was 'the workshop of the world', so when Australian manufacturers claimed to be the bearers of the future, they had history on their side. The great exhibitions of the nineteenth century exalted the machine and manufacturers were quick to claim for themselves the credit for the new world of possibilities that this amazing technology could offer.[8]

Manufacturers were practical men in search of wealth but they found a forceful barrier to their ambitions in their workers. Another English apologist for manufacturing had given them the solution. To Andrew Ure workers, especially skilled workers, were capricious, self-willed and lazy, working in cycles of work–repose–work to the detriment of productivity. The machine was Ure's answer to this problem; his ideal was the fully automated factory where machinery set the pace and rhythm of work and, more importantly, made the skilled worker redundant. He wrote 'It is the constant aim and tendency of every improvement in machinery to supersede human labour altogether, or to diminish its cost by substituting the industry of women and children for that of men, as that of ordinary labourers for that of trained artisans.'[9] Plainly what was beneficial for the manufacturer in all this developing 'science' was not beneficial to the skilled tradesman.

Machines in the nineteenth century were expensive and this limited their application in Australia because manufacturers of all kinds could sell their products only to the limited local market. Therefore many employers did not mechanise but stayed competitive behind high tariff walls, cutting costs by subdividing as yet unmechanised work processes, and organising outwork done by cheap labour. Oddly, mechanisation seemed to gather pace in the

1890s depression, partly because manufacturers could now lease machines rather than buy them, but also because they needed cost savings to stay afloat. Once they had mechanised they gained a huge competitive advantage over those who could not afford to. Their competitors, to survive, had to further sub-divide, drive their workers extra hard or sweat them at outwork. Furthermore, the application of steam or electric power to machines further improved productivity. In Melbourne, by 1890 only 30 percent of boot factories used motive power but by the end of the century practically all did. Electric power allowed employers to replace manual labour across a host of industries, increasing the volume of work that could be done and turning work away from the use of muscle power to the pulling of levers.[10]

The industrialisation of the Australian economies was, in effect, the making of an industrial workforce. The English historian, Edward Thompson, has described how an industrial workforce in Britain was itself manufactured from a population long accustomed to a kind of work in which there was a hazy distinction between work and non-work, where work was tied to the natural rhythms of the seasons, where sociability, manifest in feast days, conviviality and celebration, took precedence over work and where an adequate standard of comfort was preferable to an excessive amount of work. But clocks, rule books, whistles and hooters imposed a new sense of time on work, shaping and moulding a new workforce which was tied to the needs of the factory and to the manufacturer himself. Punctuality was paramount, and obedience, sobriety, respect and hard work were enforced by fines and dismissals. Factory workers came to have no option but to submit, for factory production quickly destroyed the handicraft and cottage industries which preceded it and indeed workers themselves began to demand regular labour and regular leisure to counter the long hours that the factory owners insisted they work.[11]

The factory system implies a workforce which sells its labour power to employers who organise it, and centralise it in places where they can mix machinery and labour together most easily. As a system it was the final result of a process which historians call proto-industrialisation. In this period, in the manufacture of cotton, for example, merchants bought the raw material and 'put it out' by the piece or on contract to people working in their homes. In the longer term they used the capital from their profits and exploited the developments in machinery and steam technology to centralise work and their workers. Proto-industrialisation did not happen in Australia but variants of it did. In the 1860s and 1870s occupations like brick making and tobacco twisting were contracted to workers inside factories who in turn employed children (usually their own) to help them. So children as young as eight or nine were employed as 'puggers up' in brickworks (fetching clay from the claypit from which their fathers made the bricks), or as fetchers, carriers, sorters and spreaders to their fathers in tobacco making factories.[12] It is not surprising that William Alderson, a Sydney manufacturer, could not say in the 1860s how many workers were in his boot factory, because he did not know how many parents employed their children.[13]

This Australian workforce was hardly the same pre-industrial one with which the English manufacturers had to deal. Yet in the 1890s tradesmen and employers could still remember how their work was done in 'the old days'. One bootmaker remembered: 'We seldom worked on Mondays. We worked as we pleased; no-one feared the boss for we lived free lives. I remember men at our factory in Fitzroy had been drinking for two days. The boss went to the hotel and shouted for them and they promised to go to work the next day.'[14] A Melbourne *Age* reporter, unaware of the standing of Monday to workers who liked to make merry on Sundays, observed in 1884 that for 'some occult reason' boot and shoe makers would not work on Mondays.[15] Craft workers were much more likely to assert their independence like this for they possessed the rare and valuable skills that precluded an unskilled worker from doing the same work.

In one sense, these were battles over time. Of course, workers and employers fought over the issue of general working hours, but they also fought over time on the job. The greater the discipline he had the greater control the employer had over time. In small workplaces, the employer himself kept discipline by a judicious mixture of example (many of the new manufacturers were former tradesmen), paternalism and fear. George Gray, a Melbourne builder, sacked a drunken worker one day in 1885 and had to do his work himself: 'So in order to push [the others] a bit and shame them if it were possible to do so I have been working very hard. And this evening I scarcely knew how to walk home. However all my work had no effect on the vermin unless it made them something worse than before.'[16] In 'marvellous' Melbourne there was lots of work for skilled artisans who, it seems, expected to be able to mix work with pleasure. Gray knew this and thought his men were 'impudent in consequence'. He would not have had the same problem in the depression ten years later.

Instead of example some employers tried paternalism. For example, in 1871 'Big' Clarke threw a party for his workers on the completion of his Sunbury, Victoria, mansion:

> The drinkables consisted entirely of immense jugs of beer and decanters of sherry, and it was noticeable that no distinction was made between the poorest guest and the giver of the feast

and his more immediate friends in the fare provided. The more substantial portion of the dinner having been disposed of, the customary loyal toasts were proposed and duly honoured, after which Mr George Browne proposed the health of Mr Clarke and, in doing so, referred to the host's well-known liberality and kindness of heart. Mr Clarke was received with tremendous cheering when he rose to respond, which he did briefly, referring especially to the thorough manner in which all the work about the house had been done.[17]

Other employers, like the Sydney plutocrat, T.S. Mort, sold shares to selected leading hands, passing on to them the responsibility for driving his men. 'I as a capitalist', he said, 'and you as workers should be bound together with the cords of common interest.'[18] But this was unusual; it was more common for employers to organise workers' picnics, retirement dinners, smoke socials, arrange for workforce photographs to be taken, or give prizes to the best apprentices. H.V. McKay, the Victorian farm implement manufacturer, rented houses to selected employees. Others simply walked about their business advising here, solving problems there, hiring and firing workers themselves. Sometimes, in factories which employed children, the boss became a father figure, a patriarch, taking, or being given by parents, authority over the children in his charge.[19]

Paternalism was just one face of the authority which employers possessed. Fear was another and the ultimate sanction by which employers disciplined their workers was, of course, the sack. In a tight labour market this was not such a problem, because a worker could always look elsewhere and employers were reluctant to lose workers. Where the labour market favoured the boss, such as during the 1890s depression, the loss of a job could be catastrophic and many employers used their position to demand long, long hours of work and instant obedience. Children, particularly, were easily replaced. 'Not wanted'; 'impudent, lazy and breaking the cutters, hitting small boys'; 'Foote Robinson dissatisfied, grumbles, etc.—cleaned them out 23/9/90'; 'One (1) oven working, dismissed all hands of no use'. These are typical entries in the engagement books of T.B. Guest, the Melbourne biscuit king, whose young workers liked the work so little they stayed on average just one month with him.[20]

The bigger the business the less this personal approach was likely to work. A report to an inquiry into the Williamstown (Victoria) railway workshops by a Melbourne manufacturer shows the directions employers were taking. He recommended much closer surveillance of the workforce and superintendence of their work by foremen. He wanted workers paid weekly to keep their minds more firmly fixed on their work. He even recommended opening up the toilets. He told the inquiry:

> The water-closets for the workmen I found to be of a far too comfortable description, as the arrangement of having a door fixed to each separate one is quite unnecessary in connection with a public workshop. From the accumulation of waste lucifer matches which I saw on inspecting these places they must be used or occupied more for the indulgence of smoking than for any other purpose.[21]

Lists of rules, too, set out exactly what workers could and could not do and fines made sure that they complied. They usually related to the tasks a worker carried out or to behaviour on the job (no smoking, drinking, skylarking or loafing), but at Ball and Welch's store in Melbourne, people arriving late for work in the morning and leaving by any door other than the one where they were checked out suffered the heaviest fine.[22] Employers thought they had bought their workers' time. Workers often thought otherwise.

Andrew Ure's inspiration, though, gave employers the best means with which to create the workforce they wanted; subdividing the work of the tradesman or tradeswoman, rendering their skills useless, opening up new jobs to unskilled workers and turning these into machine minders. This was the road employers in the clothing and textile trade, boot and shoe factories and the making of foods and drinks took.

'Gentlemen Jims' and the casual poor

Contemporary observers divided paid work in the cities into skilled trades and unskilled work. Workers themselves distinguished the 'aristocrats of labour', who had served an apprenticeship to a craft, from the factory operatives and the unskilled men and women who worked in the casual labour market. Ray Markey, a New South Wales historian, estimates that in Sydney in 1901 between 20 and 25 percent of the workforce were craftsmen.[23] Craftsmen were distinguished from the great mass of the unskilled in two ways. Firstly, their wages were higher; the wages for the unskilled ranged from 50 to 80 percent of the wages for the skilled. Thus a skilled worker in a brewery was paid about 61/- a week in 1900, a brewery labourer 40/6 and a brewery carter and driver 45/6. A skilled confectioner might earn 57/3 while a general hand in a confectionery factory might earn 34/3 and a carter 33/-.[24] But these comparisons are between men. Comparing craftsmen's wages with child labour in a clothing factory is comparing different worlds. Often children were not paid at all until after several months' continuous work.²⁵ Tradesmen were better off in their hours of work too; by the 1890s most had won the eight-hour day.²⁶ The unskilled had not, most still worked up to twelve hours a day. Tradesmen, therefore, were well off, particularly if they had stable employment and worked a full year. However, the Antipodean economy was organised in such a way as to limit the hours of work of even the most aristocratic of trades.

The typical nineteenth-century indenture bound an apprentice to a master for anything up to seven years. It enjoined the child (for apprentices began their working life at thirteen or fourteen) to avoid 'loose companions and places of debauch' and to give him or herself over to the wills of the master and his family, for which he or she would be initiated into the 'arts, mysteries and businesses' of the trade. Harry Braverman, the craftsman turned historian, tried to define for a 1970s readership what the art and mystery were, what in fact was the precise nature of the craftsman's skill. It was, he said, the application of technical and scientific learning to the routine practice of a craft. It meant that the conception and execution of a task was formulated in the one brain. It meant the acquisition of a profound level of knowledge about the character of tools and materials and it demanded the capacity to comprehend and surmount the infinite variety of problems and variations in that material.²⁷ Nevertheless, skill is a very slippery concept because any kind of job requires some level of skill in order to be performed efficiently. So why are some jobs labelled skilled and others not? Historians now agree that there are greater and lesser amounts of skill needed for different jobs, but that the label 'skill' was appropriated by craftsmen and defined in such a way as to restrict entry to their crafts, to exclude men and women whose work was similar, but sufficiently different to be labelled 'unskilled'. Plainly skill is, at least in part, socially constructed.

The learning, the tradesman's tools, the arcane language that craftsmen used to describe their work, the special kinds of clothing they wore, the initiation ceremonies they put apprentices through, and the sense of the trade's history all testified to the view common among craftsmen that in their trade lay their property. Furthermore, they put their property to use, not for the profit of the employer, but to produce an excellent product. The 'excellence of workmanship', the 'excellence of the trade' was paramount. They also valued their independence, preferring piece work to day labour because it implied that they sold their production to their employers, not their time or their labour, and because they were more able to control the rates they were paid for their work.²⁸ All these circumstances led craftsmen to distinguish themselves from other workers, the 'inferior men' as they called them. Indeed in manner and habit they seemed to ape the colonial middle-class. Cutters, the aristocrats of the clothing trade, wore top hats and frock coats to work. Printers dealt with their employers, not as worker to boss, but as gentleman to gentleman, and, if they could, they became masters themselves. However, engineers were the real aristocrats of work. Other workers called them 'tin gods' or 'Gentlemen Jims'.[29]

The possession of rare and valuable skills gave craftsmen a powerful position in the labour market. They knew more about their work than most of their masters did, a situation which many masters felt they had to combat. Boots, for instance, which in the 1850s were made from start to finish by individual bootmakers in hundreds of bespoke or order shops, were by 1900 made in factories by more than 20 separate individuals, each making or sewing a different part. Employers mechanised the trade almost completely in the 1890s in an attempt to reduce labour costs, remain competitive and reduce the power of the bootmakers union. Thus mechanisation was the conclusion of a process of sub-division which had begun in the 1860s, when sewing machines were introduced to sew the upper parts of the boots together. Sewing was defined as women's work in the 1860s, so deskilling the craftsman's trade went hand in hand with the feminising of part of the workforce.[30]

This process can be seen in other trades, such as the clothing industry, where by 1900 a shirt was made in 37 different operations, often by 37 different people.[31] Technical advances, too, destroyed some trades. When steel replaced wood in the building of ships, the shipwrights who made the wooden ships were made redundant. When reinforced concrete replaced stone in city buildings, the famous old trade of stonemasonry was sorely threatened. The linotype machines replaced the hand setting compositor in newspaper offices and eliminated more than two-thirds of compositing jobs. In the 1890s sulphide of sodium replaced the exotic mixtures tanners used to tan hides, reducing to a few hours a process which had once taken months.[32]

Craftsmen, quite understandably, resented the degradation of their skills, because both their standard of living and sense of self depended on them. Many left their trades altogether for jobs in burgeoning industries like building, transport and communications, while many became process workers in the industry they once dominated and there they fought hard to keep their wages at their previous tradesmen's levels. Others were able to grasp and keep the few skilled jobs, in repair, maintenance and tooling, that were left. Still others found a niche in more specialised sections of the trade. Employers took their opportunities too, to all but abolish apprenticeships in the 1880s and 1890s, pointing out that machine minders did not need seven-year apprenticeships to teach them how to pull a lever.[33] Craftsmen argued long and often for the continuance of apprenticeships and they did succeed in several trades in the early twentieth century, when the new arbitration bodies enforced ratios between journeymen and apprentices. This limited the employers' propensity to both sub-divide and mechanise.[34]

The factory trades were the worst hit by sub-division. What contemporaries called the handicraft trades were less so, for it was more difficult to sub-divide work done by craftsmen such as bricklayers, painters and carpenters.[35] There was little if any mechanisation and deskilling in the metal trades. In fact engineers in Australia were considered better all-round craftsmen than in Britain because the scale of operations was smaller and so the tendency to mechanise was absent. (By 1920 40 percent of all metal workers worked in workshops of less than 100 hands.) So, whereas in Britain fitting and turning were separate trades, in Australia the craftsman was a fitter *and* turner, who could turn his hand to pattern-making and smithing as well.[36] In fact the nineteenth century was good to engineers as any mechanising economy must be. Engineers worked in many industries, from gold mining to machine shops to newspaper offices, but mainly in metals, so it is not surprising that employment in the metals industry in Melbourne leapt from just 1811 in 1880 to 8329 in 1888.[37] New occupations formed, too, wherever new machines were located. Marine engineering, for example, was a new occupation dating from the 1870s. Here were highly skilled craftsmen who adopted all the accoutrements of the labour aristocracy, even refusing to join in the Maritime Strike of 1890.[38]

The sense of difference between the marine engineers and other seafarers opens the way to a discussion of the other side of the late nineteenth-century workforce, that of the unskilled. Most unskilled workers worked in the casual labour market. Their work was irregular and intermittent, often done for long hours for little pay. They did not have the training and education which gave the craftsmen leverage in the struggle for permanent work, hence they were most likely to be poor, often supplementing their paid work with help from charities, surviving by sending their children to work, relying on income generated from their homes or by hawking goods in the streets. They formed a workforce which was produced by the nature of the economy itself and for which they provided the service of being there when it needed them and just surviving when it did not.

Australia's cities were still tied very closely to their rural hinterlands. Every country person knew that rural work was tied to the seasons, the summer harvesting of wheat, the spring shearing of sheep, the autumn ploughing and seeding of crops, the annual canning of fruit and the milling of wheat. But only city workers in intermittent jobs knew just how much the country's seasonal industries were linked to the cities.[39] Work on the wharves is perhaps the best example. When the wool clip was shipped off overseas and when the grain crops were exported, there was fairly regular work for wharf labourers. They would turn up in their hundreds at the docks and wait to be picked out by stevedores (the middlemen between ship owners and lumpers) to load or unload a ship. That job would last as long as it took to do the work then they would join the pool outside the gate and wait to be picked up again. Lots of ships meant work, few ships meant unemployment. As one Sydney lumper said: 'I have seen pretty nearly all the men [in the port] employed one day and the following morning I have seen 600 or 700 sitting idly on the wharves.'[40] Stevedores had their favourite men, who they picked first and who in good times might get four days' work a week. The less fortunate might get two.[41] The work coal lumpers, seamen and painters and dockers did was much the same, it depended on the state of trade.[42] Certainly with the invention of steam-powered ships, the unreliability of sail was mitigated and work was slightly more regular,[43] but the pick-up system by which all these workmen worked kept them in poverty until the system itself was finally reformed in the 1950s.

The wharves were the last or the first stage in transporting goods around the cities. The railways employed a large casual workforce during their busiest seasons. In Victoria in 1890 there were 11 600 permanent railway workers and 3400 temporaries who were put on and put off in batches of between 200 and 500 men.[44] Multitudes of carters carried goods to and from the docks and from manufacturer to retailer. Many were independent carters with one horse and cart trying to survive in a cutthroat business. Most, though, were wage labourers, employed to drive the carts and lorries of others. Seasonality is risky for business and the owners thrust the risks it presented onto their drivers by employing them on a casual basis. If there was work they did it, if there was not they were stood down.[45] A great deal of work in the nineteenth century was done in this cycle of overload and idleness.

Building and construction workers were of course affected by the weather. When it rained work stopped and workers were not paid. Melbourne building workers must have often regretted their residence in that rain-sodden city. But they were certainly compensated up to 1890, before which the frenetic building boom saw the city spread outwards and upwards at a rapid rate. However, while the private market in Melbourne was a boom for most builders, those who worked on big government projects were not so well off. The planning of the nineteenth-century city was, to say the least, ad-hoc, because governments seemed inherently incapable of spending their money regularly over the year. Departments always ran out well before the financial year ended and so workers on public works were often unemployed in mid-winter. Generally workers were taken on for particular projects and put off when these were finished. The Sydney Exhibition Building was built in eight months in 1879 by 1500 men who worked three eight-hour shifts. They were sacked when they had built it and many of them were to be seen outside its gates for months afterwards asking visitors for jobs.[46]

Where manufacturing was tied to public works it too suffered the same problems of intermittency; and a good deal of manufacturing was also seasonal and so its workers regularly felt the sting of unemployment. Jam and pickle workers, workers in the Colonial Sugar Refinery's factories, labourers in tanneries, fellmongeries and abattoirs all suffered because their industries were linked to seasonal, rural production. Other manufacturers were linked to the seasons in different ways. Food and cold drink manufacturers took on workers in summer and put them off in winter. Gas and fuel workers were taken on in winter and put off in summer. Clothing manufacturers had their seasons too, with the peak at the start of spring and autumn and, in Melbourne, at Cup carnival times.[47]

Few of these industries or the companies in them actually closed down, except perhaps in the clothing industry. Most businesses were organised so that they could take on or shed an outer husk of labourers and tradesmen's assistants when the work justified it, while keeping the skilled and indispensable staff on more permanently. At Cole Bros, a Melbourne painting contractor, thirteen out of seventeen workers in 1881 worked an average of eleven weeks each. At Lennon's farm machinery factory the labourers averaged only 26 weeks' work per year.[48] Fred Riley, secretary of the Manufacturing Grocers Union in 1924, called the skilled workers the 'key workers', the 'skeleton into which the less skilled workers are woven'.[49]

What did these irregular and intermittently employed workers do to survive? Riley thought they went from business to business in the same industry.[50] But many went to the country to work; fellmongers, for example, went to shearing sheds as shed hands. In the winter when there was no rural work country workers flocked to the cities, filling up the common lodging houses and competing with the city workers for whatever jobs there were. Thomas Dobeson, an immigrant millwright by trade, spent several years in this casual labour market. His longest job was for ten months but most were for weeks not months and for four or five shillings a day. Once he tried self-employment but that did not work. In fact he tried almost everything, often walking eighteen miles a day to find it. 'These last five years have been thrown away', he wrote bitterly in his diary, 'I have made no progress at all.'[51]

Families in these circumstances were more likely to regard every member of the family as a worker and every income as valuable. Many, especially those with female breadwinners, were forced to turn to the charities for help, but they never got much. A woman with four or more children who went to the Sydney Benevolent Society would be given a weekly ration of three pounds of flour, three pounds of meat, one pound of sugar, six loaves of bread and half a pound of tea; she would get no vegetables or fruit.[52] Nobody enjoyed going to the charities; they were a last resort. Men were forced to break stone to prove they were 'genuine'. Everybody had to undergo humiliating inquisitions to prove that they were 'deserving' and, of course, many people had no choice but to submit. So children became 'street arabs', selling fruit or papers or matches, playing instruments, or, as one thirteen-year-old did, doing acrobatics in bars. He proudly told an inquiry, 'I can touch my head with my feet and bend my back and pick up 3d'.[53] These boys had few options, but being boys they had more choice then their sisters and their mothers. Females had very little choice indeed.

Do servant girls earn their wages?

When and where women worked in the last half of the nineteenth century was defined by the domestic ideology, the assumption that a married woman's place was in her home raising healthy children, tending to the needs of her husband, preparing him for the daily grind of the workforce. In reality married women could not have done much paid work. Fertility was still high and the ideology which excluded married women from paid work also excluded men from women's labour in the home. Paid work was men's work, men were the breadwinners, and if women had to work then they should only work while they were single. As the participation of married and single women in the paid workforce shows, the ideology had some force. In Melbourne, for instance, in 1871, 1881 and 1901 nearly 70 percent of unmarried women did paid work. In Adelaide the percentage was smaller, 48 percent in 1871, 68 in 1881 and 65 in 1891. However, in neither place did married women make up any significant percentage of paid labour—about 10 percent in Melbourne, and in Adelaide under 5 percent. Melbourne's higher rate was due to that kinked age distribution, the adult population born in the gold rushes, who reached maturity and marriage in the 1880s and who made up an abnormally high proportion of the female population.[54] So a woman's place in the family life cycle also determined how she would work.

In this period most female paid work was done by working-class women. In every colonial city over 70 percent of working women were in one of two occupations—domestic service and manufacturing—neither of which would middle-class women enter. But the proportion declined over the next 30 years. For example, in Melbourne it fell from 86 to 75 percent and from 87 percent in Adelaide to 74. Occupations in commerce and the professions opened up late in the century, but these were taken mainly by the middle class.[55]

Most women worked as domestic servants. The number was highest in places like Adelaide and Perth, where manufacturing was still in its infancy. The number was lowest in Sydney and Melbourne, where manufacturing was more developed. Across the 30 years from 1871 to the turn of the century domestic service declined as an occupation from 56.5 percent of the female workforce in Melbourne in 1871 to 40 percent in 1901, and from 61.7 percent in Adelaide to 45.9 percent.[56] Why did it decline? A brief account of what life was like for servants might explain. How hard a servant worked depended on the size of the household in which she worked, the ages of the children, if any, the number of other servants and the kind of home it was. Far from having the big below stairs staff of the great English houses, most middle-class families in Australia had just one servant, a maid-of-all-work, who cooked, washed, cleaned and looked after the children, sometimes with the help of her mistress, sometimes without.

In 1885, an 'Old Housekeeper' published a household manual entitled *Men and How to Manage Them*. It was in part advice to wives on how best to manage a home and in part a gently satirical dig at the pretensions and foibles of men. One chapter was devoted to 'Mary Ann', the servant. It set out her duties and the best way mistresses could manage her. The Old Housekeeper wrote, wives should expect their servants to work for no more than 68 hours per week; ten each day except Sunday and six on Sunday, with the extra two worked when she rose early on washing day. Mary Ann, for her rest, might have two hours to herself in the morning and two and a half in the afternoon.[57] From the tone of the chapter it seems that 68 hours was regarded as an absolute minimum and it is certain that most servants worked a good deal longer.

Long hours were 'rewarded' with low pay, although the tendency was for pay to rise as employers sought to attract servants from a declining labour market. So in 1874 a general servant's pay rose from 12/- per week to 14/-. This was on top of bed and board, but for the hours worked it was appallingly bad money.[58] However, this must have seemed like a fortune to those state wards in every colony and state who, when other domestic servants were unavailable, were farmed out to private homes. In Adelaide in 1908, thirteen-year-olds were paid 1/- per week, fourteen-year-olds 2/-, and fifteen-year-olds 3/-. At age twenty they were still only paid 10/- a week and some of this was held in trust by the state.[59]

In 1890 the feminist newspaper *The Dawn* asked the rhetorical question 'Do Servant Girls Earn their Wages?' The resounding answer was 'yes', and they should earn a lot more:

> Take the case of a general servant who does everything for a household of say six people. She has to attend to five bedrooms probably. Now to clean up everything, to refill the ewers, make the beds, and dust and sweep the room cannot take less than a quarter of an hour and no one would be likely to tender we imagine at less than 3d per room, i.e. 1/3 per day, or 8/9 per week. No washer-women would do the washing for six people for less than 9/- per week; and the household washing, the sheets, towels, etc., would be worth 10/- more. Would a waiter agree to set a table, wait on six persons and wash up all the dishes, plates, cups, glasses, tureens, knives, forks and spoons, etc., for less than 6d per meal. We think not. We add therefore 10/6 per week to the score on this item. We should also have to pay a boy 5/- a week to clean six pairs of boots daily, sweep the yard, chop wood, clean the stove, the knives, the door-steps, etc., and answer the door bell. There is the cooking and the cleaning of cooking utensils to be accounted for. Three meals a day at 6d a meal makes another 10/6 and this makes a grand total of 53/9 per week without providing for scrubbing, window cleaning, and a thousand other duties varying daily, and where there are children a multitude of odd services superadded. All this, you may say cannot be done in eight hours; true it is done in fourteen and paid, not at 53/9, but at 10/- or 12/-, plus board and lodging worth, let us say 10/-, for the worst room in the house or a bed on the sofa must not be reckoned at more.[60]

This illustrates the range of work but not the difficulty or ease with which it was done. In practically every respect the work which all women did in their homes was hard and exhausting. Kitchens were small and cramped, with no running water. An open fire made them like furnaces in summer. Cleaning, polishing and dusting were never ending jobs, especially in middle class homes, where rooms were crammed full of furniture, paintings, decorations and knick-knacks of every conceivable kind.[61] Laundry work was the worst though. The Adelaide historian, Margaret Barbalet, describes what it was like:

> First of all, fires would have to be built to heat the water for the tub or copper; sometimes a whole cake of lye soap would have to be shaved into boiling water; the clothes would be sorted into piles of different sorts of whites, coloureds, work

clothes, and rags; flour would be stirred into cold water and then thinned down with boiling water for starching; and the dirtiest spots on clothing would be rubbed on a board and then boiled or in the case of coloured clothing just rubbed, rinsed, and starched. Heavy steaming loads of clothing would have to be lifted out of the copper on poles, put through the mangle, rinsed, blued and starched, and put to dry on the lines which would then have to be winched high enough. Tea towels would be spread on lavender bushes or on the grass, old rags hung to dry on the fence, and the family underwear hung discreetly on lower lines between the larger items. Finally, the rinsing water would be used for the family's weekly baths or to water the garden, and the hot soapy water to wash the verandahs.[62]

Although some servants liked their work (this was largely dependent on whether their mistresses were kind and treated them as one of the family), most Australian domestics did not. There were many reasons why. They were worked terribly hard, and paid poorly, but they were also treated as inferiors, made to wear uniforms, expected to defer on every and any occasion and often called, not by their own names, but by names that went with the job. They had little or no time off and had precious little privacy. They were often harassed physically by men and fought with by children who were the same age. Employers expected deference, obedience, hard, uncomplaining work and respectability, but they were more likely to get resistance—day dreaming, quarrelling, sulking, fighting and a reluctance to work hard.[63] Then, too, because the demand for domestics always exceeded the supply, domestics changed jobs frequently and demanded higher pay, perhaps secure in the knowledge that if they were not satisfied with one family they could easily go elsewhere. 'Tuppence more and up goes the donkey', they might say and off they went.[64] Where there were alternatives they took them. Really the only alternative was the factory.

The Australian middle class could never understand the working girl's preference for factory work, but agreed that there were unnameable 'great inducements' (as the manager of a Victorian labour exchange put it in 1875) held out to girls by factories.[65] After all, inquiry after inquiry had discovered that the clothing and boot factories, where most girls went, were smelly, cramped, untidy, noisy, filthy, too hot or too cold, unventilated and insanitary; that girls as young as nine or ten worked for more than ten hours a day for little and often no pay; that doctors giving evidence to them swore that the girls suffered physically from too much standing or sitting and that their capacity to bear children surely must be impaired.[66] So why the preference?

What factory girls liked best was the freedom, not so much from surveillance inside the factory, but from surveillance when their work was done. They also liked the companionship of girls and boys their own age, which they usually did not get locked away as domestics. They liked, too, living with their families and working locally and not serving an alien family in an alien suburb. Their preference for a job in manufacturing can be seen by the figures. In 1871 there were 2630 women in industry in Victoria. In 1891 there were nearly 11 000. In 1886, in New South Wales, one in seven factory workers was female, but in 1907 the proportion was one in three. In 1871 in Adelaide 25 percent of women workers worked in factories. In 1891 it was 31.1 percent.[67] Obviously the increase was made possible by the rising importance of manufacturing and the sub-division of the craftsman's work, which made women and children attractive to employers. Manufacturing employment did not reach the level of domestic service until the twentieth century, but by 1900 it was getting very close.

Most women worked in clothing and textile factories. Between 20 and 30 percent of the bootmaking workforce was women and there were smaller proportions of women workers in tobacco and cigar factories, ropeworks, soap, cardboard box, pickle and jam, hat, jewellery, artificial flower factories and laundries. They worked long hours, ten, sometimes fourteen a day. The work was intermittent, clothing workers, for instance, were routinely sacked at Christmas and then re-employed when business picked up. Pay was appallingly low. Some dressmakers, who made clothes to order for the wealthy, apprenticed girls, taught them all-round skills and paid them a respectable wage. But in most factories girls were employed for six months to learn a routine task, and were not paid a penny for it. Then they might be paid 5/- a week for another six months then 12/- a week until they were adults. Then, unless they were put onto piece-work or promoted to supervisors, they were sacked and replaced by a new batch of girls. In themselves those kinds of wages were appalling but a comparison with men's shows just how low they were. Adult men in textile mills in 1875 were paid 35/- a week, about 6/- a day. Adult women were paid 10/-, boys were paid 7/- and girls 4/-.[68]

The images of women and girls working in factories in the nineteenth and early twentieth centuries invariably show them doing routine repetitive tasks like stamping bars of soap, painting cardboard boxes, folding sheets of newspaper, sewing one part of a garment, sewing one part of a boot to another or putting boot polish into packages.[69] If craftsmen were the victims of sub-divided work, then so too were women factory workers. Employers took them on because they were cheap and they were cheap for several complex reasons. Firstly there were many of them and they could be easily replaced. Secondly the employers thought that they were only temporary workers, filling in their days before their marriage and therefore without the family responsibilities which drove men's wages to these higher levels. Of course this assumption came to Australia from Britain, so employers could say that they were only doing what they did 'at home'. Therefore men monopolised the skilled jobs and excluded women from them. But the capitalist imperative also drove women's wages down. Clothing and bootmaking, particularly, were labour-intensive industries, living in the insecure world of tough inter-colonial and international competition, and that sort of competition in an unregulated labour market with no trade unions was a recipe for low wages.

So clothing manufacturing was based on a labour force of girls, usually young, single, unorganised and poorly paid. Yet it was based, too, on another female workforce, even more exploited, working sometimes longer hours, but this time usually married with children to support. These were the outworkers, the women to whom manufacturers sent work to do in their homes or who had to take work home after a day in the factory.

The materials to make coats, trousers or vests and the trousers that needed finishing (shirts and dresses were never sent out) were fetched by the women themselves to their homes, where with machines, needle and thread (which they paid for themselves) they worked extraordinarily long hours. Elizabeth Rogers, an Adelaide outworker in 1888 worked from 7.30 in the morning to 12.00 or 1.00 at night, and there were dozens like her who had to do the same.[70]

Outwork seems to have been done primarily for family reasons. A survey in Melbourne in the 1880s found a variety of circumstances among outworkers. Some were deserted wives or widows with no other income, others had husbands who were sick or who had been hurt in accidents, while others had husbands who were intermittently employed. Others were ill themselves, or had young children to look after and others worked to support aged parents. Most worked this way through sheer necessity, though there were some who did it for 'pocket money' and these usually had a husband in full-time work. Some could have worked in a factory but chose not to on principle, while others were forbidden to by their husbands. Most worked alone, but many had help from their daughters and one or two actually employed 'improvers', so becoming 'middle-men' themselves. Most worked at outwork 52 weeks of the year. The variety of situations shows that outwork suited them more than factory work.[71]

Yet when opponents of outwork pointed to the exploitation they were correct. Outwork was the cheapest alternative for a manufacturer. It meant he or she did not have to invest in plant and equipment. When trade was bad outworkers could be more easily displaced or paid less. They were not organised in a union and the Factory Acts could not protect them. They were always paid piece-rates; for example, women in the Melbourne survey were paid 4/- for finishing a dozen pairs of trousers or 2/6 for one silk coat.[72] The gentlemen on the select committees which inquired into outwork often looked at the prices of these garments in shops and gravely wondered at the huge mark ups. It is little wonder that they concluded that outworkers were the most exploited of the city's workers.

5 Work and the middle class

The aristocrats of labour in the nineteenth century took pride in displaying their respectability, their top hats and fob-watches matching uneasily with their heavy working men's boots. For the middle class, respectability was not a question of outward appearance, but of birth and breeding. Certainly it could be lost, but only by disgrace. Therefore in the context of the later nineteenth-century world of work, middle-class work was automatically respectable, and no middle-class person could do working-class work and remain respectable. But the middle class did not see their work in terms of respectability alone. They also saw it in terms of their interest in social status and hierarchy. The middle class did not generally believe in the idea of social class. Rather, its social world was one of fine gradations of status, and social mobility through this status hierarchy was what it wanted from work.

Sufficient classical proficiency

In April 1894 Paul Duflôt, 'the Canadian Healer', was arrested on Launceston's Market Green. Illuminated by glaring lights and accompanied by a band he was 'spruiking' to thousands of onlookers the virtues of 'Precious Powder', a 'perfume' which he sold for 2/6 and which, he claimed, would cure bronchitis, asthma, lumbago, rheumatism, liver complaints and many more diseases. He was later convicted on two charges—selling a drug without having a license issued by the Court of Medical Examiners, and practising unlawfully as a physician. He was fined £20. He had also been arrested in Melbourne in February, charged with pretending to be an apothecary and unlawfully assuming the title 'dentist'. Despite being cheered loudly by a full gallery, the magistrate fined him a shilling.[1] Duflôt was an outsider in a professional field and members of the professions in Australia did not like those whom they called 'quacks' and 'charlatans' practising in their areas. The following section is about the strategies the professionals used to exclude them, so it describes the way the professions created themselves.

One had to be privileged and a man to enter the professions in the nineteenth and early twentieth centuries in Australia. Professional men formed part of the upper-middle and middle class and it was their sons, or the sons of the growing urban bourgeoisie, who undertook professional work. In those days, when the title 'gentleman' meant high reaching social status, the professional man was ipso-facto a 'gentleman'. The professions remained in the hands of the wealthy because they cost a great deal of money to enter and the education system filtered out those working-class or lower-middle-class boys from the schooling necessary to get them there. Girls' education, as we shall later see, absolutely precluded them, because it aimed to educate them for little more than middle-class refinements and marriage. For working-class children there was practically no hope of entering a profession. The governments insisted they stay at school only until they were thirteen or fourteen. There were practically no state high schools which went to the level of educational achievement necessary for university and few, if any, working-class children went to private schools. They may not have wanted to, for the middle and working-class worlds of education were as far apart as any aspect of those worlds, but in any case the fees at private schools were prohibitive and children were much more valuable to working-class families as workers. So in Melbourne, boarders at most private schools had to pay £70 a year. At universities like Sydney and Melbourne, where courses in medicine, law and engineering were taught, costs were about £30 a year plus board. In England, where many students went, they were even higher. Those professionals like dentists, who were trained on the job, had to pay very substantial premiums, often of over £300. And, strange as it may seem today, students in these courses had to learn Latin and the classics of Greek literature. Not that these were of any practical use to doctors, lawyers, engineers or anyone else for that matter. They were a badge, a sign of refinement and gentility and a device by which the professions could exclude those with different social backgrounds from their own.

The jobs that we now recognise as distinct occupations in the professions are of fairly recent origin. In medicine in Britain, from where the Australian professions developed, practitioners were strictly divided into physicians, surgeons and apothecaries. Surgeons in the eighteenth century were regarded as tradesmen, members of what one historian described as a 'rough and bloody business unlikely to attract anyone of refined taste'. Apothecaries were a cross between general practitioner, grocer and chemist. They lived by prescribing and selling drugs, but in the strict social codes of the eighteenth century they were tainted by 'trade'. However, they were superior to chemists and druggists, indeed, they eventually left their shops to become general practitioners while druggists became chemists. Physicians were the top of the tree. They prescribed physic (that is, drugs) to people in high society and were untainted by the gore of the hospital or the trade of the apothecary. The Royal College of Physicians in England excluded anyone who was not Church of England and educated at Oxford or Cambridge. Initially such a student would study for an arts degree. Later medical degrees were introduced. Examinations for entry to the College of Physicians took between two and three hours, were conducted entirely in Latin and were essentially on the use of drugs and how to write prescriptions. The history of medicine is a good illustration of the essentially historical nature of the professions[2] which were not always as they are now. They became that way in the nineteenth century.

Professions are really very powerful trade unions. Their main function lies in protecting their members' interests. However, their social rank and their corporate traditions gave them far greater power than trade unions and they used that power to set up barriers to exclude pretenders to their trades. The uniform history of the professions seems to be the establishment of a professional association which registers only those practitioners who have done a registered course or passed the requisite tests. By doing this the association can control who enters the profession and say what constitutes knowledge in that field. It also sets up standards of conduct, which it calls professional ethics, and uses these to make judgements on what is proper practice. Then, too, these associations seek to acquire legitimacy, and in Australia there has been no better way of doing that than by acquiring a Royal Charter. But the real and crucial test of a profession is its ability to have legislation passed in parliament giving monopoly powers to practice to duly qualified practitioners. Professions also seek to create the knowledge in their fields, so they set up courses of training and examinations to assess whether applicants have reached the required standards. If this can be done in a 'disinterested' institution like a university then so much the better, for the profession can claim that the university is setting standards of knowledge, not itself.

All this seems rather self-seeking and self-serving. Professions exclude and devalue similar kinds of knowledge which threaten their monopoly and the obvious way in which they do this might well be expected to alienate them from the communities with which they deal. Their problem, then, is to transform this political and economic power into cultural legitimacy which their clients and the society at large will accept. Of course professions do not grow in a vacuum. They are really the products of the increasing complexity of social life which began with the industrial revolution. Accountancy rose to be a profession with the increasing complexity of business, particularly the growth of limited liability and joint stock companies. The burgeoning of the railways system brought with it civil engineers. The new technology which permitted multi-story buildings encouraged the expansion of the architect's profession. And the development of science allowed the orthodox medical profession to gain further control of medical practice.

W.M. Kernot, the first professor of engineering at Melbourne University, liked to quote the British engineer, Professor Rankine, to gatherings of engineers:

> Another evil, and one of the worst, which arises from the separation of theoretical and practical knowledge, is the fact that a large number of persons possessed of an inventive turn of mind, and considerable talent in the manual operations of practical mechanics, are destitute of that knowledge of scientific principles which is requisite to prevent their being misled by their own ingenuity ...
> The ill success of the projects of misdirected ingenuity has very naturally the effect of driving those men of practical skill who (though without scientific knowledge) possess prudence and common sense to the opposite of caution, and of inducing them to avoid all experiments, and confine themselves to the careful copying of existing successful structures and machines—a course which, although it avoids risk, would, if generally followed, stop the progress of all improvement.[3]

This is the essence of the profession. Those early engineers, gentlemen all, usually qualifying for their position in the office of a practitioner, but doing course work at Melbourne University as well, wanted particularly to separate themselves from tradesmen engineers and a range of workers such as contractors and builders whose occupations had grown since the gold rushes. Dentistry was similar. In the nineteenth century, pulling teeth was done by many people as an adjunct to jobs like blacksmithing or pharmacy, and it was also done by surgeon–barbers. Lawyers' work was done by estate agents, law stationers, conveyancers, articled clerks and trade protection associations.[4] Architectural work, too, was done by builders, contractors, tradesmen, as well as those of a higher social standing whom the historian of the profession, J.M. Freeland, describes as 'engineer architects'.[5] In Victoria in 1881 there were nearly 2000 people in the medical workforce, excluding nurses. Apart from the people we might expect to be there (medical practitioners, chemists, dentists, opticians and midwives) there were also Chinese and Indian doctors, aurists and oculists, homeopaths, hydropaths, herbalists, medical galvanists, botanists, mesmerists, chiropodists, magnetists, clairvoyants and psychopathists.[6] To the orthodox medical practitioners these were quacks and charlatans, like Paul Duflôt. To patients they were simply different kinds of doctors practising different kinds of medicine and doing it quite as successfully as the more orthodox. In circumstances where some practitioners were trained to their job and others were not, those who were trained formed themselves into associations to pursue their interests. Dentists in Victoria, for example, formed a Dental Association of Victoria in 1884 to increase their 'professional and social status'. An Engineering Association of New South Wales was founded in 1870 and the Victorian Institute of Engineers in 1883. Victoria's accountants formed the Incorporated Institute of Accountants in 1886, five years after a South Australian body was formed. A Law Institute in Sydney was formed in 1884, and in Queensland in 1903. Control of, and discipline in, the legal profession was taken into the hands of the lawyers' associations which investigated their members, disciplined them and de-barred them if they thought fit. Also, like all the associations, they drew up rules of etiquette for their members. The architects' institutes were set up in the early twentieth century and they quickly introduced another characteristic of the professions, the examination for the right to claim membership, although some institutes simply recognised the passing of a 'reputable course' as sufficient for entry.[7]

Having courses set up in universities or other high status institutions was a more difficult task. In the nineteenth century dentists served an apprenticeship with a master and learned their skills that way. In Victoria, a College of Dentistry was set up in 1897 and became a faculty of Melbourne University in 1905. The college had an unfortunate first year. A bill was passed through Parliament in 1887 which gave an elected board the power to register dentists, but it defined dentists as anyone who pulled teeth, most of whom were in fact untrained chemists. Fortunately for the trained dentists a new bill tying registration to a certified course of education was passed the next year and the process of professionalisation was completed in 1910, when legislation was passed banning unregistered dentists from practising.[8] Engineering courses began at Melbourne University in the 1860s and at Sydney in 1870, but engineers still learned their trade on the job as apprentices until degree courses began in both Melbourne and Sydney Universities in 1883. Technical colleges began to run degree courses around the turn of the century and the institutes of engineers, if they were not running their own exams, certified those courses as sufficient for entry. The apprenticeships quickly faded away, but engineers were less lucky with legislation. Only the Queensland government legislated to protect the title 'Registered Professional Engineer, Queensland'. Other Associations thought a Royal Charter might do just as well and that was granted in 1938.[9] Lawyers began learning on the job too, in clerkships with existing solicitors, a five-year apprenticeship bought at great cost. Law was taught very early at the two big universities but legal subjects, in Sydney at least, were part of a Bachelor of Arts degree.[10] Liberal and ornamental education was still the basis of a legal career. In 1838 an attorney or solicitor seeking admission to the New South Wales Supreme Court had to produce

> certificates of the tutors, or others under whom he shall have been educated, of the regularity and propriety of his conduct whilst under tuition, and of his academical acquirements under such tuition, which shall comprise sufficient classical proficiency to translate into English any part of the first six books of the *Aeneid* of Virgil from the Latin, and of *St John's Gospel* from the Greek, together with a competent knowledge of arithmetic, and of the first six books of Euclid.[11]

Barristers were admitted to courts in Queensland by a Board of Admission, but only after they had passed an examination in law, mathematics and in classics such as Demosthene's *De Corona*, Cicero's *de Amicitia*, Terence's *Pharmio*, five books of Euclid and Shakespeare's *Merchant of Venice*.[12]

Architectural education was at first an apprenticeship, but by the 1870s and 1880s there were courses at technical schools such as the Melbourne Working Men's College and subjects entitled 'architecture' were taught as part of engineering courses at universities, but only as a poor second. Courses in architecture alone did not begin until the twentieth century, differing from the college courses by emphasising artistic and intellectual skills over the merely technical ones.[13] Medicine, like law, was taught from practically the beginning at Melbourne and Sydney Universities.[14]

The history of restrictive legislation in medicine was a stormy one, more contested than might be supposed. The colonial parliaments were not always inclined to give any group a 'closed shop' over an occupation. Rather they wanted to see free competition as the way to improved health care and orthodox medicine seemed to many parliamentarians, as it did to the community, largely ineffective. Nevertheless, doctors' associations began to lobby the parliaments very early for laws governing registration. In Victoria these came in 1856, and in 1862 the Victorian Parliament gave only qualified doctors the right to use the medical title, although this did not stop the unqualified from practising. In 1908, further restrictions were made. Medicine's chief rival, homeopathy, was controlled, and a five-year course of study in a 'regular' course was made a pre-requisite for registration with the Medical Board. However, the power to de-bar doctors for 'infamous conduct' was not granted to the Medical Board till 1933. It marked the peak of self-regulation in the profession.[15]

Professions manage to acquire cultural legitimacy in a number of ways, many of which fall outside the ambit of the mere political or economic. For doctors and engineers it was science which gave them a new sense of legitimacy because it was science that came to be seen as the handmaiden of progress in the late nineteenth century (although many bogus ideas like phrenology claimed the title of science). In medicine the germ theory of contagion replaced the old miasmatic theory. Antiseptic surgery led to a decline in hospital deaths and diagnosis improved. Medical doctors often led the way in public health campaigns which reduced the heavy mortality from the big killer diseases of the nineteenth century such as smallpox, polio and typhoid. Nevertheless, as the historian of medicine, Evan Willis, suggests, the new scientific medicine was given the credit by doctors and society at large.[16]

What upholds the profession is the use of both arcane language and mysterious techniques. It is much the same as the 'mysteries of the trade'; secrecy and language. The sophistication of the concepts is mystifying. Only lawyers can understand legal jargon. Only doctors can understand medical jargon. Only chemists can understand the chemical makeup and manufacture of drugs. Only engineers can understand the properties of their materials and the complexities of their projects. Language includes the in-group and excludes the rest, and the professions have been best at using language to exclude.

A perfect substitute for pen and ink

The professional ethic of service is but one attitude which has given meaning to the experience of work in Australia. It is commonplace to refer to the protestant work ethic when discussing work in the nineteenth century, but that particular ethic was only one of many. The affection of the craftsman for his skills, the experiences of masculinity and femininity, the competition in the shearing shed and the sense of exploitation and alienation were all alternative attitudes. Nevertheless, in the later nineteenth and early twentieth centuries, something like the protestant work ethic did inform one particular kind of work, that of the male clerk in his office. Clerking expanded dramatically in the industrialising capitalist economies of the nineteenth century, a result of urban growth, the growing complexity of cities, city and country economies and of business itself. Factories needed offices and office workers. Increasing levels of private investment led to a growing finance industry. (Australia led the world in life insurance in the

1880s and 1890s.) Meanwhile, civil services increased in scale as the state took on more functions. In Melbourne in the ten years from 1881 the number of commercial clerks more than doubled.[17] To be a male clerk in the nineteenth century was to strive for the title 'gentleman'. It was not a title granted automatically to the clerk, as it was to the professional man, so clerks had to pursue it. Its outward expression was the top hat, the dapper suit and the fob-watch, each vivid symbols of the respectability that clerks wanted, for respectability underpinned much of the ideology of social class in the nineteenth century. The middle class possessed it by birth, and the working class might acquire it by the right behaviour, but it would be grudgingly given. Clerks sat uneasily in between, more middle class than working class, more clean-handed than dirty-handed, more inclined to find ultimate respectability in promotion to chief clerk, accountant or bank manager than in the lowly tasks of ledger or copy clerk. In one sense respectability came from community responsibilities. Bank tellers, for instance, had awesome duties:

> It is well also to see this officer taking an interest in the affairs of the community . . . his affiliation with a local church, with sporting organisations . . . in any amateur theatricals . . . with any musical debating or literary society all tend to his own betterment and redound to the credit of the institution for whom he is working. The reading of good literature and a course of study along banking lines, is not only recommended, but is urged as most necessary to his future advancement, and absolutely essential to his future.[18]

Clerks were walking, talking representatives for their employers. Bringing discredit on themselves brought disgrace to their employers, so employers insisted on their right to a say in the private lives of their clerks. At its most extreme, bankers forbade their clerks from marrying until they received a certain salary, usually about £200 a year. Probably realistically, bankers thought a family would find it harder to find accommodation in country towns than a single man, but they also made it clear that a clerk below that salary could not support a family to the standard that the bank required.[19] Nor would bankers tolerate employees gambling, drinking, living in hotels or being in debt, for these also brought discredit on their banks.[20] All employers expected certain things from their clerks. Punctuality, respect, thrift, patience, cheerfulness, hard work, deference and unequivocal loyalty were the bywords of the clerk's life. It is not surprising that employers demanded these qualities but it is perhaps surprising that clerks gave them so unequivocally. Certainly clerks organised themselves in trade unions but these were more social groups than bona fide unions.

Clerks associated industrial action with the working class and frequently wrote no-strike clauses into their unions' constitutions. Indeed, the Australian Bank Officers Union did not stage its first strike until 1968.[21] Clerks' work was unremittingly tedious and monotonous. Many worked long hours in damp and dingy offices. Consumption, or tuberculosis, as it is now called, was a disease clerks were particularly prone to. Their wages were small. Bank clerks, for example, did not get paid at all or were paid a pittance, during their long probationary period. (Clerks at the Bank of New South Wales were paid just 10/- per week in 1888 when labourers were getting 6/- a day.)[22] It was a standard joke in nineteenth-century cartoons that the clerk, for all his precious respectability, was much worse off than the unskilled, working-class labourer.[23]

The clerk was part of a rigid status system in the office, where deference and authority passed up and down the office like passengers on an elevator. However, if this was a problem then it was also salvation because clerking, no matter how humble, held out the promise of security (clerks had a job for life), promotion and therefore high social standing because companies invariably filled clerking vacancies from their own workforce. In banks, clerks began on routine office jobs and progressed, if they showed the right qualities, to ledger-keeping. From ledgers they might progress to the public face of the bank, the teller's cage, from there to accountant and from there to the peak of their career path—branch manager.[24] Clerks in other offices began their careers as office or messenger boys and worked their way through the various levels of authority to, if they were lucky, a partnership in the business or a business of their own. Clerks in the civil services might aspire to a high position in the public service.[25] It was the promise of a job for life, higher status and their own respectability which kept clerks under the heel of their bosses.

For many working and lower-middle-class boys, clerking put their feet on the ladder of social mobility. It offered slow and steady advancement—at least that was how it was presented to the upwardly mobile job applicant. In fact three things stood between the working-class boy and social mobility. The first was the self-selecting nature of clerking. Because they were paid so poorly in their first few years, the clerks' families had to support them and this was often beyond the reach of working-class families who needed their sons' wages in their homes. The education system, too, filtered out the sons of the poor. The high degree of literacy and numeracy required was not readily achievable by working-class boys in the state education system. Moreover, lower-middle and middle-class boys had little alternative but to enter clerking. They could not do apprenticeships or labouring jobs because their status forbade it and most were precluded from the professions because they did not have the connections for successful practice. Hence the supply of clerks always exceeded the demand.[26] Sadly, connections were crucial in business, too, for family interests often stood in the way of an aspiring clerk on his way to the top. As the Melbourne merchant E.T. Derham put it: 'I do not feel very much inclined for fresh partnerships. As long as our boys can be made all snug, that is all I care about.'[27]

While family connections were a barrier to some, it was the increasing size and complexity of the office in the late nineteenth century which stood most in the way of promotion and social mobility. Certainly opportunities increased at the lower level of clerking, but these were often in newly routinised jobs. In the early twentieth century, as office work became systematised, more and more jobs became de-skilled. Business systems usually replaced the idiosyncratic book and accounting systems that gave clerks some sort of value to their own business. Standardised systems of accounting and bookkeeping made clerks more easily replacable as they made them less skilled in the literate and numerate skills they previously needed and relied on.[28]

The other side of promotion was patronage. Recruitment was often made on the basis of kinship, promotion on the basis of influence, and nowhere was this more obvious than in the colonial civil services. As the Melbourne *Argus* pointed out, public servants 'were exempt from the pressures and stress which private individuals must face if they want to get on in the world', in that they had permanent employment.[29] They usually worked from 9 am to 4 pm and were given three weeks annual leave at a time when most workers got a week, or nothing at all, or the sack.[30] Then, too, public service appointments were more often than not dispensed as patronage by ministers of the Crown or by departmental heads, and so were almost impossible to get.

The patronage system was a product of nineteenth-century politics. In no colonial parliament was there a fully fledged parliamentary party system with a strong extra-parliamentary party. Instead there was a 'system' of shifting alliances between factions whose members might unite behind a powerful figure or who might coalesce around a particular cause. The extra-parliamentary groups were held together less by ideology than by the pork-barrelling nature of politics and patronage.[31]

In the early civil establishments most people were nominated by powerful sponsors for their jobs, and this lasted in New South Wales until 1855 when a Constitution Act vested all big appointments with the Governor, advised by the Executive Council, and minor appointments, such as letter carriers, watchmen and the like, with heads of departments. This made scarcely any difference to the patterns of patronage, though, and reformers of the civil services knew that until recruitment and promotion were based on merit departments would remain less the administrative arm of government and more the preserve of jobbery and corruption.[32]

Reforms of the various civil establishments, pushed through the several colonial parliaments, provided for recruitment by competitive examination and promotion by either merit or a combination of merit and seniority. However, the acts always left a loophole through which patrons could pull their clients. In Victoria, an 1862 Act allowed people to be appointed as 'supernumaries', without the examination. In New South Wales an 1884 Act allowed ministers to make temporary appointments of up to two years, and this they did. In 1894, out of a total of 21 363 civil servants in several departments, 7072 were temporary, and these did not have to produce evidence of either skill or education. Success in examinations did not guarantee appointment either, as ministers could still pick and choose among the successful.[33] Such was the extent of patronage in New South Wales that one member of Parliament said that he felt little 'better than a perambulating labour bureau'.[34]

Taking appointments and promotions out of the hands of the politicians was the aim of the reformers and their solution was to vest control in the hands of public service boards. Victoria set up its Board in 1883, New South Wales one year later and Queensland in 1889.[35] The Commonwealth Public Service Board was established by Act of Parliament in 1902 and appointments and promotions were even further removed from politicians when this Act laid down that heads of departments be responsible for their departments. Entry to the clerical division and promotion from division to division was made by examination, and promotion through the grades in each division was made annually, except in cases of merit.[36]

These initiatives did undermine the patronage system, but two other factors contributed. In the first place, the political system itself changed as party politics developed and the need and opportunity for patronage declined. And as governments took on more responsibilities, the size and complexity of their civil establishments increased until it became quite impossible for politicians to wield the sort of influence they had hitherto had.

Histories of offices in the USA and Britain point to rapid technological change in the last few decades of the nineteenth century and to reorganisation in the first few decades of the twentieth. Carbon paper was invented in the USA in 1869 and the fact that a copy clerk might now write only one copy of a letter reduced the monotony of the work considerably. The cash register was invented in 1879, and the calculating machine in 1892.[37] Then there were stenotypes, dictaphones, addressographs, billing machines and more. But the machine which did most to change office work was the typewriter, invented in 1864. As one early American advertisement put it, typewriters were 'a perfect and practical substitute for pen and ink ... One person can do the work of two and in some kinds of work, three to five ... The machine will more than pay for itself in every three months that it is used.'[38]

Some historians argue that the typewriter caused that revolution in the office which changed the clerking workforce in Australia from 100 percent male to 60 percent female in the space of little more than 50 years. This is not so. The typewriter first appeared in Victoria in 1885, but small numbers of women, doing filing, mailing and other routine tasks, clearly preceded it into bigger offices, and women doing a wider range of tasks preceded it in the smaller.[39] Nevertheless it is certainly true that typewriting quickly became typecast as women's work, as 'typewriters' took over the work of the copy clerk. Historians disagree on the meaning of this. Some say that employers gave women the jobs on the typewriters because they were cheaper to employ than male copy clerks. Others say that copy clerking was already becoming women's work because it was routine, unskilled and could be done at home as a form of outwork, hence women continued to do women's work. Still others argue that typing began as men's work and only changed to women's work much later. In each of these cases it soon became women's work partly because it seemed to be suited to women's skills, the typewriter being constructed and shaped something like a cross between a piano and a sewing machine, two instruments long associated with women's work.[40]

Women typists began to appear in the late nineteenth century in Australia and male copy clerks began to find other work. At first women set up businesses doing contract typing for other firms, but as the cost of typewriters fell, firms began to employ their own typists. Women moved into offices much faster in the first years of the twentieth century as office and clerical work expanded and the demand for office workers increased rapidly. They consolidated their position during World War I, when they replaced the men who had enlisted in the military.[41] In Perth, for example, fully half of the men in the public service between 18 and 44 years old enlisted, and similar if not such dramatic stories could be told of most offices across the country.[42] Women moved into banks too. One banker later gave figures:

> 1915 the war period commenced. 21 girls came in and two left. In 1916 we took in 41 girls, and three left. In 1917 we took in 24 girls and 5 went, and in 1918, our peak year, we put in 63 girls and four left. 1918 was the termination of the war, although things did not come back to normal immediately afterwards. I am taking the year from June to

The paid workforce

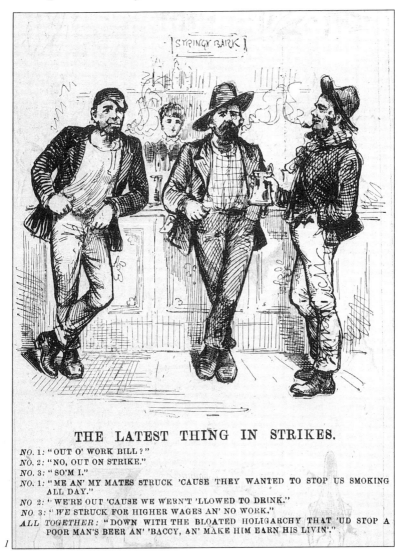

Australian men hard at work at their leisure, a common observation of Australian work habits. *Bulletin*, 20 June 1885, p. 12.

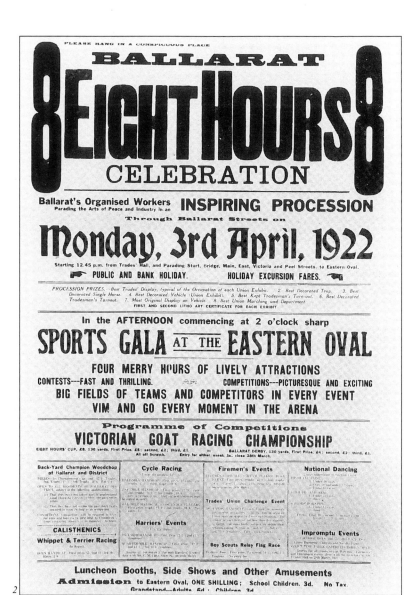

Ballarat eight-hour day celebration poster.

Right: Gender at work in the Great Depression. *New Idea*, 2 December 1932, p. 35.

Betty Bright Keeps *Her* Job with BEAUTY TABLETS!!

Capable—Alert—Efficient . . . She's Highly Paid because she is Bright—Attractive—Full of Energy—EVERY DAY . . . since Doctor told her About Myzone.

NEW!—Only Way to Banish Headache-Pain—Quickly and Certainly —Without Adding AGE to Your Face.

THERE is nothing so surely kills beauty as the left-over waste products of drugging "pain killers" and depressing headache powders. You know your own self how dull . . . and aged-looking they leave you until these nerve-numbing drugs wear out of your system.

Here's a wonderful new way, a delightful—"beauty building" way, discovered by celebrated medical specialists, . . . utterly different . . . safer than anything you've ever known. When blinding headache, sickening pain, or dragging backache comes along—take a modern Myzone instead of beauty destroying "pain-killers." The most tormenting pain or headache will disappear in seven (7) minutes and won't come back! . . . Just think! . . . Myzone means keeping on your feet four (4) more active days. Myzone relieves the pain,—not by drugging the system,—but by quickly restoring normal balance in nitrogen metabolism to the system,—speeding up Nature's processes by regulating and equalizing circulation, so that congestion, or blood pressure, on the nerve centres (the primary cause of pain) is cleared away. Thus, impurities are oxidized and swept from every cell and organ of the body.

Therefore Myzone cannot possibly leave you feeling doped and old-looking—irritable or impatient. In fact, this amazing tablet goes further . . . actually takes away any usual pain-lines, dark shadows, pallid skin—transforms the whole day into one of happy attractiveness.

When You Suffer—

Didn't "Go down" to it . . . .

At times I fear for my position, feeling quite incompetent, and always tired. I am very thankful for Myzone. The relief from pain was wonderful, and I felt so well. I know, only for the tablet, I would have had to "go down" to it.—Miss I. McN——.

"Was Always Pale . . ."

says another girl, Miss D. M. A———, of Bowning, N.S.W. "I suffered dreadful pains, and was always pale. Now scarcely a pain. My skin is much clearer and healthier—quite a colour. I am very satisfied with Myzone."

Remember—14 million other modern women now depend on the new Myzone formula,—a product of the world-famous International Laboratories. Prove for yourself how different—how better it is. So harmless dentists are now also prescribing it to rest and soothe the nerves after extractions, etc. At all chemists and leading department stores, two or three months' supply in dainty silvered cases, costing but a trifle.

NOTE: Every Genuine tablet is branded M-Y-Z-O-N-E—your safeguard against imitations containing habit-forming drugs. There is NOTHING "just as good."

—
Ask for
"A Box of MYZONE"
—Take One
—Watch Your Mirror.
—

4

... and the office, and the home!
Perth office, c.1960s. B.A. 287/221, Battye Library, Perth.

Right: A prosperous farming family. Nicholls family with labourers and domestic servants, Palmerston Cressey, Tasmania, c.1900–19. Archives Office of Tasmania, NS 507/6.

Class differences

Master of all he surveys. Mine manager's house, Mt Lyell Mining and Railway Company, Queenstown, c.1905. Mt Lyell Collection, University of Melbourne Archives.

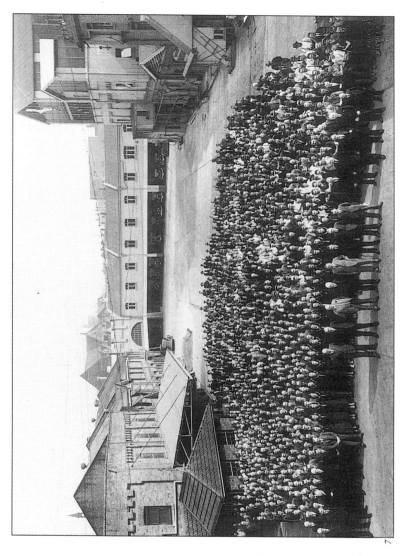

The workforce at Tooths Brewery, Sydney, c.1950s; a carefully staged hierarchy. Company Staff File, Tooths Brewery Collection, Z223, Box H, No. 3784, Australian National University Archives of Business and Labour.

Work at home

HE THINKS WOMEN DON'T COUNT.

Working-man enthusiastically — 'Ah, my dear, it's a grand way the Eight Hours' Movement is spreading in Foreign parts; our glorious principle will soon be recognised the world over!'

Working-woman — 'Yes, and then perhaps you'll begin to do something for the wives who work sixteen hours a day!'

Melbourne *Punch*, c.1860s. La Trobe Collection, State Library of Victoria.

Sausage making as household production, Gus Hoffman and family, Glenmore, Victoria, c.1900. Museum of Victoria.

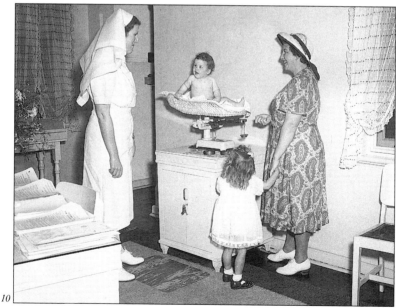

Measuring progress. Perth Infant Health Centre, c.1950. 816 B. Series C/3560, Battye Library, Perth.

The office

> 1 Victoria St
> 45 Bream St
> Surry Hills
>
> H. L. Partridge, Esq.
> Tooth & Co. Ltd.
>
> Dear Sir, I beg to make application for a position in the Kent Brewery.
>
> I have been connected with the produce trade for the past 6 years, and seeing an opening for improvement hence my application for a position.
>
> I have a good knowledge of typewriting & shorthand and I have also had a good deal of experience in the Motor trade.
>
> I shall be pleased to hear from you if I am successful in obtaining a position.
>
> I am, dear Sir,
> Yours truly,
> Athol Blair.

A redundant skill. Copperplate handwriting in 1911. Company Staff File, Tooth Brewery Records; Z223/57, 4128, Australian National University Archives of Business and Labour.

12 Celebrating respectability: Speech night at Zercho's Business College, 1906. University of Melbourne Archives.

13 Typewriters arrive and the office is changed forever, Kalgoorlie, c.1900. 3728B/163, Battye Library, Perth.

14 The 'assembly line' office of the 1930s. Reprinted from *Rydge's*, 1 June 1934, pp. 575-6.

15 Rubberplanting the office. The landscaped office at Qantas, Underwood House, Sydney. Reprinted from *Modern Office*, November 1978.

Work and technology

16

Muscle power at work. Feeding the blast furnaces, Mt Lyell smelters, Queenstown, c.1910. N.S. 872/23, Archives Office of Tasmania.

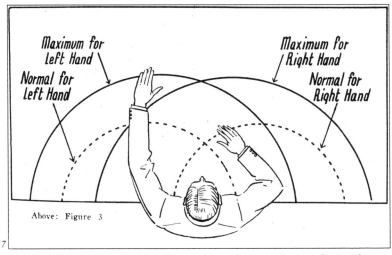

17

Scientific management at work. Reprinted from *Rydge's*, 1 September 1937, p. 720.

Computer numerical control at work. *Australian Technology Review* 3, 1 February 1989. Reproduced with permission of Riddell Publishing Pty Ltd.

Work and race

Inside the Great White Walls (1). Japanese pearlers in North Western Australia, c.1915. 28080 P, Battye Library, Perth, A. Richardson Collection.

Inside the Great White Walls (2). Chinese seamen on the Perth–Northern Ports–Singapore route, c.1890s. 5323B/1558, Battye Library, Perth.

Early schooling for the unskilled labour market, Moore River Aboriginal settlement, Western Australia, c.1930s. BA 368/5, No 27, Battye Library, Perth.

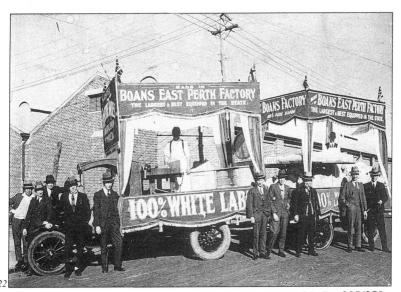

Keeping furniture manufacturing white, Perth, c.1925–27. BA 287/270, Battye Library, Perth.

Unemployment

The future of work? Late 1970s poster; Victorian Trades Hall Council Collection, University of Melbourne Archives.

December. Our sum total at the end of 1918 shows 154 girls in and 15 went out, leaving a total of 139 at the end of the year.[43]

Problems began when the war concluded and the men came home expecting to return to their old jobs. Women workers had been told that where they had replaced men their jobs were only temporary. Nevertheless, they were not inclined to give them up, nor were many employers inclined to dismiss them, as they were cheaper to employ than men and equally efficient.[44] However, many of the jobs had changed as new technologies continued to make old jobs redundant. Employers got around the problem by extending a process that had begun before the war, strictly segregating office work into men's jobs and women's jobs. Jobs like accounting, legal work and other skilled work which fulfilled the demands of traditional clerking were reserved for men. The jobs which were now being done by women, like typing, stenography and routine book and account keeping were turned into dead-end jobs with no career paths. In the Commonwealth public service women were excluded altogether from jobs in the 'administrative' third division, and in the 'general' fourth division each sex was excluded from the others' jobs.[45]

Women were always considered to be working only to fill in time between school and marriage. They were thought certain to leave paid work on marriage, never to return. Employers therefore gave them work suited to short and temporary stays, such as the routine clerical work, typing and shorthand, and refused to train them beyond demanding that they acquire skills at any one of the mushrooming business colleges, such as Stotts. Nature was sometimes called to the cause of this segregation, even to excluding women altogether. One banker, anxious to avoid employing women in his bank, claimed that they did not possess the capacity for secrecy and responsibility necessary for bank work. Further, they were mentally incapable of doing any other than routine work, of which there was very little in banks. Their presence in banks, he argued, would cause gossip and delay and their feminine frailty meant that they were unable to work under stress. Indeed, he concluded, they 'have to be treated gently. They cannot be ordered about summarily like men and this is not conducive to discipline.'[46]

Women office workers were in most circumstances paid less than men, and that is to be expected. Only in the Commonwealth public service was equal pay granted to women. Although typists and telephonists had their own low pay rates, men and women doing equivalent work—post mistresses and post masters, male clerks and female clerks—got the same pay. However, in 1916 the Commonwealth Arbitration Court set different minimum rates for men and women (and incidentally for married and unmarried clerks) and then refused to grant equal cost of living increases to men and women. Again the grounds were that a man's responsibilities were greater than a woman's as he had a family to support and she did not. So what was probably the only avenue of employment where women got equal pay was put on the same basis as practically every other job.[47]

Women liked the new jobs that the office had to give them. They certainly preferred them to factory work, and they were considered far preferable to domestic service. As one middle-class Perth woman found in 1919:

> The daughters of the working classes are taking up anything but domestic service to give them a chance of advancing up the social scale. I saw it stated the other day that a man who advertised for a typiste had nearly 100 applications for the job, while his wife who advertised the same day for a domestic had none.[48]

This is not surprising. After all, the working conditions in the office were infinitely better than in domestic service or the factory, so young women flocked to the new commercial schools to learn the trade. In 1910 in Melbourne the commercial college Stotts enrolled over 1000 students, while in much smaller Perth the number was 348.[49] In these schools students, increasingly young women, learned general and standardised skills that could be used in the systematised and standardised offices. And if Australia was like other industrialised countries, most of these young women were middle class, and had stayed at schools which, in the early twentieth century, began to teach skills useful for employment.[50] Like their brothers, they became literate and numerate in a practical way, but unlike their brothers they were excluded from the professions because they were women. This new and expanding labour force, unable to work in factories or domestic service because they were middle class, had to go into office work, and office work provided them with status, respectability and femininity, part of being middle class.

When you manage a man

Two ideologies informed the work of Australian middle-class women. The first was that domestic ideology which developed in early nineteenth-century England which constructed woman as the 'angel of the home', the cooling, restraining hand on the fevered brow of nineteenth-century commercial life, the builder of husbands' and sons' emotional life. The second was that brand of class consciousness which put most kinds of paid work for women beyond the bounds of respectability. To be middle class and to do paid work smacked of poverty, genteel poverty perhaps, but a poverty which in the nineteenth century spoke of moral and social failure. Hence, paid work for middle-class women was described less as work and more as a vocation, a service to humanity.

The first ideology was beautifully expressed by 'An old housekeeper'

> What you have to manage when you manage a man is not only the creature himself, but that belonging to himself which he has to confide to your charge, his house, his children, his friends, his good name, his reputation for hospitality, his property, his comfort, his standing in society and his servants.[51]

This was 'the ideal bourgeois family', in which the husband was the breadwinner and his wife and children were dependent on him for their physical survival. Each had their space, their sphere. The public sphere of paid work and politics was the husband's. The private sphere of the home that of the wife and mother. Both were supreme in their own domains—the wife as carer, nurturer, and civiliser—and this she was, in one sense, because her civilising influence spread from her home to society and gave her the responsibility for reproducing, on a society-wide scale, the domestic contentment and security of the home. In reality it condemned women to a glorified slavery—*his* home, *his* children, *his* friends— the world is the man's, the woman his servant.

This ideology really did not have to develop here, for it arrived in Australia ready made from England.[52] It took hold in the 1870s and 1880s for much the same reasons it did in England, where there was a strong evangelical movement, a middle-class striving for power, a decadent ruling class and a working class beginning to flex its muscles. Although in places like Melbourne there was an endless optimism about the future, there was a sense that the whole of society was still unsettled, still a frontier, its social order still fluid and solidifying. In Australia the home became the 'haven from the heartless world', the place where the husband was re-created each night for the next day's work, the place where the manly and feminine virtues which underpinned work roles were created and developed, the place where consumption, leisure and display were a measure of a man and his family's status.[53]

In this idealised picture, middle-class women did little work because they had servants to do it for them. Servants gave her time for accomplishments and moral example. In practice, the amount of work they did depended on the family's wealth and the number of servants. However, by 1901 only 10 percent of New South Wales households employed domestics, the bulk of them employing just one.[54] Housekeeper, parlourmaid, cook, scullery maid, kitchen maids, still room maid, head housemaid, second and third housemaid, ladies' maid and children's nurse—this is the image of the below stairs staff we get from television shows like 'Upstairs, Downstairs'. Of course it was quite anachronistic by the turn of the century. Maids-of-all-work had all but replaced such specialised staff in Australia.

Such was the strength of the belief that a civilised and civilising family needed servants that the migration of working-class women to Australia in the nineteenth century was based largely on their presumed use as domestic servants. Middle-class women led the crusades for women's immigration for they saw in every servant the basis of their way of life.[55]

The relationship between mistresses and servants was a class relationship. Servants were working or, occasionally, lower middle-class women or girls, their mistresses middle class and above although occasionally lower middle class and artisan's families might employ them. The core of the relationship was that unequal employer–employee one, which, however, as that keen scholar of nineteenth-century urban life, Richard Twopeny, reported, was of an archaic sort. He sympathetically quoted an article in the Melbourne *Argus*, which asked 'why the relations between mistress and servant should continue as they were in feudal times, when the relations of other classes of society to each other have been settled on an entirely different basis'.[56] That 'entirely different basis' was the supposed egalitarianism of Australian society, which allowed servants to be both independent and impudent. Nevertheless it is well to remember that for every example of a servant leaving her employment for better wages there were plenty of examples of arbitrary dismissals.

The 'servant problem' was solved in Australia in the twentieth century by several developments. New labour-saving devices filtered slowly into middle-class homes, which were themselves transformed from the showy and over-decorated places of the Victorian age to the more sparsely and functionally fitted out places they became in the new century; hence they were easier to clean. That demographic transition which saw the average number of children born per woman decline so radically gave middle-class women the time that their servants had formerly given them. Most of all, however, middle-class women became housewives because of the sheer unwillingness of working-class women to work for them.

Servants gave middle-class women time and time gave middle-class women the capacity to display their accomplishments, and the time to engage in 'good works'. Married middle-class women did not, by and large, do paid work, so those with the energy and the inclination engaged in philanthropy, unpaid work which on the one hand gave assistance to the poor and on the other made sure the poor stayed exactly as they were—poor. They organised and ran charities like the Ladies' Benevolent Society, hospitals for women, such as the Women's and Queen Victoria hospitals in Melbourne, and refuges. Most of these dealt with poor women from whom the lady committee-members maintained a discrete social distance. The aim was, by a judicious mixing of assistance, instruction and threat, to turn those poor women into mirror images of their benefactresses, upright, responsible, respectable, home-loving, dependent wives.[57] Sometimes their philanthropy was more blatantly self-interested. The Tasmanian Society of Friends petitioned the Governor for funds for a 'servants' home':

> There can be only one opinion as to the importance of having good female domestic Servants, and of their influence on the comfort of our homes, the morals of our children, and the prosperity of the general community. And whereas young Females leaving the mother country and their natural guardians, when they arrive in the Colonies, finding themselves friendless, and their high hopes disappointed; and sometimes proving incompetent for situations so different from their former occupations, too often become the victims of the designing and depraved, and sink into poverty and vice: Your Petitioners, therefore, are deeply impressed with the conviction, that a Lodging House, or Home, for the accommodation of female domestic Servants, is greatly needed in this city.[58]

Given the ideological construction of middle-class women as carers and mistresses, it is not surprising that jobs which middle-class women could do were constructed in the same way. The domestic ideology prohibited any but single women or those in dire straits from taking paid work, but a very pronounced sense of propriety restricted them to a very narrow range of jobs. Factory work and domestic service were quite beyond the pale (a middle-class domestic servant to a middle-class family would have caused great social problems). Nineteenth-century education hardly fitted them for paid employment, because they were taught accomplishments designed to make them interesting companions; so beyond moderate reading, writing and arithmetical skills they learned needlework, drawing and painting, French and how to play the piano. It was not until late into the nineteenth century and early in the twentieth that some schools began to teach literary, scientific and commercial skills.[59]

Teaching and nursing were the occupations into which most single middle-class women went (and they were expected to give these up on marriage). Nursing was made respectable in the mid-nineteenth century by Florence Nightingale. The 'Nightingale system' of nursing took previously untrained nurses and trained them. It took previously lax hospital administration and transformed it. And it transformed the image of nurses from the Dickensian 'Sairy Gamp' to the 'ministering angel'. Lucy Osborne, the first Nightingale nurse in Sydney, regarded the character of the nurses in Sydney Hospital with contempt. When she arrived she found

> dirty frowsy old women, slatternly untidy young ones all greasy with their hair down their backs with ragged stuff dresses that required no washing [sic]. The doctors habitually stamped and raved at them. In the wards the patients called Betsy and Polly to do the most menial work for them. The dirt, in spite of all the stamping and raging, seemed ever increasing. The noise and prank in the wards were too dreadful; I was several weeks in understanding it all—weeks simply amazed.[60]

Under the Nightingale system, nursing became a 'gentlewoman's occupation'. Although in theory it was open to working-class girls, the very selective entry requirements and the fact that first-year student probationers were not paid and only paid paltry wages thereafter meant that most nurses needed the financial support of their families. It was the middle-class contempt for monetary reward for women's work and the Nightingale ideology of selfless and devoted work that kept the occupation mainly in the hands of the middle class. It was also an occupation that was kept subordinate to male doctors. Nightingale herself would not attend patients unless doctors were there.[61]

Teaching was the second major occupation open to middle-class women and it took two forms. Governessing was the smaller and more idiosyncratically middle class, really derived more from the home than the school, for governesses taught middle-class children in their homes. Governesses were usually educated and unmarried emigrants from Britain, where, in the nineteenth century, their employment prospects were declining. They worked in all parts of the colonies in quite large numbers until the Compulsory Education Acts of the 1870s and 1880s made parents send their children to schools.[62] However, it was much more common for middle-class women to become teachers in the colonial and state teaching services. Compulsory education created the need and the vast spread of schools across the country offered the opportunities for women, opportunities which increased as the meaning of 'compulsory' was tightened and the number of schools increased in the twentieth century. By the end of the nineteenth century about half of state school teachers in New South Wales were women. Before and after World War I women made up nearly two-thirds of state school teachers in Western Australia. Typically they were under 30, unmarried, assistant teachers, working in the city or the bush.⁶³

Yet strict rules and regulations combined to tie women teachers into patterns of respectability and domesticity. Colonial education departments kept tight reign over the private lives of their staff. In Victoria women teachers who married or 'engaged in unseemly conduct' were dismissed. For example, this is what they were not allowed to wear: '1. A bathing costume; 2. skirts split to expose the ankles; 3. bloomers for cycling; 4. bustle extensions over 10 inches.'⁶⁴ This gendered discrimination also kept women teachers at the bottom of the teaching scale. In New South Wales in 1902, although half the teachers were female, only one quarter were in charge of schools. And as might be expected their pay was also substantially less than men's.⁶⁵

Another, and perhaps the final kind of job open to middle-class women was in the drapery and millinery trades. 'Trade' to the socially conscious always had vulgar connotations of the lower-middle-class. Nevertheless, some middle-class women did work in the new and big department stores, where they dealt only with women and then only with women of their own class. Again status was important to such 'shop girls', separating them from women doing manual work and tying them into the structures of authority and patronage exercised by the owners of the department stores.

For these workers, as well as for nurses, teachers, middle-class housewives and mistresses of servants, the combination of the ideologies of domesticity and respectability, which they had been told gave them moral and ethical power, really did little more than segregate them into a constricted area where their talents and interests and capacities seemed to be frustrated at every turn.

6 Control and protection

From the beginning of 'free' work in Australia there has been a sense in which workers asserted their common identity. That unions were established in the 1830s and 1840s is well known, as are the campaigns which workers fought over issues that were important to them. However, the sharing of information about pay rates among rural workers, the widely held assumptions about which wages were fair and which were not, and even the riotous way workers celebrated good fortune or simply escaped the dreariness of their work, illustrates a common ethos. Yet the mobilisation of workers as a real industrial and political force did not begin until the 1870s and 1880s. To be sure it was exclusive and restricted to white, male workers; nevertheless it was strong enough to change the course of the history of work. The period from 1880 to 1910 is crucial to that history because it represented a consolidation of class consciousness and the flowering of a movement strong enough to wield its influence in the arena which had hitherto been closed to it—the state. The arbitration system was plainly the most important result of this, up until the time that labour was able to take hold of government itself. People have long argued about the nature of arbitration, its virtues and its faults. Nevertheless, turn-of-the-century unions by and large supported it, for it did give them some of the protection they needed following their heavy defeats in the great strikes of the 1890s. Yet the arbitration system helped to consolidate the changes in the labour process that workers disliked, and helped to solidify the unequal distribution of work and wages between men and women. So while it was playing a part in creating a strong union movement, it was also institutionalising its inequalities. For the working class as a whole, then, the advances it made over this period were a mixed blessing.

We have come 16 000 miles to better our conditions

The origins of trade unionism go back to before the gold rushes, to those first concentrations of working men in the colonial capitals. Skilled craftsmen like tailors, shoemakers, printers, weavers, cabinet makers and carpenters were among the earliest to organise. Watermen, clerks, drapers and brickmakers were among the first of the semi-skilled, but there were signs of organisation among the unskilled too. A recent survey of organisations in the smaller colonies shows that among the 22 occupational groups in Tasmania, the 19 in South Australia and the 9 in Western Australia that engaged in some kind of collective action there were whalers, rural workers, miners and wharf labourers. Most of the early unions were weak, and their existence precarious. Those in the colonies without convicts were the more aggressive because they did not have to compete with unpaid convict labour, but in economies which boomed and broke with depressing monotony, no union could guarantee its survival, nor the full protection of its members.[1]

The early craft unions were rather different from unions as we know them. They provided benefits to members to tide them over sickness, injury and unemployment and they also paid for funerals, all from the funds which they accumulated from members' dues. However, they were also concerned with pay rates (especially falling pay) and hours of work, so they tried to impose their 'working rules', their codified conditions of work, on employers. And like all unions they tried to restrict entry to their trades by controlling the taking on of apprentices, and by establishing 'houses of call', informal labour exchanges where employers had to hire unemployed union members. They had other interests as well. They fought against transportation and assignment of convicts and the assisted emigration schemes. They campaigned against the Masters' and Servants' Acts and the importation of non-white labour. They did not seek the intervention of the state except in their political campaigns probably because, by their very existence, they were breaking the anti-union Combination Acts, inherited by the colonial governments. They did not seek to change society, although some of them established short-term cooperative production enterprises. They had, too, a sense of their own status, they despised unskilled workers, and women workers were completely beyond the pale.[2] This then was the character of the early movement, and its interests, forms of organisation, tactics and style continued to typify unionism for many years.

James Galloway, the British born stonemason whose name is remembered in Melbourne for his role in the eight-hour-day campaign, once said:

> We have come 16,000 miles to better our conditions, and not to act the mere part of machinery; and it is neither right nor just that we should cross the trackless regions of immensity between us and our fatherland, to be rewarded with excessive toil, a bare existence and a premature grave.[3]

Migrant workers saw migration as an escape from the old world and old-world conditions of work in the early years of the industrial revolution. They had seen the effects of machinery on their trades in Britain and their rhetoric speaks of this knowledge.

The chance of a new start in a new world did not come about through the promise of a reconstructed society, nor through the independence promised by gold or land. The early trade unionists were practical men, not given to theorising. They were committed to their trades because their trade skills were their property. They had worked their way up from apprentice to journeyman to craftsman, and some had gone further, from employee to capitalist. In their trades and their property lay their self-respect, developed in the long years they had served as apprentices, learning the arts and mysteries of their trades.

They were upright, proud and respectable. They demanded to be treated with respect and that meant being treated with fairness, for it was this sense of fairness which characterised the early struggles of the craft unions, especially in their campaign for the eight-hour day. Eight hours work was one of the three intertwined 'eights' which adorned many a trade union emblem, eight hours work, eight hours rest and eight hours recreation. However, it was not just a question of reducing hours. Many of the working men's leaders were hungry for education, moral and intellectual advancement. In circumstances where education certainly was not regarded as the right of working people, the eight-hour day was an assertion of such a right.[4]

The Sydney stonemasons won the eight-hour day first in 1855 and their Melbourne brethren won it next, in 1856. It spread quickly in both cities, at first through the building trades then slowly across the other skilled trades. Sydney workers compromised with their employers and had their wages reduced, but the Melbourne men did not, so they won a real wage increase as well. However, most workers never worked an eight-hour day. Unskilled men, women, children, and the Chinese still worked very long hours, often until well into the twentieth century. Even those unions which had won 'the boon' frequently lost it and had to begin the fight all over again.[5]

It was not until the 1870s and 1880s that the unskilled male workers began to organise—miners, shearers, shed hands, lumpers, seamen, transport workers, gas-stokers, clothing workers and railway workers. Contemporaries (and historians) observed this phenomenon and their propensity to strike and called these new organisations 'new unions', to distinguish them from the older craft-based ones, but they were not so dissimilar.

In the first place, they had benevolent functions written into their constitutions and used them as a way of attracting members just as the craft unions did. Secondly, to call their members unskilled is to underestimate the training and knowledge needed to become, for example, a shearer or a miner. Many shearers and miners were paid piece rates, so the more skilful the worker the more he was paid. Thirdly, these unions were also exclusive in two senses. They all opposed the entry of non-British workers into their occupations, claiming that they would undermine hard-won wages and conditions. In fact, like most white Australians at the time, they were violently racist. For instance the Federated Seamen's Union in its original objectives urged its members to 'manly resistance to Chinese Labour' and the Shearers' Union refused to accept Aborigines as members. These unions were also restrictive in the more usual sense that they allowed only workers of a kind into the union. 'I hate the smell of a rouseabout', shearers might have hissed to station hands, and this reflects the distinctiveness shearers felt, which caused shed hands to form their own union. Seamen, too, had different unions based on occupations, and the Sydney Wharf Labourers' Union had strict laws governing with whom members could work. Working with non-union labour was right out!

The new unions were also less radical than has been supposed. Certainly they were prepared to use strike action, but as any analysis of the shearing strikes of the 1880s and early 1890s shows, most of these were strikes over recognition of the union and its log of claims. That is, they were tools of collective bargaining, just as were the strikes of the craft workers. Certainly they were sometimes violent. The tactic the shearers used, of abducting strikebreakers, certainly was not common to the nineteenth century but it was an expression of the outright hatred that all union members felt towards those who were taking away their livelihood. However new and innovative these may have been, they were not the tools of a general strike or a class war. The new unions, therefore, were not so dissimilar from the old. It is not surprising, then, that a sense of common identity between workers' unions of all sorts was being forged. In Sydney, unions formed their Trades and Labour Council in 1871; in Melbourne, the Committee which had been managing the old Trades Hall took on the functions of a TLC in 1879; and the Brisbane unions followed suit six years later. In 1879, the first inter-colonial trade union congress met in 1884 and again in 1885.[6]

The crucial moment in the history of unions' wage demands in Australia was the adoption of the living or family wage. Throughout most of the nineteenth century wage levels had been arrived at by a combination of custom and practice and the relative strength of bosses and workers in the shifting labour market. The living wage seems to have been based on the presumption that wages should be high enough to support a family in reasonable comfort. As it was used in Australia, the concept was more a moral demand by unskilled workers and their sympathisers to raise their wages to a 'fair and reasonable' level. Adopting the language of 'fair and reasonable' was to claim the high moral ground and the appeal to a public long indoctrinated in the relationship between fairness and right.[7]

A fair day's work meant the eight-hour day. Fairness in wages meant, for unskilled workers, 7/- a day. Tactically unions began their campaigns by urging governments to lead the way and pay their unskilled workers the 7/- a day minimum on government works or have the 7/- minimum written into work given out to contractors. (Better still, unions thought contractors should not do government work anyway.) They then hoped that the 7/- would be carried over to the private sector. They used workers' representatives in the new post-depression parliaments to argue their case and, in New South Wales at least, they were so successful that by 1901 governments had all but done away with contracting and were paying 7/- as a standard rate.[8]

Private employers were under no such compulsion and very few paid the 7/- minimum. In the context of weakened unions and a disrupted labour market, collective bargaining was more a matter of uncollective impositions. Unions, in Victoria particularly, won very little from the wages boards, which ignored the living wage and instead made their judgements on the 'capacity of industry to pay', the wishes of the employers or as a plain compromise between the conflicting claims. In the states, in the private sphere, the 7/- a day standard was not universally accepted until 1921, and then only for male wages.[9]

If there was one issue other than wages and hours which preoccupied the nineteenth-century unions it was unemployment. They first attacked the problem at what the unions thought was its source, immigration, and they also tried to cope with it by lobbying governments to protect local industries. Restricted immigration, unemployment relief, and many more union demands needed the state for their institution. The state in Australia has been one of the most powerful in the capitalist world. Its stature was, in part, a cause of the unions' engagement with it and in part a product of it. The extent of the states' engagement with work is the subject of the next section.

A fair and reasonable wage

If we call the parliaments, the governments, the bureaucracies, the police, military, prisons and the courts 'the state', then the state has been the third party to the organisation of work from 1788 until the present. At the time of transportation the state set up an apparatus to constrain and control the convicts' work, and the early governors established regulations to fix the wages of free labourers. Reluctant governments used relief works from the 1840s to mop up seasonal unemployment. Assisted immigration programmes were designed to sway the labour market to the advantage of the employers of labour. There were also the Masters' and Servants' Acts, the anti-trade union laws and, of course, the use of the police and the courts to break strikes and destroy unions, of which there is no better example than in the great strikes of the 1890s. But let us begin with schools.

By the 1870s elementary education was available, in principle, for all parents in Australia who wanted it for their children, except in country areas, where there were few schools and where few children received little formal education of any kind. Even in cities and towns education was not compulsory, so many children's attendance was irregular to say the least. Many parents did not want to send their children to school, and it is not surprising when we remember just how many worked from the age of eight or nine and how many families depended on this work for the family's survival.

In New South Wales by the end of the 1870s the average attendance of children at schools was just 152 days out of a possible 230 per year. 'Compulsory' education instituted in each colony between 1870 and 1890 meant attendance for a minimum number of days each quarter or half year. In South Australia this was 35 days out of 55 per quarter, and exemptions and fees made the term 'compulsory' seem even less real. Nevertheless it did affect work in three ways. Firstly, it took many children out of the labour market and put them into school (and progressive increases in the leaving age have had the same effect). In theory this should have benefited older workers who would suffer less competition, but employers still employed armies of children twelve and thirteen years old. Secondly, schooling took the children's pay out of the family income, reducing that family's standard of living. Thirdly, it played a part in destroying that transitional stage in the development of wage labour, the sub-contracting phase, where parents took their children to work with them.[10]

The child protection Acts passed in several colonies in the later years of the nineteenth century were similar in effect to the compulsory education acts. In New South Wales, for example, one Act passed in 1892 prohibited the employment of children in public performance or exhibition when they were in physical danger. In

1905 a Neglected Children's and Juvenile Offender's Act prohibited children under ten from street trading unless they had a license and they could only get a license if it could be shown that their 'moral and spiritual welfare' was not at risk.[11]

The Acts which regulated Aboriginal employment were also couched in the language of protection. Protection of Aborigines has a long history in Australia, based on a confusion of motives. Humanitarians urged that Aborigines be segregated from white society both for their physical survival and to protect them from 'contamination' by 'low whites'. Employers wanted to secure a regime of discipline over their employees. Governments, anxious to cut costs anyway, were convinced that the best solution to the 'Aboriginal problem' was Aborigine's rapid social and racial absorption into white society. New South Wales and Victorian policy tended towards the last programme, and Acts of Parliament in 1886 in Victoria and 1909 in New South Wales evicted part-Aborigines from reserves to force them to fend for themselves. In the other colonies and states the Parliaments did the opposite and set up a system of reserves, giving themselves the power to forcibly send Aborigines there, where they were subjected to rigid rules which regulated practically every aspect of their lives, forced them to work on prescribed jobs and educated them in Christianity and British culture.[12]

In part these acts segregated Aborigines and white Australians but they were also labour laws, and some of them regulated the employment of Aborigines outside the reserves. The Parliamentarians who passed the 1886 Act in Western Australia not only set up that colony's rudimentary Aboriginal protectorate, they also established a system of contracts governing Aboriginal employment. Henceforth no one under fourteen years of age could sign a contract, government administrators had to certify that the recruit had signed willingly and, a regimen of rations, clothing and medical treatment was set out. But the Act did not prescribe that all employment relationships had to be under contract so, when in 1905, a Royal Commission counted the number of contracts, it found that only 10 percent of Aborigines were covered.

By the 1890s Western Australian pastoralists had begun to use the Masters' and Servants' Acts to control and discipline their Aboriginal workers, however, in 1892, the colonial government excluded Aborigines from that Act. But, Parliament, acting at the pastoralists' behest, passed new legislation imposing heavy punishments on Aborigines who absconded. An 1886 Act had reduced the penalty for absconding from three months' imprisonment to one. The 1892 Act restored the original and added a flogging with a cat o' nine tails as an extra incentive to Aborigines to stay put. A later Act allowed pastoralists who were also Justices of the Peace to hear cases and deliver verdicts against their own workers, a practice which was unknown elsewhere in Australia and which law makers throughout the nineteenth century had carefully avoided.[13]

Protective legislation was also applied to the work of some of the imported non-European groups. The outcry over the tragic death rate and the gross abuses of the Kanaka labour trade forced successive Queensland governments to regulate it. In 1868 the Polynesian Labourers Act obliged employers to notify the government of the number of its workers, to guarantee their wages, provide them with food, shelter, tobacco and medical care, to pay their costs to and from their homes and guarantee their return and to enter a bond with the government to make sure this was done. In 1871, government agents were sent on each recruiting mission to ensure that the recruits were both willing and aware of the implications of their jobs. Later acts tightened up on the conditions of work, food and accommodation, recruiting vessels were licensed and could be banned and recruiters had to pay for each recruit they signed on.[14] In one sense these were responses to the abuses in the trade, in another they were reactions to the anti-labour trade humanitarians who depicted Queensland as a slave-trading colony. However, the end of the trade was not a response to the abuses but part of the development of the White Australia policy. In 1901 the new Commonwealth government, in one of its very first enactments, introduced legislation to phase out the trade by 1904 and deport all the Kanakas (with some exceptions) to their islands by the end of 1906. A tariff would henceforth protect the industry—£3 per ton excise was placed on sugar, with £2 of it to be refunded if the sugar was grown by white labour. (This was later increased to £4 and £3.) The overwhelming sentiment in the Commonwealth government was that all work in Australia should be reserved for white workers, that all 'coloured' labour should be excluded from the country.[15] By 1906 the Kanaka period had all but ended, only 1000 were permitted to remain in Australia, while white workers, particularly southern Europeans, began to do the work the Kanakas had done for the previous 40 years.[16]

Only in the 1880s did the Western Australian administration begin to insist on proper contracts between master and men, into which were to be written provisions for adequate wages, rations, working conditions and repatriation, although the frequent use by masters of the Masters and Servants Act reminded the Malay and Japanese pearl divers that the state was not wholly their friend. Later legislation restricted the Malays and Japanese to the northern half of the state. There was also provision for repatriation, which seems benevolent, but it was in reality a way of maintaining the pearling labour force and of making sure its members did not 'sully' white Western Australia by staying on permanently. In its defence it must be said that the government was on the horns of a dilemma. Pearlers had convinced it that a white Australian workforce was not available to do the work. Trade unionists assailed it for allowing the pearlers to undercut white workers' conditions by employing Malays, and humanitarians accused it of countenancing a system of slavery. In the end the colony's and the Commonwealth's Immigration Restriction Acts resolved the problem. Henceforth only Japanese pearl divers were allowed to remain in Australia because the pearlers persuaded the Commonwealth government that the industry could not survive without them.[17]

For white Australian workers the Factory Acts were the most important of the state's interventions in the paid workplace until the introduction of the arbitration system. The first Factory Act was launched in Tasmania in 1874 and the second in Victoria in 1875; like most of their successors these Acts came about because of public exposure of the working conditions of women and children in factories. Victoria led the way in this kind of legislation probably because it was the first colony to introduce a comprehensive tariff and because Victoria was the most industrialised of the colonies. Given the protection granted to industry by tariffs and the poverty and exploitation exposed by anti-sweating campaigns, the conditions in these workplaces seemed even more reprehensible. Each colony passed Factory Acts in the 1890s and 1900s, as and when conditions in their own factories were exposed.

Factory Acts regulated the construction of factories and restricted the employment of women and children. Standards of lighting, heating and sanitation were set. The number of workers to a room was regulated. Standards were set for the fencing off of machinery. Factory inspectors were appointed to oversee these improvements and to prosecute backsliders. Restricting the work of women and children began with the first Victorian Act, in which they were forbidden to work more than eight or eight and a half hours a day, but later Acts actually forbade boys and girls under specified ages from working at all, which was an extra encouragement to parents to send their children to school. Night work for women and children was also banned. Some of the later Acts tackled the difficult problem of outwork, requiring that employers register their outworkers and keep records of their names and wages paid to them.[18]

The early Factory Acts were ineffective. The first Victorian Act, for example, defined a factory as a workplace with more than ten workers, so some employers cut their factories into smaller units to reduce employees' numbers to below the limit, and others reduced their numbers to under ten and sent the rest home to do outwork. Some of these early Acts were 'voluntary', so employers ignored them; and when inspectorates *were* set up, they were small, understaffed and often too friendly with the people they were inspecting. Later Acts became somewhat more effective as the number of workers deemed to comprise a factory was reduced and the inspectors were given greater powers.[19]

The Royal Commissions and select committees from whose reports the Factory Acts came were obsessed with sex. Certainly women and children workers needed protecting from exploiting employers, so there was a great deal of chivalric language from the sponsors of the Acts.[20] They were also concerned about the 'promiscuous' mixing of women and men and boys and girls in factories, in circumstances the committees were convinced would cause vice and immorality. They worried, too, about the effect of factory work on family life. Their ideal was the bourgeois family, their nightmare a family where working wives and children undermined and subverted the authority of the husband/father and the 'proper' role of the wife/mother. Outwork, done in the home, they believed made it a home no longer. They also wanted to make work for white men, so the Acts also placed several petty barriers in the path of Chinese factory owners.

The proponents of factory legislation were good liberals. They were worried that sweating and outwork would bring down the wages of the factory trades as factory owners reduced their wages to compete with the 'sweaters'. At the heart of liberal thinking, in Victoria especially, was the belief in the identity of interests of labour and capital, particularly as it was shored up by the tariff. Unrestricted competition might break that link and send workers and bosses from consensus to conflict.[21]

In addition to regulating the hours and conditions of work in factories, several of these Acts reduced the hours during which shops could open. Long hours of work, six days a week, was the lot of the shop assistant in the nineteenth century, despite the succession of early closing movements in the 1840s. This memoir of an employee of a boot retailer recalls a working day of thirteen hours:

> Fifteen years back, when I made my first bow to the world (ahem!), as an incipient boot retailer, the working hours of the employees were cruelly long. For seven years I toiled in that ancient shop—squeezing copper toed boots onto chubby feet and pulling lasting elastic-side boots on feet of old ladies who were too stout to stoop and pull them on themselves—from 8am to 9pm on weekdays, and till 11.30pm on Saturdays. It was not until I had been in the place more than four years that I even obtained a single early night off. When I was allowed the privilege of one evening off every week at 5pm I nearly went mad with joy. A night off—to be able to leave off work in broad daylight—seemed too utterly grand to be true.[22]

In the 1885 Victorian Act shops were required to close at 7pm each weekday and at 10pm on Saturday. In the 1896 Act a limit of 52 hours a week was set on the hours women and boys under sixteen could work, but, peculiarly, municipalities were given the right to vary hours, so powerful retailers on municipal councils could, and did, make by-laws to allow themselves to stay open. The half-holiday did not eventuate for shop assistants until the twentieth century; 1901 in South Australia and 1907 in Victoria, although retailers could choose whether this might be on a Saturday or a Wednesday.[23]

The state's most important intervention in the workplace began in the 1890s with the creation of wages boards and courts of conciliation and arbitration. Most trade unions wanted a system of conciliation and arbitration. They were greatly weakened by the 1890's depression and the defeat of the unions in the big strikes of the 1890s. Humanitarian liberals, too, were anxious for some means to minimise the class conflict which characterised the 1890s and clearly saw arbitration as such a means.[24]

As part of the Victorian Factory Act of 1896, four wages boards were set up to provide minimum wages and conditions for the clothing, furniture, baking and butchering trades. Just five years later there were 27 such boards in Victoria, on which an equal number of representatives from employees and employers met under the stewardship of an independent chairman.[25] Victoria ran second to New South Wales, however. Its 1891 Royal Commission on strikes had recommended conciliation and arbitration courts for New South Wales, and a system was established whereby a dispute would go first to a conciliation board, then to an arbitration court if conciliation failed. The system itself failed but New South Wales tried again in 1901, and an Act was passed which gave the court real teeth. It could make an award for a whole industry. It could compel the production of books and accounts and, in what was a triumph for the union movement, it would hear only unions as representatives of workers.[26] The other states took various routes to arbitration. Western Australia and Queensland followed New South Wales; and South Australia and Tasmania followed Victoria.[27]

The Commonwealth system was introduced in 1904, in a different context from that of the colonies and states. Robin Gollan argues that the context was the creation of a new, isolated and anxious white nation, half a world away from the Europe with which it identified itself, and arbitration was but one of a package of measures designed to keep alien worlds and cultures at bay. The Immigration Restriction Act was passed to keep Australia white. Other acts created the Australian navy and conscripted men for military service. And 'new protection' promised to keep foreign goods out so that Australian industry could grow.[28]

The new Australian constitution declared that there would be free trade between the states but that the Commonwealth would have power over foreign trade. New protection would do more than just keep foreign goods out. In one sense it was the liberals' answer to industrial regulation. As the Prime Minister, Alfred Deakin, stated:

> The 'Old' Protection contented itself with making good wages possible. The 'New' Protection seeks to make them actual. It aims at according to the manufacturer that degree of exemption from unfair outside competition which will enable him to pay *fair* and *reasonable* wages without impairing the maintenance and extension of his industry, or its capacity to supply the local market. It does not stop here. Having put the manufacturer in a position to pay good wages, it goes on to assure the public that he *does* pay them.[29]

A series of tariff Acts made up the new protection, but the most important for the history of work were the two which regulated protection for the farm machinery industry. They were the Excise Tariff Act and the Customs Tariff Act. The latter set high tariffs on imported farm machinery and the former imposed duties on agricultural machinery made in Australia, but it stipulated that manufacturers could get rebates or exemptions only if they paid their workers a fair and reasonable wage.

What was a fair and reasonable wage? Who would decide? That job was given to the Commonwealth Arbitration Court and to one of the most influential men in Australia's work history, Henry Bournes Higgins. Higgins, like Deakin, was a radical Liberal. He had been shocked by the conditions in Melbourne's clothing industry in the 1880s and 1890s, and had long believed that it was the state's duty to advance the welfare of the underprivileged. His first protagonist was quite the opposite. H.V. Mackay was the wealthy manufacturer of the Sunshine combine harvesters and he hated unions and loathed wages boards. In 1904 he applied to the Arbitration Court for a rebate on the excise duty on the grounds that the 6/- a day he paid his unskilled workers was 'fair and reasonable'. Higgins found that it was not, and after a detailed investigation settled on the 7/- a day which the trade unions proposed, a daily rate which would support a man, his dependent wife and three dependent children. Mackay's application was refused.

The judgement was an historic one, but Mackay appealed against it to the High Court, which agreed with his submission that the Excise Tariff Act was unconstitutional on the grounds that the Constitution expressly gave this power to the states. Higgins' judgement was struck out and new protection collapsed. However,

Higgins' commitment to the 'fair and reasonable' wage continued and for many years the Commonwealth court applied the principle of need to its judgements on wages. State courts took ten years to come around, but eventually need became the basis of wage fixation throughout Australia.[30]

Arbitration courts went much further than imposing a basic wage. They erected a superstructure of margins for skill, rewarding, as a succession of judges said, the long period of instruction that turned apprentices into artisans. The difference in pay between skilled and unskilled work had long categorised paid work, so the arbitration systems in this case simply ratified existing customs. Nevertheless they did intervene in the way technological change and the reorganising of work affected pay by setting up systems of classifications into which they fitted new jobs. They also set limits on the ratio of apprentices and improvers to tradespeople in various industries. In some industries these protected trades threatened by de-skilling. In others the courts deliberately undermined the trades by increasing the number of juniors without apprenticeships, so facilitating the replacement of the skilled by the unskilled.[31]

The courts had other functions too. For example, they were given power over unfair dismissals, an interesting and important intervention in the arbitrary powers of management.[32] Many unions were given complete closed shop coverage of workers in their industries and others were awarded preference clauses in which employers had to give preference to unionists.[33] However, one of the most important decisions regarding workers came not from the tribunals but from the governments which established them. Most tribunals would hear only unions as the representatives of workers. When people marvel at the percentage of Australian workers in unions and compare them to the equivalent figures in the USA, for example, they should look to this system of representation for a substantial part of the difference. An arbitration system depends on the organisation of both sides to make it work. Workers flocked to form and join unions in the early years of arbitration, as the table on the following page shows.

Trade union membership in selected years from 1891 to 1926[34]

Year	Number of unions	Members	Total members as % of workforce
1891	124	54 888	4.1
1896	134	55 066	N/A
1901	198	97 174	N/A
1906	302	175 529	6.1
1911	573	364 732	27.9
1916	392	546 556	47.5
1921	382	703 009	51.6
1926	372	851 478	55.2

Born to cook

It is very difficult to chart the progress of women's unions and women in unions in the nineteenth and early twentieth centuries. Edna Ryan shows that in Sydney there were separate unions of telegraphists, tailoresses, barmaids and waitresses, laundry workers, general workers, shop assistants, cooks and pantry maids. Only the telegraphists survived the Depression of the 1890s, although others were revived later. The Tailoresses' Union was one of these; in 1901 it had 1500 members. A Laundry Employees' Union was formed with 200 members in 1903, but it is difficult to say whether there were any more.[35]

The tailoresses were first to organise, in Victoria in 1882. Indeed, the Tailoresses' Union was the first women's union in Australia and it had 2000 members at its peak. However, by 1891 it had all but collapsed, weakened by the twin pressures of outwork and the Depression. It recovered slowly until it amalgamated with the tailors' union in 1906. After the Depression, others were formed, such as the Female Confectioners' Union, the Victorian Ladies' Teachers' Union, the Women's Public Service Association and the Women's Post and Telegraph Association; and the Women Bookbinders and Stationers' Union, formed in 1911.[36]

Other unions had women members. In Victoria, the boot, textile and tobacco workers' unions admitted women members but only into certain classifications of membership. Probably twelve of the 101 unions registered with the Arbitration Court in New South Wales had women members; they were among workers like straw hatters, broom makers and textile workers. The Australian Workers' Union had special women's divisions in New South Wales and Queensland, which it set up in 1892. In fact, it was the first union to employ women organisers, which it did in the same year.[37]

The history of the Melbourne Tailoresses' Union exemplifies the history of women's unions and the position of women in unions. Domestic service and the clothing trades were the two biggest sources of paid work for women in the late nineteenth and early twentieth centuries in the big colonies. From time to time there were attempts by the labour movement to organise domestic servants into unions but they invariably floundered on the isolation of servants in the houses of their employers and their invisibility to the organisers.[38] This was not the case with the tailoresses, who were often employed in big factories, and could be organised more easily.

The Tailoresses' Union actually originated from a strike in the Beath Schiess and Co. factory in December 1882 in protest at a reduction in piece rates. At first the strike was run by the Victorian Trades Hall Council, but on 15 December a 500-strong meeting of tailoresses formed the Union and rejected the company's offer to re-employ the strikers at the old rates. Beath Schiess and Co. quickly accepted the union's log of claims but the other big manufacturers did not, and in February the next year a general strike of tailoresses took place. The strike seemed to have been successful. As manufacturers progressively accepted the log the women called off the strike in their factories.

The effects of the strike were not as the tailoresses had wished. Most big firms reneged on the log, and began sending work to outworkers. As one tailoress put it, 'Everywhere the work went out [and] the hands inside had nothing to do.'[39] Perhaps this is the reason why membership declined so dramatically. In 1883 it had 2000 members. In 1890 it had 100 and in 1906 its remaining members amalgamated with The Tailors' Society.[40]

The sexual division of labour and the structure of the industries women worked in acted against the success of women's unions. What stood in the way of a strong clothing industry union for women was their weakness in the labour market. The subdivision of work meant much clothing manufacturing was becoming relatively unskilled work. And because there were so few options for women in employment other than the clothing trades, this opened up the labour market to the great benefit of employers, who could say to women struggling for better pay, 'If you won't work at our pay scales there are plenty who will'.

The other side of this problem was that of outwork. Clothing manufacturers adapted their operation to the easy availability of outworkers and used outworkers as a way to undermine factory organisations. As one tailoress told an 1883 Royal Commission into factories and shops: 'Every other house in the suburbs is a tailor's shop; and people who would not acknowledge themselves to be tailoresses are carrying it out on the quiet. They take it out from our places far below our prices and then they laugh at us'.[41]

Factory workers, both male and female, understood the threat of outwork to their jobs, yet many women unionists also understood why so many women worked at home. After all, it was always an alternative that might one day be forced on them.

Outwork reduced factory wages as well because employers cut costs to compete with the sweaters. When the wage boards and arbitration courts were set up unions urged them to set minimum wages for outwork, or to set outwork piece rates higher than factory pay rates. The courts were anxious to do this, for the abolition of outwork had long been the central concern of that liberal humanitarianism of which Higgins and Deakin were representative. For unions, abolishing outwork meant that when work returned to the factories they could keep a much closer eye on the pay and conditions of their members. The big manufacturers were not unhappy either, for it disposed of cheap-cost rivals.[42] However, this had long-term effects which the unions could not or did not foresee. Employers, unable to cut costs by putting work out, reorganised their factory operations, cutting costs by introducing new machines and speeding up work.[43]

Male unions were also a barrier to women's employment. Men regarded women as a threat to their conditions of work, but there was much more to it, as a revealing 1890 editorial in the Melbourne printing union's journal showed. Responding to an article by the Brisbane socialist, William Lane, it argued that not only *would* women replace male printers, but *had* already replaced them. The editorial concluded:

> We feel convinced that it will be much more to the permanent advantage of women that they should be able to cook, sew and make their own dresses than learn a smattering of a trade which will probably be of no use to them in after life. We plead guilty to possessing ... 'the slavish idea that one half of the race is born to cook for the other'. We simply want the 'other half' to be in a position to get something to cook. Surely our Brisbane friend does not want the woman to print and the man to stop at home and make the beds.[44]

Excluding women from the workplace also meant excluding women from the unions.

Whenever the state intervened in the workplace it intervened in women's work. However, its most important role was in institutionalising the sexual division of labour through the pay relativities it granted to men and women. We have already encountered the family wage. In 1908 Justice Higgins said of it, 'a wage that does not allow for the matrimonial condition for an adult man is not fair and reasonable. It is not a living wage'.[45] The concept of a fair and reasonable wage was tied to the ideal bourgeois family.

Higgins, his fellow judges and many of their contemporaries believed that women in paid work fell outside the natural order of things, that it was men's place to be in the paid workforce. As Higgins' co-judge, Mr Justice Powers, observed in 1921: 'It is better in the interests of the community generally that men who are called upon to support wives and children should be employed at work suitable for them than girls and women should be tempted to take up men's work in factories and workshops.'[46]

The arbitration court had to confront the question of equal pay in 1912 when the Rural Workers' Union asked for equal pay for men and women fruit pickers. Higgins gave them equal pay but refused it to the workers who packed the picked fruit. He had made a clear distinction between what he regarded as men's work and women's work. Because men picked the fruit they had to be given a living wage. Because women packed the fruit they only needed a wage sufficient to support themselves and that was set at 53 percent of the male wage because it was assumed that women workers were single with no dependants. Women were given equal wages with men pickers because he suspected that employers would replace male pickers with women if he granted them a lower wage.

Where unions began to call on employers to pay equal wages for women, it was plain to see that like Higgins they had in mind the threat to their jobs, and they were usually motivated by a desire to keep women out of their work rather than to welcome them in. They obviously thought that no employer in his right mind would employ a woman to do a man's job.

The influence that the arbitration system had on women's work did not end with the structuring of women's and men's wages and the institutionalising of the division of labour. When the various systems were established they took over a wages system which separated skilled from unskilled work and paid them differently. Most skilled workers were men, and when in some cases women began to do men's work the male unionists applied to the courts for higher classifications for those jobs, again hoping that employers would not employ women to do them.[47] Cutting and pressing in the clothing trades had always been men's work. So heavy was pressing work (wielding heavy irons) that pressers thought women were physically incapable of doing it and, even if they could do it, they should not. Light irons and pressing machines introduced around the turn of the century meant that women could now do the pressing as easily as men. In Victoria the wages boards granted women equal pay even though the jobs were being de-skilled and hence employers were even more inclined to employ men because equal pay had obviated the cost advantage of employing women.[48]

The courts also discriminated against women in another way.

When skilled and semi-skilled male workers found new technology changing their jobs they were sometimes able to win margins for skill. Unions did not often take women workers in this situation seriously enough to pursue *their* claims in the courts and the courts did not take women's work sufficiently seriously to pursue them either.[49] The judges were also conservative men who could not bring themselves to recognise women's skills, let alone to pay for them.[50]

The way in which the state finally organised women's work was as employer itself. The state's functions today are vast, it is by far the biggest employer in the country. The state was smaller around the turn of the century. Nevertheless, there were six colonial governments and, after 1900, one Federal government, all employing women in similar jobs of extremely limited range. In 1899 in South Australia, for example, most women in the public service were state school teachers and nurses. There were several 'matrons' of various government bodies, laundresses and cooks at hospitals, assistants at girls' and boys' reformatories, several postmistresses and telegraph operators, some 'folders and sewers' in the government printery and just a few clerks in the Education and Postmaster General's Department.[51]

There is nothing particularly surprising about this. Nursing and teaching were 'women's jobs' of long standing. Clerking was still dominated by men. Postmistresses usually worked in post offices attached to their homes, so in terms of the contemporary constructions of women's work, they could legitimately run them. Telegraph operators did 'finger work', and so were similar to clothing workers, that is they did work allegedly suited to women's physical capacities.

The pay of practically all female government workers fitted that model whereby women were paid about half the wages of men. In the Commonwealth, however, women telegraphists and postmistresses were given equal pay to men doing the same jobs. At least they were in 1902, when the first Public Service Act was set up. Indeed equal pay for men and women engaged in the same occupation was one of the Public Service Board's early principles. Postmaster–postmistress and male clerk–female clerk were given equal pay. For women doing 'women's work', things were different. Telephonists and typists were given relatively low pay. Then, early in the century, the Commonwealth reduced the number of postmistresses and telegraph jobs available to women, gave them instead to men, and shifted women down the scale to switchboard attendants, work without prospects.[52] The state in this period was not kind to its women workers.

7 Managing the paid and unpaid workforce

Employers have always used their authority to press their workers into harder work, higher productivity and increased profits. The power to hire and fire is their ultimate sanction and in labour markets which favour them it is a very powerful one. However, most keep this in reserve and use other methods to achieve their aims. Sub-dividing the work process and mechanising the work are two, and paternalism is a rather different third. Just before and during World War I, a fourth emerged in Australia, inspired by new ways of thinking about work in the USA. These became known as the 'management revolution' and arose in the particular historical context of mass immigration, urbanisation and industrialisation in North America. The emergence of trade unions and bitter class conflict towards the end of the nineteenth century engendered a sense of crisis among many middle-class people, with which they felt their familiar social and political institutions were incapable of dealing. Management, or its contiguous ideology, efficiency, was one powerful response to this. It promised to solve the country's problems, to bring social and moral renewal, by the application of scientific principles to national concerns. Applied to the workplace, from where much of this crisis was thought to emanate, its enthusiasts argued that it would increase productivity and reduce prices. It followed, they claimed, that wages would increase and working hours would fall, while the general standard of living would rise. It was a panacea, they boasted, for the USA's problems, and a patriotic contribution to the national welfare.[1]

To many Australians, feeling a similar sense of crisis during World War I and the political and industrial strife which the war generated, these ideas seemed to have some applicability. The idea of national efficiency was taken up and applied to many areas of social life, and the paid and unpaid workplaces were two of them.[2] However, their application was uneven, to say the least. Australia's manufacturing was inching towards heavy industry, with a good deal of help from the state. Manufacturing employment was rising rapidly, but most workplaces were still small, producing goods for a limited local market which severely restricted their capacity for innovation. Yet the 1890s Depression had shown many employers the benefits of closer attention to the reorganisation and mechanisation of their factories, and these new ideas from the USA applied science to the familiar need for enhanced supervision and control. For their workers it meant yet another area, another facet of working life, to try to negotiate.

Hiking in the factory

David Baker was not a scientific boss. He was an old fashioned union-buster from the USA, which was why Broken Hill Proprietory Ltd (BHP) hired him in 1913 to develop and manage its new Newcastle steelworks. Advanced production techniques, a complex system of job classification, tough American superintendents and foremen and a driving hostility to workers' organisations characterised Baker's early years. His approach built on BHP's tradition as a hard and harsh employer, as workers at Broken Hill and Port Pirie well knew (foundry workers at Port Pirie worked a seven-day week). At Newcastle, however, Baker did not face the unskilled and semi-skilled workforce BHP used at these other places. The workforce here was largely skilled, strategically placed, organised and recalcitrant.[3]

Baker's techniques were honed to the confrontationist methods developed in his home country. He brooked no challenge to his authority, so the company rejected union calls for preference to unionists. It barred union representation and shop stewards from speaking to workers except at meal times, and then only with permission. It provoked strikes to flush out militants, employed spies to identify them, then sacked them. It sacked workers who went on strike then re-employed them on worse terms. It used the arbitration system to de-register striking unions. It employed scabs to break strikes, then used them as the membership of company unions. If this didn't work it insisted that workers join the 'tame' unions like the AWU.[4] Then finally, in 1922, it shut its steelworks down. By breaking the unions it hoped to reduce wages and increase hours— and it did both, while incidentally throwing the town of Newcastle into chaos. The main game, though, was busting the steelworks unions. Union coverage of workers in this strongest of working-class cities fell from 85 percent before 1917 to just 28 percent after World War I, at which level it remained until the outbreak of World War II.[5]

Union busting was one management strategy in its quest for control of the workplace. Scientific management was quite different, for it wrapped the quest for control in the beneficent rhetoric of easier work, better pay, shorter hours and a higher standard of living. Scientific management grew from the efficiency movement, and in the paid workplace it took shape in the context of massive changes in mass production techniques, the ever-increasing size of corporations and the creation of a mass workforce which made the workplace too complex for the eyes and ears of the authoritarian paternalist boss. So scientific management developed a new bureaucratic structure, levels of management and supervision which it inserted between the boss's office and the factory floor. The manager became the expert, using the new ideas both to control the work and make a space for him or herself in the company.

The son of a well-to-do Philadelphia family who wanted to be an engineer/patternmaker epitomised the movement. Frederick Winslow Taylor was an engineer, teacher and management consultant who wanted to weld together science and work in the cause of productivity and social advancement. As he saw it, in his way stood the craftsmen, who controlled the labour process in the factories because they knew more about their job than did their bosses, and used their knowledge to restrict output, maintain the exclusiveness of their craft and so keep their pay high. For Taylor, efficiency became a question of breaking these craft skills, and removing that knowledge to management. Then he could separate the execution from the conception of work leaving the former with the worker and relocating the latter with design and layout specialists. Then these specialists would lay out, in the minutest detail, how each job would be done. Exit the craftsman, enter the detail worker. Exit craft skill, enter the mindless monotony of repetitive motion. This was Taylor's legacy to work.

Not that Taylor thought workers would not get used to the new regime. They would be bribed by incentive payments to increase output after having been chosen 'scientifically' to suit the work. It was often said of Taylor's detail workers that they did not need brains to do their work, and he and his followers certainly agreed. They thought brains on the shop floor a positive menace. A brainless worker, an automaton, a human robot could be pushed and pulled about in any way management wanted, so scientific managers developed time-and-motion studies to measure wasted moments and unnecessary movements. A wasted moment might be lifting an arm vertically rather than horizontally. An unnecessary movement might be reaching too far for a tool. Then work was reorganised to get rid of the unnecessary movement and abolish the wasted moment. Time-and-motion experts, armed with stop watches and job cards, became the right arm of scientific management. Layout and design engineers became its left. The workers became the object, the raw material.[6] In its pure, unadulterated state Taylorism probably de-skilled only a small portion of the workforce, but historians agree that Taylor's philosophies provide the principles on which management has based nearly 80 years of labour process organisation and reorganisation.[7]

The impact of scientific management before World War II in Australia is difficult to measure, because historians have only just begun to sift through company records. But Taylorism seems to have entered Australia before World War I. In 1912, workers at the Lithgow Small Arms Factory complained about management's 'American hustling methods', and in 1916 and 1917 some other companies seemed to have taken it up.[8] For many years, however, it was busily promoted by trade and management journals like the *Australian Manufacturer* and *Rydge's* and by enthusiasts like Bernard Muscio, a Sydney university academic, who wrote a booklet entitled 'Lectures on Industrial Psychology'. The early writing on Taylorism was mainly explanatory. It expatiated on its general principles, defended it against its critics and boosted its potential for improving the lives of workers by, among other things, compassionately reducing fatigue.[9]

Once the business public had become used to the idea, Taylor's Australian followers began to provide advice on the actual implementation of the time-and-motion studies, showing managers how to acquire 60 minutes work in every hour by the 'scientific' use of stop watches and time sheets; how to stop 'hiking in the factory' by removing the need for workers to work in different places; and how to apply wage incentives to the reorganised work. The language used in some of these articles was quite extraordinary. Some made a pretence of beneficent concern for the workers. Others did not:

> The amount of time lost to production by unnecessary walking is incalculable. Walking in the average factory is sheer waste. Both time and energy are lost. One has suggested, almost seriously, that hiking clubs be formed, packs issued, and the thing done properly.
>
> Why is hiking in the factory worth eliminating? Why is it waste? Because time away from the bench or machine is lost time—red ink time. It is just as unproductive as lunch time. More so, in fact! At the least, lunch time re-creates.
>
> If the ordinary factory operative is compelled by the managerial policy to do constructive thinking in the course of his work, then that policy is wrong! 'Legs and arms out in the factory, brains in the office': that should be the slogan. The more brain the operative has to use, the more money he wants. (Which is not bad in itself.) But he is less efficient! Why? Because he cannot 'think' as well as the man whose entire job it should be; and he is probably holding up production somewhere else while he is thinking 'a way out of the trouble'.
>
> The better the factory organisation, the less the need for operative thinking. Of course, if he wants to think, we cannot—and don't want to—stop him—provided he doesn't stop work to do it.[10]

Promotion is one thing, implementation another. One company which introduced Taylorism, apparently root and branch, was the Melbourne clothing manufacturer Pearson Law (later Pelaco). Prompted by inadequate output from its cutters, the company 'took a lot of timings to get at the actual time required for each motion and found it was possible for a cutter to cut a great many more than 250 to 300 dozen [collars] per week with a great deal less effort'.[11] Cutters no longer worked out how to cut their cloth. Patterns were designed in a planning department. Boys and girls marked the patterns and cutters simply cut them out. They were encouraged to improve their output even more by bonus payments, the other end of the Taylorist process. Shirt making and pressing suffered the same fate, so by 1920 each shirt was made by 37 different machinists.[12] And the machinists were selected according to Taylor's principles. In 1927 James Law told an arbitration hearing how he hired his young female workers:

> Our employment girl downstairs has been well taught and has read a great deal of psychology, and knows the type of individual who would fit the different jobs ... She knows by looking at a girl's head and hands, the shape of her mouth, eyes, etc., and can tell to a certain extent what any girl is particularly useful for.[13]

Pelaco's case is less well known than the events which sparked the 1917 general strike in New South Wales—the attempt by the railway department to introduce time cards into its workshops. We will return to this a little later.

At the other end of the de-skilling process was the moving assembly line. A full car was not made in Australia until the 1950s. Till then local car makers only made bodies and fitted them to imported chassis and motors. In the early days of the industry the bodies were custom made in workshops where, if a body builder did not make a whole body, he certainly put together a solid part of it. The Holdens, father and son, wanted to change all that. They wanted to reproduce in Adelaide something of the US mass production of cars. This meant introducing standardised designs, labour-saving machinery and a subdivided labour process for which they needed, not the old skills of the coach maker (in any case there were not enough coach makers in Adelaide to staff their new factory) but a new, large and unskilled workforce. To get it the Holdens made a deal in 1918 with the local coach-builders' union. If the union would permit the 'dilution of the work' (that is, its subdivision for the production of standardised cars), the company would give it a closed shop and let it do the hiring when it could. And just as Henry Ford did in his North American plants, Holden's sweetened the pill with a pay rise to 5/- a week above the award rate.[14] The result was a factory the size of which had never been seen in Australia before.

Skilled jobs were broken up into parts, body builders became assemblers, or glazers or welders or sandblasters. New jobs like leather cutter, machinist and paster were invented, but they had nothing of the mystique of the old. A panel beater for Holden's remarked in 1929:

> ...coachbuilding was more varied work. You would be called upon to do many different things. I found it was not so monotonous. It was more interesting and you did not feel so languid; as in the motor trade, you are compelled to stand and work in one position all day long and it becomes more wearing than the heavy lifting in the coachsmith trade... it is considerably more monotonous... it is the most harassing work I have met with...[15]

This monolithic monotony had moved into other trades too. A moving assembly line, or rather a dis-assembly line, was introduced in the 1930s into abattoirs in Australia. Previously each carcase was butchered by an individual tradesman butcher. In the chain system introduced into some Tasmanian, Melbourne, Sydney and South Australian abattoirs in the 1930s, 'one cut slaughts', as they were disparagingly called, performed only one task, hacking at each carcase as it groaned past them on a moving chain.[16]

Taylorism was but one of these management strategies, Fordism but one other. There were other workplaces in which employers thought Taylorism inappropriate or in which they thought it needed supplementing. In these a 'welfarism' was sometimes introduced. Again, welfarism was a systematic programme and set of ideas, just as scientific management was, but it was based on different principles from Taylorism. Welfarists did not agree that the worker's primary motivation was money. Instead they believed that workers responded to a range of monetary and other considerations. Welfarism was not new to the inter-war years, what was new was the propagation of welfarist principles in management journals and government publications and the systematic application of these new ideas to the paid workplaces. So big companies like BHP at Port Pirie, the British Tobacco Company in Sydney and Australian Paper Mills in Victoria established cooperative stores, refreshment rooms, playgrounds, sporting clubs and in-house magazines. The Commonwealth Bank, the Postmaster General's Department and the New South Wales Railways provided libraries and reading rooms for more refined and educational pursuits.[17] Big stores, too, with their own paternalist traditions, introduced a wave of welfarist ideas. The usual dining rooms, social and sporting clubs, and libraries were supplemented by discounts on purchases, insurance schemes and medical services,

'Happy Staff... Healthy Sales' was how Boans in Perth put it.[18] But as historians have argued, welfarism was really paternalism with a remade face. It tried to tie workers into a pre-existing authority structure by presenting that structure as caring and humane.[19]

Workers responded to these initiatives in a bewildering variety of ways, from outright rejection to complete acceptance. By and large any response took place within very clearly defined divisions between management and worker rights. Unions and workers did not seek to trespass on managerial prerogatives over the organisation of work and the introduction of new technology. Workers certainly knew the disemployment effects of both (after all, they had been telling sceptical Royal Commissioners about it for years). But management, although it was prepared to negotiate over wages and conditions, would not otherwise compromise. The arbitration systems, too, divided their judgements into go and no-go areas. Pay and conditions, yes, the shop floor and new technology, no! Unions which crossed such boundaries did so at their peril.

In retrospect, the defeat of the New South Wales railway workers seems to have been almost inevitable. Fourteen unions in the railways struck over the introduction of the time cards, which looked innocent enough. Management claimed that the information workers would write on them was only for the record. It seemed a very mild form of Taylorism, but the fact that foremen had to write down the exact time it took each worker to do each job meant, for their unions, the 'Americanisation of the service', and could only mean that fast workers would henceforth set the standards for all work.[20]

1917 was a terrible time to stage action against the state. The New South Wales government was fully committed to an unfettered war effort and branded the men as traitors and saboteurs. With police help and scab labour it broke the strike, the Arbitration Court de-registered the unions and the railways department sacked the strikers. It then rehired the less militant on lower pay and rank, and formed its own loyalist union, while the cause of the strike, the card system, was confirmed. It was a harsh beating indeed.[21]

Some workers took the Taylorists at their word. The Victorian Clothing Trades Union supported the introduction of scientific management in Melbourne's clothing factories, believing that increased output could be transferred into higher wages, shorter hours, easier work and better factories,[22] and management was more than surprised when unionists argued that productivity was obviously a product of improved organisation. So, the unions continued, who needs a 48-hour-week when output could be increased with a shorter working day and better planning![23]

The argument had another side, for the Clothing Trades Union soon found out that the turnover in some of the new efficient factories was quite phenomenal. Speeding up, de-skilling, monotony, stress and pressure and an increase in the number of juvenile workers seemed to follow the new Pied Pipers of industry, the methods engineers around. Alf Wallis, the Victorian secretary of the CTU, remarked fatalistically, '... in every industry, everywhere, no union or strike has been able to prevent new methods and machines... and... if employees struck against acceptance of the new machines they would not have one chance in a hundred of preventing new methods'.[24]

His members in several factories disagreed. In 1935, women machinists in three big Melbourne factories struck over plans to reorganise trouser making, and in 1936 workers in another factory declared that they would ignore new time cards and not fill them in. Then the union hierarchy itself seemed to have a change of heart. By the late 1930s it, too, was opposing time-and-motion studies.[25]

Raelene Frances argues that there was more to the CTU's acceptance of scientific management than the optimistic hope for more pay and shorter hours. The union had long been cosy with big clothing manufacturers, collaborating with them over tariffs and sweating, for big manufacturers and the union wanted the cost-cutting and low-paying sweater out of business. In addition, many trade union leaders themselves were ambitious to become capitalists. More importantly, though, the union was not all that interested in helping those most affected by new techniques. 'Let the women look after themselves', one union leader was heard to say, 'for they have taken our jobs'.[26] It was a case of male union leaders looking after the skilled male workers, those who could negotiate from some strength or who had gone on to supervisory jobs in the factories at the expense of the mass of unskilled, de-skilled women workers.

Workers reacted differently, too, to the moving assembly line. The slaughtermen at Angliss's in Melbourne were militant craftsmen, members of a radical union, linked to other workers at Angliss's by a strong shop committee. The export slaughtermen were the ones whose jobs were threatened by the chain. They had struck often in the early 1930s against wage reductions and they struck too against the introduction of the chain. At least the slaughtermen did. Others in the factory, unaffected by the chain, kept working.

Slaughtering was seasonal work. It began each year in September and finished in February. Then, the 2000 strong abattoir's workforce was reduced to a skeleton crew of 500 who killed animals for local butchers and maintained the works. For local

Footscray workers it was a case of 'report to the gates' and join the mass of men hoping to catch the foreman's eye. In the midst of the Depression, the number of volunteers at the gates was such that no strike could succeed, and that against the introduction of the chain failed and the meatworkers' union slid into bankruptcy.[27]

The introduction of the assembly line at Holden's in Adelaide illustrates a different union position, in the deal struck between the Coachbuilder's Union and Holden's in 1918. The union was craft based, a combination of skilled artisans who could see the implications of mechanisation and standardisation for their work, and who were told by Holden's that there were simply not enough skilled workers to man the plant that was envisaged. Therefore it listened receptively when Holden's approached it with the deal in which it exchanged the dilution of the work for the closed shop. New hierarchies of wages were developed, and despite paying 5/- above the award rate, Holden's reduced its labour costs so much that it gained a huge benefit over its interstate competitors, still tied to older craft pay systems. The results of the deal were that Holden's became the biggest producer of cars in the southern hemisphere and it enjoyed 26 years of industrial harmony. The cost to the workers was the mind-numbing monotony of the assembly line.[28]

The other side of Taylorism was the incentive payment system. Incentive payments were usually rigorously opposed by unions. They were paid to workers for each piece of work they produced above a number set as a base standard by management. Unions believed that incentive payments, piece rates and bonus systems were anti-social, at the most general level pitting worker against worker by encouraging competition for the highest pay. More immediately, they recognised that employers tied time-and-motion studies to incentive payments, turning the fast worker into the basic standard unit and then expecting everybody else to catch up. Bosses used piece rates in similar ways. By cutting the rates, people had to work harder to maintain their pay. Such was the opposition to incentive payments in 1927 that the Australian Council of Trade Unions (ACTU), in one of its first ever pronouncements, black banned them. Nevertheless, as the discussions at ACTU congresses showed, piece work, at least, was common.[29] As a delegate from one union pointed out:

> His union fought piecework, and took every action to see that a member did not work piecework under the lap ... There were moulders in South Australia working piecework who had been expelled from the Moulders' Union, yet these men had been taken on by other unions.[30]

The ACTU campaign counted for little. Jim Hagan estimates that

20 percent of Australian jobs were being paid by the piece by 1937 because many workers liked piece work.[31] Generally they were highly skilled and exercised considerable control over their work, thus being able to negotiate high standard rates. Unorganised workers, though, found that it was not so much the method of payment that it was important but how the rates were set.[32]

The response of workers to welfare policies is much more difficult to measure. It is easy to assume that there was a close link between welfare policies and docile workers. For example, the management of Pelaco's provided a dining room, tea breaks, a social club and an in-house paper for its women workers, as part of a deliberate policy to keep them out of the union. This seemed to be effective, because the CTU had practically no members there and on one occasion, in 1932, visiting union officials were actually counted out by Pelaco workers.[33] Similarly, workers in Sydney's big retail stores seem to have relished the new opportunities that social and sporting clubs and welfare programmes gave them. This is not really surprising, because these represented a real improvement in working conditions. One shopwoman at David Jones observed in 1934 that it was 'impossible for an outsider to realise the privileges enjoyed by the staff and the consideration they are shown'.[34] The result was little enthusiasm for industrial organisation, let alone action.

Both of these examples are from a largely female workforce. The response of men in the New South Wales railways was rather different. Lucy Taksa argues that the Railway Institute libraries and other welfarist provisions were an attempt to incorporate workers into the ethos of hard work, loyalty, sobriety and respectability. But railway workers ignored these. The libraries were unused and the books unread, as workers used other places, other sources for their reading. They also preferred to read labour and union papers rather than those of the railway department; and this is not surprising, given the bitterness engendered by the 1917 strike.[35]

Resistance and accommodation cannot be related only to the strategies management might use to acquire control or obedience. They relate also to the strategic place of workers in the local labour markets, that is, how easily they can be replaced. When the option is unemployment workers will do practically anything to keep their jobs.

The cuddling hour

The sense of crisis that pervaded the Australian middle class around the turn of the century provides the context for the second site of the application of the new doctrines of efficiency—the home and the work of the wife and mother. The context was not particular to Australia, for the sense of crisis was felt in many western countries, Britain of course, the USA and the white Commonwealth countries like Canada and New Zealand.

Australia in the 1910s and 1920s was going through what demographers call the great demographic transition. The birth rate in Australia fell from 43 live births per 1000 total population per year in the 1860s to just 16.4 per 1000 in the 1930s. Translated into everyday language this means that from the 1860s to the 1950s the number of live children a married woman would bear fell from an average of seven to between two and three. In hindsight we can see good reasons for this; delayed weddings, an increase in the number of women who never married, better knowledge of and use of contraception.[36] But authorities in the 1910s and 1920s saw more sinister motives and far more sinister results. Selfish women were not bearing children. Their self-interested wish to work and their self-indulgent pursuit of political equality were driving them to forsake motherhood for the public world of work and politics.[37]

The white Australian race had, it seemed, stopped growing. Racists like those in the eugenics movement feared that whites would be outbred by the more freely populating Asian and African races. The language of 'race suicide' was freely used. Not only were white Australians being outbred, but, as one eugenicist put it, 'the unfit' were outbreeding 'the fit', that is, the 'lower types', the mentally deranged, the morally deficient, were outbreeding their superiors. The solutions for the eugenicists ranged from the 'lethal chamber' (those ideas later circulating in Nazi Germany were also circulating in Australia), to family planning clinics in poor suburbs, to legislation to prohibit the 'unfit' from breeding.[38]

The eugenicists had a rival school of thought, however, which fortunately proved to have greater influence, perhaps because it combined both theory, ethical explanations and practical solutions to the perceived crisis. Historians call them environmentalists, and they argued the point with those early eugenicists over the real cause of the crisis. The unfitness of mothers and children they did not dispute, but the cause lay, not in their breeding patterns, but in their environment. Here the environmentalists linked up with a common thread in European thought that accompanied the process of urbanisation—the belief that the degraded cities rendered city boys unfit for the 'manly life' and city girls unfit for motherhood. Hostility to the city is, of course, as old as the city itself. Images of crime, larrikin gangs, factory girls, stunted and shrunken slum dwellers and dirty and uneducated children clouded the minds of social reformers. Building noble youth in the festering cities became their programme, and we can see their work in a wide range of reforming causes in the late nineteenth and early twentieth centuries; in public health, slum reclamation, sanitary reform, food and drug laws, town planning and parks. We can see their monuments in the inner city pocket handkerchief parks, the grandly ornate public baths, the free kindergartens, the infant health centres, the garden suburbs, and, later, in the multi-storey housing commission flats.[39]

These movements allied themselves with a third stream of social reform, the charity and philanthropic organisations, whose interests lay less in reforming the environment than reforming the individual through strengthening the family unit. They wanted to re-define the ideal male as sober, hard working and caring and put out of his way those devilish temptations of drink, gambling and prostitution.[40]

Into these overlapping interests, these crises of confidence, came the experts, turning the home, the family, the housewife and the mother into a series of problems to be solved by rational and scientific methods. They 'discovered', in the early twentieth century, the inefficient home, the unproductive family and, from closer observation, the incapable housewife and the incompetent mother.[41] Reforming the woman, then, was the priority in a number of movements, and the solution lay in scientific motherhood, the application of the scientific method to the problem of motherhood. Of course the movement was predicated on the familiar ideal—the dependent wife, the home-bound mother. These movements promised hardly any change to women's circumstances.

The formation of the new woman meant the destruction of the old, so, to begin at the beginning, with childbirth itself, the experts began to reform the age-old practices which had kept childbirth as a quintessentially woman's event. Male doctors began a process that the historian Kerreen Reiger calls the 'drive to make childbirth a medical event'.[42] It was a process which was completed only by the 1940s but it entailed an attack on midwives who, in the nineteenth century, delivered most children and delivered them in the houses of their mothers. Midwives were eventually displaced, not only by doctors, but by nurses too, who, in their own drive for professionalisation, increasingly incorporated midwifery in their skills. Midwives then became the resort of country and poor women who could not afford hospitals.[43]

The implications of this process for the women having the babies are clear. Childbirth became less a home-centred, women-centred, neighbourhood-centred practice. The oral evidence tells us that some women found it alienating, but others found the usual two-week stay in hospital after the baby was born restful and the birth itself less worrying, knowing that medical attention was close by. Whether this had much affect on maternal and infant mortality under one week is doubtful. These rates declined hardly at all over the first three decades of the twentieth century.[44]

What did decline was the infant mortality rate for infants under one year of age. In Sydney, for example, it fell from 120.4 per 1000 births in 1901 to 74.2 per 1000 births in 1920, and in the whole state the decline was nearly as startling.[45] On the one hand this can be put down to great improvements in public health and the decline of many of the big baby-killing diseases like gastroenteritus, smallpox and the bubonic plague. But it seems probable that the improvement in general child care associated with the infant welfare movement played a part.

The infant welfare movement began around the turn of the century, by 1927 there were nearly 140 baby clinics in Victoria and New South Wales alone.[46] It was a movement of public health officials in local and state governments, of doctors and middle-class social reformers. The clinics were staffed by nurses and there was both a retreat from and a return to the belief that motherhood was natural in women. On the one hand it disparaged the old ways in which child care had been passed on from mothers to daughters, but on the other it insisted that women's natural function was as mothers. It demanded the application of scientific principles and practice to the raising of infants, with the baby clinic as the centre of operation; testing, weighing, advising, propagandising, until the 'common sense' knowledge of women was discredited and what it regarded as inefficiency, bad habits, unhealthy and unhygenic practices had been replaced by scientific motherhood.

The way forward was in regularity. Babies should be fed not when they wanted to be but at regular three or four-hourly intervals. They should be breast fed rather than bottle fed but when they were bottle fed, it should be with systematically calculated quantities of mixtures of calories, fats and proteins. Regular measuring, charting and weighing of babies would record their progress. Hygienic, short clothing, no dummies and regular sun-baths would make them healthy. A 'cuddling hour' would replace random and unsystematic playing and cuddling. What could be done at home should be, but regular visits to the baby clinics should become part of the new mother's weekly routine. System, routine and regularity. These were virtues that the followers of authorities like Dr Frederick Truby King hoped the baby would internalise. It would become a more disciplined and orderly child and ultimately a more disciplined and orderly adult.[47]

Visits to the infant health centres did become part of the routine of most mothers. Some, however, rebelled. 'Ridiculous, stupid nonsense', was how Molly Taylor of Tumut in New South Wales described the clinic's advice.[48] Women became more confident, too, with their second child and tended to rely on their own experience rather than the clinical manifesto.

Doctrines of efficiency were also applied to housewifery. Interestingly, the new courses were first called 'domestic *economy*', then 'domestic *science*', and later 'household *management*'.[49] The language of Taylorism was being used because the principles of Taylorism were being applied to the home. In the minds of its proponents the pressures of urbanism were threatening social stability, where the separate spheres of home and work, the sexual division of labour in the family and the health of the family itself were at risk. Who's fault was it? Not the men's, who still indulged in their bad habits, but 'wives and mothers':

> In the schools an attempt is being made to combat with the evils of drink and smoking for juveniles by theoretical lessons on the result of indulgences in these practices. A superficial knowledge of the matter is sufficient to prove that a very common cause which drives a man from his home to the hotel is a badly cooked dinner or a mismanaged washing day. Therefore it seems to be of more importance to provide instruction in practical cookery and laundry work for the girls who will develop into wives and mothers than to teach theoretically the evils of excessive drinking and smoking.[50]

Then there was that old chestnut, the servant problem, for the upper-middle-class family, of course, more than anyone else. The solution to both these problems was to educate girls and women in the principles of scientific housework. It would create a steady supply of qualified domestic servants yet would also train the middle-class girl in home management and housewifery should she have to do the work herself. In schools and similar institutions across the country, the social and educational reformers set up courses in domestic economy or home science.

The kitchen, it was stated, also needed to be scientifically planned. More space, less need for movement ('hiking in the home'), better lighting and ventilation were the central pillars of scientific management and were increasingly applied to the new Californian 'bungalows', which seemed to dominate the 1930s Australian suburban landscape. And in these new model homes were to be the very latest labour-saving devices. An article in a *Real Property Annual* in 1922 sets out the possibilities very nicely—an electric cooker, which was not only smokeless, fumeless and didn't need fuel, but which cooked roasts perfectly; a 'general kitchen machine', which beat, whipped, chopped, minced and mixed; a vacuum cleaner which cleaned a room faster than two maids could, and so on. Electricity 'has wonderful possibilities'. And plainly it had.[51]

The real impact of new technology on the home was nothing like this of course, except for the relatively small number of women who could afford it. Electricity and gas only gradually replaced wood and kerosene, and not in any linear progression. Electric lights, wood stoves, kerosene fridges, petrol irons were all found in a mix of technologies in the one home right up until the 1970s. Chip heaters were still used in the best homes even when electricity was commonplace. The only pattern seems to be that city houses got electricity and gas first and that wealthy houses got the new technology first. The real age of the labour-saving device was not between the wars but in the 1950s and 1960s.

There are two questions which we now need to consider. The first is whether these labour-saving devices, and this scientific and expert instruction did indeed reduce the work of housewives. It seems self-evident that it did, and any number of housewives will say so. But others argue that it did not. One Kew housewife, explained that better lighting and lighter coloured paints showed up the dirt. Modern cooking demanded a knowledge of calories and vitamins, which meant more study and care (although oral historian Ruth Barton's informants didn't recall any interest in them). Modern clothing meant more mending and making. Rather wistfully she wrote: 'I would rather see a decrease in the standard of living and an easier and less exacting life for each of us.'[52] The influence of these technological changes depended on the extent of their distribution. I suspect it was small and that most women still did the housework they had always done.

It seems that one intent of labour-saving devices was to reduce middle-class housewives' dependence on domestic servants, and there is a theory that the absence of domestic servants caused middle-class families to invest in new technologies. It has been suggested, too, that the new technologies made servants redundant, which might explain the rapid twentieth-century decline in domestic service.[53] Both assumptions are wrong. The number of domestic servants fell right away between the 1933 and 1947 censuses, and it is to World War II, the manpower directorate and the new opportunities for women's work that we need to look.

8 Unemployment and full employment

Australia rode the roller coaster of depression and war in the 1930s and 1940s. Even earlier, collapsing international wool and wheat markets, a devastating drought in the late 1920s and the drying up of overseas investment following the Wall Street Crash in 1929 meant that Australia had to face the music for an economy far too dependent on investment from overseas. In terms of government economic policies, however, what was impossible in the context of the social devastation of the Great Depression, as it became known, was not only possible in war, but wholly admirable. The contrast is stark. A largely unregulated economy delivered high unemployment in 'good times' like the 1920s and chronic unemployment in the 1930s. The demands of war, a strictly directed economy, and positive labour market policies turned the economy from one where hundreds of thousands of workers could not find jobs to one in which there were not enough people to fill the jobs created.

Many Australians expected that there would be another depression after the war but this did not eventuate. There was not even the heavy unemployment that was expected when one million war workers returned to peace-time jobs. War-time experience and the new Keynesian economics showed the way to what the Labor Prime Minister Ben Chifley later called 'the light on the hill'.

We want work!

That unemployment could reach the level it did in the 1930s was partly a product of the high levels of unemployment in the 1920s. For thousands of workers caught in the casual and seasonal labour markets, permanent employment was only a dream. Unskilled men formed about 60 percent of that permanent 7 percent unemployment average which characterised the decade. It would probably have been much higher had not state and local governments spent so much money on developmental public works.[1]

The seasonal character of much of the economy continued in the 1920s and 1930s. Farming, fruit picking and shearing still had their linkages through the economy. Fruit canning, meat processing and the jobs transporting produce to local and overseas markets were still the most seasonal of jobs, and it is clear that the big, and bitter, waterfront strikes in 1929 were as much a product of the insecurity of the waterfront job market and the pick-up labour system as they were of wage reductions. In building and construction, work could not continue when the weather was too wet. In the food industry the consumption of cold drinks still increased in summer and fell away in winter, and the clothing trade was, as ever, one of the most intermittent for busy and slack periods. Slackness meant a fall in production, fluctuating demand for raw materials and spasmodic ordering. In the final analysis it meant intermittent work, insecurity and poverty. In addition, credit movements, changes in prices and exchange rates, rising and falling demand for exports and instability in the balance of payments still caused that pattern of boom and bust which contemporary economists called the business cycle.[2]

The point at which recession, depression and the lives of workers met were unemployment and a floating population of reserve labour. Workers were taken on during recovery and shed during recession. They were dependent on short-term jobs and often chance selection. For many Australians, therefore, unemployment was not unfamiliar. Through years of an unregulated labour market they had learned to live with it. However, only those old enough to have lived through the 1890s Depression could have had any idea of the extent of the disaster that was to come in the third decade of the twentieth century. The latest estimate of unemployment in the 1930s puts its peak at 35 percent of wage earners (see table below[3]).

Unemployment in the 1930s

Year	% of wage earners
1929–30	16.7
1930–31	27.0
1931–32	35.0
1932–33	31.3
1933–34	24.5
1934–35	21.0
1935–36	16.5
1936–37	14.2
1937–38	11.4
1938–39	11.9
1939–40	11.7

Unemployment hit industry unequally. A quick analysis of just one state shows this. In June 1933, at the Commonwealth Census, there were 98 000 males and 21 000 females out of work in

Victoria, 24 and 13 percent of male and female wage and salary earners respectively. Some 24 percent of the men, 23 000 in all, were normally employed in the making of roads, railways and earthworks. They made up nearly half of that workforce, a fact which illustrates just how drastic was the drought of capital which dried up government funding of public works. Men usually employed in manufacturing also made up about 25 percent of the unemployed. Nevertheless only 21 percent of those previously employed in manufacturing were unemployed, though this was in 1933 when manufacturing was recovering comparatively quickly. Over the whole period, some 43 percent of job losses across Australia were in manufacturing. Some 13 percent of those out of work were normally employed in building, that is nearly 50 percent of its workforce. About 9800 shop assistants and clerks were unemployed, 10 percent of the total unemployed, but only 16 percent of those specific workers. Seven percent of unemployed men worked in agriculture, and were only 13 percent of those who worked on the land. Of those in mining and quarrying, 31 percent were unemployed, as were 26 percent of those in water transport. In personal and domestic service, it was 17 percent, but it was next to nothing in public administration, the professions and property and finance. There was no unemployment among the religious orders or in social welfare.

Over 60 percent of the 21 000 unemployed women came from the two big employers of female labour, light manufacturing and domestic service, 37 percent from the former and 24 percent from the latter. In terms of the two workforces 16 percent of women previously in manufacturing were unemployed and 11 percent in domestic service. The 5196 unemployed clothing workers made up fully 25 percent of unemployed women.[4]

Faced with such a scale of unemployment, people looked for scapegoats. The New South Wales Labor Party Premier Jack Lang dug deep into the Australian character for its anti-semitism and made his scapegoat an imaginary Jewish financial conspiracy.[5] Others believed that women were taking men's jobs so there was a barrage of propaganda in the 1930s designed to drive married women from the paid workforce. The error in this prejudice is now commonly accepted, but that was not so in the 1930s. The Melbourne trade unionist, Muriel Heagney, presented a devastating critique of it in 1935, in a book called *Are Women Taking Men's Jobs?* Her arguments are now commonplace. Women were not taking men's jobs because they were segregated into restricted areas of paid employment, and their unemployment was lower than men's because the occupations they were segregated into were less affected by the Depression. They were, for instance, excluded from the worst hit industries—building, heavy manufacturing and mining. So, although the clothing industry was hit hard earlier in the Depression, the sex-stereotyping of their jobs gave women workers a measure of protection.[6]

Plainly working class, most of the unemployed men were from the poverty stricken inner cities. Not that unemployment was confined to the cities. Australia-wide, there were 226 000 men and 52 000 women without paid work in the cities and 179 000 men and 23 000 women unemployed in the country.[7] Only in Queensland and Tasmania were there more country unemployed than city unemployed, although the unemployment *rate* in Brisbane and Hobart was higher in every case than in the country. However, it was highest in those metropolitan working-class suburbs like Bassendean and North Fremantle in Perth, Fitzroy and Collingwood in Melbourne, in Port Adelaide, in Balmain in Sydney and Fortitude Valley in Brisbane. In these places the proportion approached or exceeded 30 percent on Census day, and that was nearly a year after unemployment began to fall.[8] It was in fact a year earlier when unemployment had reached its peak. That it could be so high was because most workers in these suburbs were in industries like manufacturing and the construction of roads; work in which unemployment was highest. The average length of time for an unemployed Melbourne man to go without regular work was two years. Women were marginally better off. It was 1¼ years for them—fifteen months of day to day uncertainty.[9]

The location of unemployed women presents a striking contrast to that of the men. In Melbourne, although the raw number of women unemployed in working-class suburbs was very high, the *rate* of unemployment was often not much higher than that for many middle-class suburbs. Plainly the timing of the Census has something to do with this, because by June 1933 the clothing trade was two years into its recovery, and the clothing factories were all located in working-class suburbs. Conversely, in those suburbs where most women were normally employed in white-collar jobs, unemployment was lower because they were protected by the continuing demand for that type of work.[10]

Many workers lost only part of their jobs, that is they had their work rationed out among their workmates. Work rationing meant that they could keep their jobs only if they agreed to work fewer hours a day, or fewer days a week, or fewer days a month. There is little hard evidence about the extent of work rationing in the 1930s, although the economist E.R. Walker observed in 1936 that 'it was quite a common experience in the worst period of the Depression'.[11] It was certainly widespread in certain South Australian industries, and a 1930 Trades Hall survey in Melbourne showed that out of 58 unions which received the questionnaire, 34 replied that their members were being rationed, 14 replied that they were not and 10 (including the Builders Labourers' Federation and the Waterside Unions whose members *were* rationed) did not reply. The Female Confectioners' Union reported that 60 percent of its members were losing one week in four and some 60 percent of Furnishing Trade Union members were reported to be working 'one, two or three days a week'.[12] The Census in 1933 showed that about 12.2 percent of the male and 6.9 percent of the female workforce in Victoria were doing part-time work.[13]

Rationing was an invidious option for workers. They had to weigh up the relative possibility of keeping their full-time jobs, accepting a cut in hours or joining the queues at the dole office door. Where they had the choice they naturally preferred the second to the third. In 1931 outdoor workers at Melbourne's Collingwood City Council agreed to ration themselves one week in ten rather than allow the Council to dismiss ten of their fellows. The dilemma which faced employers is illustrated by the decision of Melbourne's Sandringham City Council in 1933 to reorganise its outdoor staff. It decided to end rationing, but sacked half its staff to put the other half on full time.[14]

The Council's dilemma was as nothing compared with the future which faced its sacked workers. This episode may have occurred well into recovery but those workers joined the 25 percent of the workforce competing for jobs. This search for work was often the most miserable part of unemployment, especially where neighbours and friends were losing their jobs with frightening frequency. All the studies of the unemployed in the 1930s refer to this situation. When workers lost their jobs their first reaction was to undertake a frenzied search for a replacement. In September 1930, for instance, 1800 women and girls applied for eight jobs at the Melbourne Royal Show refreshment rooms. One paper reported 'The first arrived at 6.00a.m. From then the number increased until at 10.30a.m. the advertised hour for opening, there was a struggling mass, blocking the stairway leading to a disused iron foundry where the applications were received.'[15] In the face of this sort of competition and constant rejection the search for work became increasingly routine. Eventually, as months and years passed, most workers became embittered at the pointlessness of it all.

The mainstay of the family of the unemployed worker was government or private relief. For those breadwinners whose pride prohibited such help the alternative was to rely on other family members for support or to scrape a living selling bits and pieces door-to-door. Every memory of life in the Depression recalls streams of men (and some women) knocking on doors selling bottles, rags, pins, flowers, home-crafted dolls and toys, offering to clean windows, weed gardens or chop wood.[16] The recollections of wives of unemployed husbands show, too, how many took on cleaning, washing and cooking in both the formal, paid economy and that informal economy centred on the home. Daughters, often more employable than sons because of their lower pay, became more important to this economy, often giving all their wages to their mothers for the sake of their family's survival. All too often though, that income made the family ineligible for government assistance.[17]

It became obvious by 1930 that the private charities could not cope with the distress. Therefore each state government set up its own relief system, paid for with special unemployment relief taxes (except in South Australia, which used money from its ordinary revenue). Each scheme combined relief work with a new measure—sustenance, popularly known as 'susso' or the 'dole'. This was usually paid in the form of an order on shopkeepers for goods (although in Western Australia it was part cash, part goods and later in New South Wales it was cash). It was family based, usually paid to the man of the household. Single men were sometimes given sustenance, sometimes food and bed tickets and relief work.[18] Several governments set up special camps to house and control them, such as at the Exhibition Building in Adelaide and the Blackboy and Hovea camps on the outskirts of Perth. From these places they were sent off to look for gold or to work on farms for a pitiful wage. Single girls were sometimes given sustenance or work in sewing centres but were more often completely ignored. Conservative governments thought single girls could and should find work as domestic servants. In some states, such as New South Wales and Western Australia, unemployed Aborigines were not given unemployment benefits at all.[19]

The 'dole' was not an unemployment benefit in the strict sense, because one could be unemployed and yet get nothing. One was ineligible if any member of the family earned an income above a certain limit and if one still had realisable assets apart from the family home. So never in any state did more than a small proportion of the unemployed receive relief,[20] the underlying assumptions being that the relief system would be much the same as the old charity network. Applicants were investigated by private or government inspectors or the police. In Queensland they had to sign a declaration: 'I hereby declare that I am indigent'.[21] In Melbourne, from 1932, they were forced to work for their sustenance to prove their 'genuineness'.[22] Even when unemployment was at its peak, the jobless could not escape that suspicious inquiry: 'Are you really looking for work? Are you genuine?'

Plainly, the new relief systems were used to control the behaviour of the destitute. Any kind of political agitation or moral failing invariably resulted in losing the dole. The old charity network had extended class domination into poverty relief and the new mass forms of relief in the 1930s institutionalised that domination. The new relief networks were largely administered by the same people who ran the old, even down to the police, who gave out relief in country towns.[23]

In the 1930s, thousands of men, women and children experienced unemployment for the first time and were thrust into relationships they had never before encountered. Yet many understood that their subordination was a product of their isolation—that individually they were supplicants, but together they could be powerful. Ironically, it was usually the relief system which brought the unemployed together and it was at the local sustenance relief centres, at ration dumps, on the job at sustenance and relief work sites, at single-men's camps, and at labour bureaux that experiences were exchanged, the inadequacy of the dole condemned and the government's neglect exposed. It was here, too, that new ideas about ideology and change were disseminated, the rudiments of organisations were laid, alliances formed and costs and benefits debated. The way the capitalist state treated unemployed workers helped them to organise resistance.

Unemployed politics was extremely complicated, but for the sake of clarity it can be divided into radical, moderate and conservative streams.[24] The radical stream was associated with the Communist Party, and included groups such as the One Big Union of the Unemployed, the Unemployed Workers' Movement, the United Fronts of Employed and Unemployed, and the Dole and Relief Workers' Council. These radical organisations had branches in most capital cities and the big industrial and mining towns. The moderate stream was associated either with the Labor Party or local trades halls. The Central Unemployed Committee in Victoria was an affiliate of the Trades Hall and the Queensland ALP rank-and-file committee was, as its name stated, allied to the state Labor Party. These were federated groups with no interstate connections. Then there were the conservative groups with no labour movement connections, such as the organisations of unemployed returned soldiers. Another example was the Western Australian Relief and Sustenance Workers' Union, which had links with the Douglas Credit Party. There were also many suburban and town groups which, hoping to impress conservative municipal councils, stuck to providing relief and odd jobs for members and steered clear of working-class politics.

Still, common to all unemployed groups was the desire to improve the range, quantity and quality of relief. Generally they sought full-time work at award wages and conditions or sustenance paid at basic wage rates. They wanted to stop the evictions of the homeless and the harassment of the unemployed by police. This was crucial, because police often used vagrancy laws to jail militants and a range of other laws to harass strikers, marchers and picketers.

Within these general aims were a multiplicity of specific campaigns with more immediate objectives. The range is huge, from agitation by itinerant unemployed men in north Queensland for decent shelters in country towns to fights with railway police in the Victorian Mallee District for a free ride on 'the rattler', and from the Adelaide Beef Riot in 1931 (a protest against government plans to replace beef with mutton in men's rations) to mass protests for free speech in the Melbourne suburb of Brunswick. Day-to-day, these groups fought constant battles with local councils over the right to use council premises and the right to collect relief. This too was crucial. Practically all unemployed groups, no matter how large or small, supplemented government relief through their own efforts. Not only was this necessary, but leaders well knew that producing extra relief meant more members.

The success or failure of the unemployed movement in the Great Depression can be measured in several ways. First of all, it never captured the permanent loyalty of all the unemployed, instead it constantly struggled against a chronic inertia. Nevertheless, at times it could mobilise extraordinarily large numbers. For example, the entire sustenance workforce in Victoria struck for a week in 1935 to wring increased sustenance out of an unwilling government. Secondly, in countless individual cases, the unemployed movement forced concessions, withdrawal or retreat from local councillors, landlords, police, sustenance administrators and others, who held the fate of the individual unemployed workers in their hands. Thirdly, large-scale agitation forced concessions from governments. In Victoria, for example, practically every improvement in government relief came about as a result of a specific agitation. The abandonment of a Victorian scheme to replace coupons with goods given in bulk (the unemployed believed that the 'bag system', as it was known, forced them to parade their poverty) was the result of a black-ban on the local depot by the unemployed of Richmond. The institution of an eight-shilling a week rent allowance was the product of a sustained agitation against eviction. The two big increases in sustenance rates in 1933 and 1935 were granted after strikes by sustenance workers. One strike involved 3000 men and lasted fully five weeks. The passage of legislation ending police harassment of street meetings came about after a campaign of civil disobedience in 1933. And a long agitation in 1932 forced the United Australia Party government to restore basic wage rates on relief works. Another strike by single men in 1934 forced the government to give them more relief work, which increased their 'wages' by 50 percent.

On the other hand there was no revolution in Australia, though the radical unemployed struggled hard for it. Even in their more immediate aims, the unemployed organisations' achievements were mixed. No government anywhere ever introduced full-time relief work at award wages and conditions or paid sustenance at the basic wage rate, or called off the police and the bailiffs. And just as there were countless little successes, so there were also countless little failures. But all this is politics in practice for the role of the unemployed movements of the 1930s in developing a consciousness of identity among the unemployed was one of their greatest achievements. The Great Depression was an experience which might have encouraged passivity, fear and inaction on the part of its victims, yet a creative, often extensive and vigorous unemployed movement was born and sustained by the victims of the worst poverty Australia has known, and this is where the success story lies.

Take a war job!

When they reflected on their lives in the 1940s and beyond, many old diggers used to wonder why capitalism in peace-time could not give them jobs, but capitalism in war-time could. There was plenty of work in the 1940s because the military needed men to fight and the war effort demanded production. However it was the way war was organised at home which finally put to rest the spectre of a new Depression. Unemployment fell to about 1 percent and there was a huge and unmet demand for workers in strategic war work.[25] This demand, coupled with the iron fist of a state directing the economy to war production, saw the beginning of a 30-year reign in Australia of the doctrine and reality of full employment. The jobs which went missing in the 1930s returned in abundance in the next decade.

A country at war needs two things above all: soldiers and munitions. The demand for both of these was met initially by mopping up the unemployed and by people shifting jobs (some 720 000 people moved from civil to military work in this period).[26] At first this was voluntary. There was conscription only to fill the ranks of the citizen militia, and after their training the militiamen went back to their old jobs. Nevertheless, there was compulsion in the sense that people's right to move from job to job was restricted. Skilled workers in essential and war industries were the most affected. They could not leave to join the military, nor could they leave to work in munitions factories.

The major shift in investment and production was to munitions and many non-essential industries lost workers to the new and expanding munitions factories. Farm labourers, clerks and even some professionals were attracted to these not so much by the work, but by the war-time pay loadings. So many people turned up to places like Lithgow in New South Wales and Maribynong in Melbourne to work in munitions factories, that the local infrastructure could not keep up. Tent and shanty towns sprang up as governments struggled to provide transport and services. And still these factories were short of workers.[27]

The shortages became much more desperate when Japan entered the war. Till then it had seemed distant, in far-away Europe. But when the Japanese armies began sweeping down through Asia towards New Guinea, the conflict metamorphised into a defensive war, with the security of Australia at stake. Labour shortages became much more serious, not just in the services or munitions but in the whole range of war-related projects. One response of the new Curtin Labor government was to introduce conscription for both military and civilian war services. A Civil Construction Corps was set up, comprising some 60 000 men of all ages, which built much of the necessary war infrastructure such as roads, new munitions factories, airports, camps, gun emplacements, warehouses and hospitals.[28] But the demands of war continued to grow. In January 1943, despite the fact that nearly one million people were employed directly in war work, there were still labour shortages.

The responses of the Commonwealth government were quite revolutionary in the context of the history of work. It set up a new Directorate of Manpower, with the power not only to direct people to stay in reserved occupations, but also to direct people into jobs, although this did not become extensive, as no more than 500 a month were ever told to move. Nevertheless, some industries were hit hard. After 'Manpower' had 'combed out' banks, the number of male bank workers fell by nearly 40 percent.[29] 'Manpower' also raided places of recreation, like race tracks, dance halls, clubs and hotels, looking for people it labelled 'shirkers and slackers'.[30]

The government also tackled a problem which had been created by the Depression—the collapse of apprenticeship and the shortage of skilled labour. It persuaded the craft unions to let semi-skilled workers do the work of artisans where these were not available. All told some 38 000 'dilutees' (as they were called) entered trades covered by the Amalgamated Engineering Union during the war. Governments upgraded and shortened apprenticeships too, and set up training courses, and old, retired workers were brought back to work as well.[31]

In 1942 the government used its powers to peg wages and prices. Hours of work were lengthened considerably, and so much overtime was being done that the average working week rose to between 50 and 60 hours. Later that year a worried government pegged hours at 48 for workers under 18 and 56 for adults.[32] In late 1942 and 1943 the government began to call up fit, young, male munition workers, who had till then been exempt, and replaced them with old men and discharged soldiers. So great had been the decline in the rural workforce, as rural workers rushed to better paid city jobs and the services, that the government suspended the call up of rural men altogether.[33]

The war shook up the labour market in a way wholly new to Australians. It caused government to involve itself in the economy in ways that it had never previously done. However, there was still one revolution to come. There were still, in 1943, labour shortages in all areas of war work, but the government had till then sought the solution in controlling and directing male workers. After a great deal of soul searching, it finally turned to women—in the first notable shift in the strict gendered segregation of work. Although women had taken up new jobs during World War I and kept them, they were jobs which fitted quite easily into existing notions of women's work.

The first noticeable change was the shift in women's participation rate in the wage and salary-earning workforce. In 1939 it stood at 25.3 percent; by 1943 it had increased to 33.5 percent.[34] This rapid increase took place, not by compulsion, but by persuasion. Until 1942 the government had to a degree sought out single women, but after 1942 it turned to married women. One advertisement read:

> Lonely? No more breakfasts to get in a hurry—a quick 'see you tonight' kiss as he rushed for the bus. No more need to get his dinner at night. Yes! The place is darn lonely without him. The best way to make the time pass ... is to take a war job.[35]

'Manpower' wanted single women most, but any married women without children, or even those with older children would do. Still it was a little reluctant to take young mothers.[36] Prior to the war only 5 percent of married women were doing paid work. By 1943 this had increased to 11 percent.[37] In terms of raw numbers this is not huge, but the implications were. For the first time married women were called to do paid work where previously they had been vilified if they tried. For the first time a crack appeared in the wall which imprisoned married women in the family.

Women went into three areas of work. The first was in the auxilliaries of the three services—navy, airforce and army. There had been nurses for the army since Florence Nightingale but now women became telegraphists and some did unskilled work in the airforce on planes. However, there was not a gender revolution in the services. Most women ended up doing the same work they had done previously—cooks, stewards, domestic servants, clerks or chauffeurs. Nance Kingston from Melbourne was typical. To avoid being sent to a munitions factory, she enlisted in the Australian Women's Army Service. She wanted to become a signaller but spent most of her time working as a domestic in a Townsville officers' club and as a clerk in an office in Melbourne.[38]

More women went to work in heavy industry, making guns and ammunition in munitions factories and building aircraft and ships.[39] At first only single women and widows were taken on, but after Pearl Harbour the factories took any woman they could. For many this kind of work was a new and strange experience. One analysis of 800 new munitions workers in a ten-week period in Melbourne showed that 268 were formerly domestic servants, 190 had already worked in factories, 89 were shop assistants, 74 were waitresses, 47 had not worked in paid jobs, 41 were dressmakers, 38 were nurses and receptionists and 31 were formerly clerks or typists.[40] Rose Cruikshank and Rosemary Davies became rivet gun operators in an aircraft factory. Rose had formerly made feather decorations for hats and Rosemary had been a dressmaker.[41] It was quite a change.

Women shifted into other kinds of strategically important work as well. Over 55 000 women went into the metal industries, trebling women's share of the metals workforce. In Sydney the number of women working in factories increased by 24 percent from 1939 to 1943.[42] Domestic service was the biggest loser in the war effort. Domestic servants fled middle-class homes for the new work. In 1939 nearly 19 percent of female workers were domestic servants. By 1943 this had fallen to 4.4 percent, just 80 000 people, and these were mainly old.[43] 'Manpower' regulations played a big part in the fall because they set a limit of one servant to a household. Domestic service in war-time could hardly be called a reserved occupation.

The third destination of women war workers was into organisations like the Women's Land Army. Women from cities and towns enlisted voluntarily. They were full-time workers who did all kinds of farm work; picking cotton or tomatoes, cutting asparagus, and so on. They filled the gap in the rural workforce left by the men who had joined the military or fled rural work for the cities. What they did, therefore, was critical, but it became even more so from 1943 onwards, when Australia agreed to take over the production of food for the Pacific allied forces.[44]

With so many women going into jobs previously thought to be 'men's' work, the question of pay became important. On Australia's entry into the war women were still being paid 54 percent of the male basic wage, although in 1941 the ACTU and various feminist groups began to clamour for equal pay. The Curtin government responded in 1942 by establishing the Women's Employment Board (WEB) and told it to consider the pay of three kinds of work—that which was usually done by men, that which had been done by men since the war began, and altogether new work. It was empowered to set rates of between 60 and 100 percent of the male rate of pay.[45]

The impact of the WEB was relatively small. It awarded increases in pay to only 90 000 women out of a female workforce of 800 000, the rest being in jobs still considered women's work. For example, servicewomen got only 57 percent of male pay rates and women in asylums, hospitals and woollen and cotton factories still got only 54 percent. Nevertheless, most of the lucky 90 000 had their pay increased to 90 percent of the male rates. Rose Cruikshank recalled, 'I never had so much money in my life'.[46] The WEB also dealt with working conditions. It restricted the weights women could lift. It kept women from dangerous machines and set knocking-off times (in fact it repeated much of what the old Factory Acts had done).[47]

Nevertheless, working conditions in these new jobs were often poor. Women worked the same hours as men, often up to 60 hours a week. In the munitions and metals trades the work was dirty, exhausting and dangerous. Absenteeism was correspondingly high, usually twice as high as the men's rate.[48] This was taken by some men to mean that women could not do the work, but they ignored the fact that women still had to run their homes and that there was precious little child care available. Governments were wary of child care, although 'Manpower' wanted it in order to release more married women for war work. In the end the Commonwealth government funded 850 places, when for children under five alone over 9000 places were needed.[49]

Women entered the workforce over the opposition of many men. The New South Wales Tramway Union tried to keep women off the trams and in 1940 the Sydney City Council refused to employ women to replace men gone to war. They failed. Women entered both.[50] Other unions argued for equal pay, hoping to keep women out that way. Other unions, like the Amalgamated Engineering Union, refused to accept women members.[51] However, most accepted the inevitable for the duration of the war but prepared plans to eject women once the war ended. John Curtin had already foreseen this. He promised in 1943 that 'The government gives the undertaking that all women employed shall be employed for the duration of the war and shall be replaced by men when they become available'.[52]

In 1945 the government legislated to give returned soldiers absolute preference in work. It stopped funding child care, wound up the dilution agreements and launched a media blitz to persuade women that they should return to their homes to care for, succour and readjust their men to post-war life. So by 1947 women's participation rate in the workforce had fallen to 27.3 percent.[53] Some women were happy to return to the home but others were not. Many wanted to stay in their jobs and others wanted to be retrained. Others had to return to jobs that paid the usual 54 percent of male pay rates and many resented the end of their chance to learn and use trade skills and to choose from a much wider range of options. At least in the short term, the pre-war division of labour and the gendered ideologies had been reasserted.

A high and stable level of employment

Post-war reconstruction in Australia really had its genesis in the mid to late 1930s, as progressive liberals began to search for ways to make capitalism work. Many younger economists had been emotionally scarred by the Depression, and began to argue for a greater degree of state intervention and planning. Within the Labor Party there had long been a conviction that an unregulated economy was bad economic thinking. The common Labor Party solution was to nationalise the banks and use their control of credit to expand consumer power and productivity. The economic historian Rick Kuhn described the typical ALP approach as 'under-consumptionism':

> Stated crudely, underconsumptionist economics holds that the productive potential of society is not matched by its purchasing power or effective demand. At times resources—machinery, land, and labour power—are idle, even if social needs remain to be satisfied. Underconsumptionist theories differ over the reasons for the deficiency of purchasing power and the best solution to the problem. Most of them can have, at least, a superficial appeal to the working-class interests, through the identification of inadequate purchasing power with workers' concern to improve their own living standards.[54]

The reconstruction division of the Department of Labour and National Service set up by the Menzies Government in 1940 began the planning of the post-war world. However, the Curtin government took the matter more seriously and created a new portfolio, Post-War Reconstruction, for the Treasurer, Ben Chifley. Despite a suspicion that it was set up only to boost morale during the darkest days of the war, the new department was given a strong staff of energetic, young and progressive thinkers. Chifley referred to them as his 'long-haired men and short skirted women' and put at their head the talented bureaucrat H.C. 'Nugget' Coombs.[55] The Department's brief was no less than to refurbish capitalism in Australia by planning the conditions for full employment, directing programmes to channel investment into production, which would lead to a higher standard of living and develop a system of social security to protect those who needed protection. Ben Chifley said:

> ... the primary aim of our post-war economic policy must be a high and stable level of employment ... It means placing permanently within the reach of every one of us, freedom from the basic economic worries, the realisation of some of our ambitions for personal development and the opportunity of bringing up happy, healthy, well-educated families.[56]

That these could be more than just pious hopes was due to the extraordinary work of the British economist J.M. Keynes. His Australian followers used Keynes to criticise the uncontrolled play of market forces, blaming these for the Depressions of the 1890s and 1930s. Previous economic orthodoxy had held that the free play of supply and demand would produce full employment of all available resources, that capitalism was a self-adjusting system which would tend to balance out into economic growth and high employment if only it were left alone. It was a theory which in practice insured that Australia had a permanently high level of unemployment, that economic activity went through a short-term cycle of booms and recessions and endured a major depression every fifty years.

Keynes' solution to the problem of unemployment was to use government expenditure to drive the economy out of the bogs of recession and depression. Since the private sector could not do it governments should encourage investment and private spending by both deficit financing and expanding government expenditure. This would increase aggregate demand for goods and services, stimulate production and so maintain high levels of employment. Boosting the economy when recession loomed would flatten out the trade cycle and put to rest the ever-present prospect of another depression. Planning for the peace, then, meant the implementation of the Keynesian economic agenda.

The Labor Party took to Keynesian thinking with alacrity. There had for some years been a nascent Keynesianism in some elements of Labor thinking. The Scullin government's Treasurer, 'Red Ted' Theodore, is often described as a proto-Keynesian for his plan to revive the Australian economy in 1931 with a fiduciary note issue. However, Ben Chifley himself may have been the first major ALP figure to turn to Keynes. His minority report from the 1936/7 Banking Royal Commission, of which he was a member, illustrates his early understanding of, and commitment to, the new economics. To Chifley and to other social democrats Keynes offered a way of 'civilising capitalism', and an alternative to more radical social visions like communism or state socialism. Peter Love was correct when he wrote that Keynes' dislike of 'unrestrained capitalism, particularly the human waste occasioned by unemployment, was a moral stance shared by Labor people'.[57]

This moral stance, ironically, gained immeasurable practical support from Australia's war, because the war clearly demonstrated the benefits which government control could bring to the economy. Government spending, argued the progressive economists, had maintained a high level of demand and, hence, a high level of employment. The government already had control over prices, wages and rents as well as over imports and exports, exchange rates and the issue of capital in a way that had put to rest people's fears that increasing government control meant an equivalent decline in freedom. Real freedom lay in abolishing insecurity and real involvement lay in organising community consensus to get it done. The war, they argued, had shown how the nation could pull together.[58] If it could happen in the war then it could also happen in the peace.

The Australian welfare state appeared in these war years. In 1943 Ben Chifley unveiled the National Welfare Fund, the fund from which social security was to be paid. It was itself funded from progressive taxation (the Commonwealth had just taken over the states' income taxing powers), and it was used to pay what seemed like a social security bonanza. Widows' pensions were introduced in 1942, maternity benefits for Aboriginal mothers in 1943, and funeral benefits in the same year, and unemployment, sickness and pharmaceutical benefits in 1945. The Commonwealth Employment Service was set up as well in that last year of the war.[59]

How far the Curtin government was animated by feelings of social justice or plain political opportunism is a matter of controversy. Curtin himself said that the new programmes would support those who could not support themselves, and a generation of historians has agreed that the new social welfare policies were born of Labor's deep commitment to equality, fuelled by the human tragedy of the previous decade. The historian Rob Watts thinks differently. It was a question of political tactics, he argues. Widows' pensions was a bribe to sweeten the states when the Federal government wanted to take over income tax in 1942. When Curtin wanted more money for the war effort he sweetened the population with the promise of a social security programme. He had to do this, claims Watts, because he had promised not to increase taxes nor introduce new ones. But he did! In 1943 he introduced the National Welfare Fund Bill and an Income Tax Assessment Bill which increased rates of tax *and* lowered the tax threshold.[60]

The Full Employment White Paper was the cornerstone of the government's post-war strategy. The White Paper plainly had its origins in the Depression experience, but its inspiration came from similar ideas emanating from Britain in 1944. What was full employment? The White Paper itself was vague about this, and contemporary estimates ranged from an unemployment rate of between 3 percent and 8 percent. The second figure, in the opinion of the economist Douglas Copland, would hardly have pleased the workers, for 8 percent was above the average level of unemployment in the 1920s.[61] The actual post-war figure of about 1–2 percent was unforeseen by the government and its public service advisers and it delighted workers, bureaucrats and governments alike.

The full employment objective was the centrepiece of Labor's welfarism. The welfare state was always to be secondary to it, to catch those who could not otherwise cope. Plainly the employment policy, the new welfare policies and the adoption of Keynesianism were intended to resuscitate and accommodate capitalism. Nevertheless, among business and the press there was great opposition to it. It had, said *The Sydney Morning Herald* 'socialistic implications'.[62] It meant regimentation, the continuation after the war of war-time controls. Some opponents thought it would give organised labour more power. Others thought that it meant more public and less private employment.[63] On the other hand organised labour was enthusiastic. But the reaction of business was surprising; after all, the policy represented a commitment to stability and planning, two things business had never had in Australia.

The full employment policy also represented full employment for men. The White Paper came out not long before the government passed its Re-establishment and Employment Bill giving absolute preference in employment to returned servicemen. The propaganda offensive which forced women back to their homes was the ideological cement which held the legislative proposals together. Reconstruction, therefore, meant different things to men and women. To married women it meant security of employment for husbands and fathers and a safety net for their family in times of trouble, but it said nothing about their position in the paid workforce. The Labor government's policies for women concentrated on housing, so in terms of work, reconstruction re-emphasised women's domestic work. It was the beginning of the suburban dream, for the new houses were not the flats and tenements of the inner cities but the brick or fibro bungalows of the suburbs. Electricity, piped hot water and labour-saving devices were depicted as every woman's right. The provision of child care, pay for housewives, equal pay and women's right to work all were swamped in the campaign to return women to the home.[64] The ultimate aim of this, of course, was to increase the birthrate, a need made even more urgent, in the minds of the reconstructors, by the Depression and the war. The slogans of better housing and full employment certainly had a moral and political force and they certainly captured the imaginations of many Australians with memories of fifteen years of social dislocation. Nevertheless, the reality was an attempt to return Australia to the pre-war sexual division of labour and to the ideal bourgeois family of the breadwinning husband with his dependent wife and children.

9 The changing workforce 1945–1974

The end of the war ushered in nearly 30 years of prosperity in Australia, known as the second long boom. Economic growth measured by gross national product rose annually by between 4 and 5 percent. Keynesian economic management and constant labour shortages delivered seemingly ever higher living standards. The real average weekly earnings of workers after overtime and over-award payments are taken into account increased by 78 percent between 1947 and 1971. And when unemployment dared to reach just 2.6 percent in 1961 the sense of crisis was such that the Menzies government nearly lost office. As Australian cities became suburban conglomerates and the suburban dream turned Australia into a consumer culture, manufacturing boomed, increasingly financed by multinational corporations. Its share of national production rose from 17 percent in 1928–29 to 28 percent twenty years later, and it stayed at that level well into the 1960s. Finance, banking and property also flourished to provide investment for the reconstructing and expanding economy and for the cities, which spread rapidly up and the suburbs which spread rapidly out. New industrial suburbs were built too, when mass production factories demanded more space than the traditional home of manufacturing, the inner-city suburbs, could provide. Obsessed by ideas of development, governments poured money into economic infrastructure; the Snowy River hydro-electric scheme was not only the biggest of the post-war development projects, its scale and its conception symbolised the vision of which it was part. Agriculture boomed too, especially in the 1950s and 1960s. New machinery, fertilisers, heavily funded research, taxation concessions and new markets increased farm production in the 1950s by fully 50 percent. And if agriculture's share of Australian export trade fell from 80 to 50 percent in this period it was only because of the mining boom when mineral exports began to take its place.[1]

The office, the factory, the big building and infrastructural projects all needed workers. Administrative functions became a greater part of productive enterprises and new levels of management, with their attendant paperwork increased demand for office workers. The growing complexity of government, the growth of hire purchase and the increasing size of the banking and finance sector opened job opportunities for people with white-collar skills. On the other hand the continuing de-skilling of factory work, the building boom and the backward state of technology in mining and infrastructural development created new demands for manual workers. Yet in agriculture, technology was advancing so fast that the farm workforce was actually declining. The proportion of the workforce in agriculture fell right away, from 20 percent at war's end to just 10 percent by the 1970s.[2] The future of those who normally laboured for pay on the farms looked increasingly bleak.

The boom broke in 1974. Oil prices rose by 1000 percent and Australia, being an importer of oil, suffered dearly. The end of the Vietnam War destabilised the world economic order, as the world's most powerful economy, the USA, ground from a war to a peace economy. Unemployment returned to Australia, but this time it was accompanied by inflation. The Keynesian panacea, it seemed, had failed and economists and governments turned to the reactionary policies of the free marketeers for the answers to the new problems. The prospects for work after 1974 were very different from those of 30 years earlier.

Reshaping the office worker

There were revolutionary changes in both the structure and staffing of offices after the war. In the big nineteenth-century offices, workers usually had their own rooms, lined up on each side of a corridor. By the 1930s the open-plan office was the norm. The clerks worked in one big room designed to facilitate a 'continuous flow' of work. Today these offices looked like school rooms. The desks were lined up in rows so that one clerk, having finished his or her work, passed it on to the next. The work itself was fragmented and subdivided, each person having a particular function and doing nothing else. Desks were positioned to eliminate walking and office managers had separate offices positioned so that they could see what their clerks were up to.[3] The office was beginning to look like the factory, which is not surprising because the Taylorists had turned their stop watches to office work.

Offices were labour intensive and seemingly inefficient, so were ripe for reconstruction. Time-and-motion men had begun to 'engineer the office' in the USA in the 1920s. Just as they had done to process workers in the factories, they pounced on secretaries, and timed and measured their work until they had eliminated every wasted movement:

> In one very large company, having more than 1000 office employees, the manager is proud of the fact that he has eliminated 21 key-strokes on each letter, and thereby saves

620 strokes of the typewriter operator each day—each operator writes a daily average of 30 letters. This is equal to 10 lines, or 100 words a day. Multiplied by 100 operators, it is a saving of 1000 lines or 10,000 words a day. Again, multiplied by the working days in a year—300—this means a saving of 300,000 lines annually or 3,000,000 words, with a cash value of perhaps $2000 a year. An excellent saving to be sure.[4]

Type-strokes were measured, basic levels set by fast typists, the slow ones that did not improve were sacked, and the rest given bonuses for fast work.[5]

There was another revolution in office layout in the 1970s in Australia inspired by German models of office structure. The engineered office was transformed into the landscaped office. The 'continuous flow' was abandoned for the 'work group'. Desks were now clustered in groups, colour and pattern appeared on walls, and planter boxes, rubber plants and screens separated the groups from each other.[6] Groups were given responsibility for whole sections of the work, which itself was organised to allow them to rotate jobs and use more skills and talents. The internal layout also became much more flexible. If the work needed changing then it was much easier to move desks and screens about than it was previously. The landscape enthusiasts hoped the new system would result in improved attitudes to work and an enhanced sense of commitment to the firm. And it seemed they were right, for workers liked their new environment (some said it allowed them to work with a greater team spirit) and productivity did increase.[7] The introduction of work stations, which followed from the use of personal computers and in which an office worker had all he or she needed close at hand, did not really change the principles behind the landscaped office.

Historically, white-collar workers had shown a greater sense of community with their employers, a greater commitment to middle-class values than have blue-collar workers. However, the 40 years of Taylorism had threatened to destroy that consensus by turning clerks into an office-bound version of the industrial proletariat. Office landscaping was designed to repair the damage, nevertheless it should not be thought that it was not influenced by the urge to control. Job descriptions were formulated which set out exactly what an office worker had to do and the advent of computerisation made it easy for managers to see in an instant if a worker or a work group were slacking. Electronics also made it easier to measure key strokes on word processors (operators called one such system 'the spy in the typewriter'), and the old Taylorist tactics have been used to set fast rates.[8] As well work groups and autonomous workers control themselves. Historians of work sometimes call this 'responsible autonomy' but it is just one more strategy in the continuing battle management wages to impose on workers the hegemony of its aims.[9]

It was women who staffed the new offices, swamping male clerks in ever increasing numbers. But this was part of a much wider movement in which women's participation in the labour market rose from a fifth to a third in the 30 years before 1975. The percentage of women doing paid work in 1961 reached 32 percent, and in 1976, 50 percent. This is dramatic enough, but not as dramatic as the participation rate of married women. Only 3.4 percent in 1947 (it actually fell after the war—in 1933 it had been 5 percent), it rose to 16 percent in 1966 and then to 42 percent in 1982. In 1947 15 percent of all women workers were married, but the figure rose to 60 percent in 1981.[10]

Why was there such a change? Plainly the tight labour market and the feminisation of work was important but the supply of women was a product of demographic changes. More women were marrying but were having less children, so the constant labour of child rearing which dominated women's work in the nineteenth century had long since passed. The average issue of live births had fallen to around two, and most women had their babies by their mid to late twenties and then returned to the workforce. Between 1966 and 1980 married women between 25 and 34 made up nearly three-quarters of the increase in the female workforce.

Another result of the increase in married women in the workforce is the corresponding increase in part-time employment. Married women have taken most of the part-time jobs the economy has produced. Figures for the 1940s and 1950s are hard to find, but in 1979 when over 15 percent of the workforce worked part time, 80 percent of these were women and 45 percent of all employed married women were working part time.[11] Most women who worked part time were happy doing it. In the early 1980s an Australian Bureau of Statistics survey showed that nearly 90 percent of married women doing part-time work did not want to work more hours and nor did 77 percent of single women working part time. Part-time work obviously is good for mothers who want to mix paid work with time at home, but it also is a reflection of difficulties with child care.[12]

The rapid post-war growth in the manufacturing sector was also largely responsible for the increasing participation of women in the paid workforce. Ever more of what women once produced in the home was being produced in the factories and sold back to the home cheaper than what it cost to produce formerly. Women on farms made and sold butter and cheese less frequently. Commercial laundries took up some of the weekly washing. And young men and women who might have lodged or boarded were increasingly likely to set up house themselves. As Ann Curthoys suggests, women's value as producers of goods continued to decline and as that part of their housework became redundant they were forced to join the paid workforce to recoup their loss. Many one-income families had to become two-income families to afford the new labour-saving devices which became a 'necessity' in every good home. Hire purchase made the difference. Most hire purchase in this period was taken out on cars, but in 1959 for example, of the £260 million advanced on 'the never-never', 25 percent of it was spent on household goods.[13]

The expansion of women's paid work after the war made precious little difference to the way work was divided between the sexes. To give some examples, in 1971 every stenographer, typist and receptionist was female, but every plasterer, electrician and bricklayer was male. These were sex-typed jobs par excellence. Beyond these, as the economist Margaret Power has pointed out, over 80 percent of women worked in occupations which were disproportionately female and just under 80 percent of men worked in jobs that were disproportionately male. Six years later just eighteen occupational classifications covered 85 percent of the female workforce. Bookkeepers, cashiers, stenographers, typists and clerks made up 34 percent; domestic workers 17 percent; shop assistants 13 percent; teachers and nurses 7 percent each; clothing, boot and textile workers 2 percent; and telephonists 2 percent.[14]

The feminisation of the office took off after the war. Three sets of figures show how quickly this developed. In the ten years after 1966 the proportion of women in the census category 'clerical' increased from 60 to 67 percent. In the years from 1947 to 1966 the number of women typists, secretaries and stenographers increased from 71 000 to 162 800. Whereas in 1950 women comprised only 11.5 percent of bank staff, in 1978 they comprised 46.3 percent.[15]

Inevitably, women were fitted into offices at the lowest level. The Commonwealth Public Service is a good example of this. From 1903 women were concentrated in the general division of the service, the divisions which employed typists, telegraphists, clerical assistants and manual workers. They could not enter the next division up, the clerical division, in the usual way, through competitive examinations from outside, instead they had to be promoted from the general. Then in 1915, the government excluded women altogether from the clerical division and they remained on the outer until World War II, when labour shortages allowed them back in. Despite the big expansion of the service after the war, women were still compressed in the fourth (formerly the general) division. In 1972 the fourth division employed 72 percent of the service and women made up 82 percent of these. Of the clerical division, which was finally opened up after the war, 16 percent were women, but 90 percent of these were confined to its lower grades.[16] In part these circumstances were a product of women's family responsibilities, the unequal division of labour in the home, and the assumptions that women were short-term workers and that men entered the public service for a career. It was also due in good part to the marriage bar, which until 1966 barred married women from working in the public service at all.[17]

Once clerical public service jobs were opened up, in principle at least the public service career structures were opened to women. A division began to develop between typist-stenographers and administrative secretaries whose superior office skills, responsibility and organisational experience were more valued by employers and who were able to open a career path (of sorts) for themselves.[18] In 1970 the Secretaries Forum, an organisation of administrative secretaries, began to assert its members' professional status. Their aim was to

> impress on the business that every girl who can do shorthand and typing is not a secretary and that the top-flight secretary is more valuable than to be used as a general office dogsbody ... As long as she continues to be lumped together with thousands of others who have nothing more than stenographic skills and as long as business men continue to see secretaries as a homogeneous breed who merely type or take dictation, then the girl with the potential to make the ranks of the executive secretary will remain one of the most frustrated members of the whole business hierarchy.[19]

As for married women, the greatest barrier to their full participation in the office workforce was their families. It is indicative of the ideas about women's place that one of the first post-war child minding centres was set up in central Sydney for the use of women shoppers in 1950, fully 20 years before governments took any interest in providing child care for women workers.[20] Once again child care was a case of the state catching up with the extent to which industry depended on women's labour. By 1969 fully a quarter of all working women also cared for children under the age of twelve years. Most did then as they do now, they left their children with families, neighbours or friends, or did shift work so either they or their husbands would always be at home, or they worked part time so that they could look after their school-age children after school.

In the 1940s, 1950s and 1960s most organised child care was provided by voluntary bodies, or by local councils, state governments and private, profit-making companies. Only in the late 1960s did the Federal government begin to fund child care and, especially under the Whitlam government, this expanded rapidly. In 1970 the Commonwealth funded just 40 centres and 2171 children out of the 555 centres already running. Seven years later subsidised places had increased to 20 000 and commercial non-subsidised places to 45 000.[21] Most of these centres were in middle-class suburbs, however, providing relief for middle-class families, and it has been only since 1985 or so, that the Commonwealth, under another Labor government, has consciously been directing its funds towards working-class families who need child care most.

The slow pace of change was a product of many factors. Despite the clear commitment of government to increasing women's participation in the workforce, there was still a widely held belief that a married woman's place was in her home, particularly looking after her children. Any number of social problems were blamed on working mothers, juvenile delinquency being the most obvious one. Employers, anxious as ever to keep down their costs, refused to provide child care at their workplaces, despite the fact that they knew that their working mothers were anxious about their children, were less inclined to work efficiently and were more likely to take 'sickies'. Unions, too, accustomed to fighting for improved wages and conditions, were very slow to see and appreciate the particular needs of their women members. Child care is now a hot political issue. Should parents pay for it, or employers, or the state? Should it be run for private profit or should it be regarded as part of the social wage? As the car stickers say: 'Childcare. A right not a privilege'.

Doing the dirty jobs

The clean, shining and feminine office was another world to Australia's unskilled labourers. Their lot was dirt, smell, dust, heat, noise and pressure in an infinite variety that was tied together by monotony and fatigue. The screeching and pounding din of a motor vehicle assembly line, the bloodied clothes in an abattoir boning room, the incessant clatter of sewing machines in a clothing factory, the raw, red heat of a steel plant's blast furnace, the dry heat and dust of a paddock on the margins of good farming land and the different and deadly dust of an asbestos mine, the nauseous stink in a small-goods factory. Boring, tedious, monotonous, stressful, dirty and sweaty. These were the circumstances and the adjectives most often used by unskilled workers to describe their jobs.

Factory work on an assembly line came to represent the characteristic kind of unskilled work in Australia's consumer culture.

De-skilled workers in clothing, boots and textiles, long the basis of small manufacturing, were joined by the workers on the line making fridges, washing machines, irons and an endless range of other goods. Employers had discovered the productivity advantages of de-humanised work and adopted them with a vengeance. As it was in light, so it was in heavy industry. Iron and steel production, paper and cement factories employed thousands of workers in subdivided tasks, but it was the manufacture of motor vehicles and its associated industries, rubber, glass and petroleum, which dominated the industrial landscape. The massive car assembly factories like Ford's at Broadmeadows in Melbourne came to symbolise both the possibilities for output and the degradation of work.

Many post-war workers in Australia were modern manifestations of the nineteenth century navvy, the pick and shovel workers who built the colonial railway networks. Power generation, irrigation works, the construction of more railways, roads, bridges and other earthworks employed armies of men to do the work which underpinned Australia's post-war development. Thousands more cut timber or dug asbestos and tin to provide the raw material for the housing boom. Their skill lay in their strength and endurance and the dexterity with which they wielded their implements. Australians might have considered themselves a technologically advanced people, but they still relied to an extraordinary extent on good, old-fashioned muscle.

Unskilled work, therefore, was very much like it had always been. Unskilled workers received less pay than their skilled counterparts, but could perhaps make up some of the leeway by working overtime. To be a labourer was to stay a labourer. Unskilled workers had no career paths. Their only mobility was from job to job (many factories have very high staff turnovers), or was geographic, searching the country for higher pay in a probably more isolated workplace. They were at the bottom of workplace hierarchies too, impossibly distant from owners, managers, white-collar 'staff' and (all too frequently) their skilled counterparts. Hence they suffered neglect, ignored by the office (except when they did something wrong) for whom the shop-floor was as foreign as the office was to the labourer. Yet there were new aspects to the post-war labourer's working life, which distinguished them from their pre-war counterparts. Work was easier to find, because of the tight labour market, hence incomes were higher and unions stronger than, for example, in the 1920s. Then there was shift work, where the horror of the 'dog shift' (midnight to 8am) was amply illustrated by the fact that shift workers regarded the day shift as a holiday.

The workers in these jobs faced their bosses (if indeed they ever saw them) across the chasm that is social class in Australia. But after World War II they faced them across an ethnic divide as well. Unskilled work was done less and less by white Australian-born workers. Instead it was done more and more by migrants from Southern and Eastern Europe.

Post-war migration was immensely significant to Australia. By 1986 about 3.2 million of its residents had been born overseas. In 1981 the nearly 3 million foreign born made up 23 percent of the population, double the number in 1947. In 1947 over 98 percent of the Australian population were native English speakers. In 1981 this had fallen to just under 90 percent. Most migrants to Australia in this period were British, as they had always been, but large numbers of Italians, Greeks, Yugoslavs, Germans, Poles and Balts, Asians from India, Turkey, Vietnam and many more had significantly altered the demographic character of Australia. From 1947 to 1985 five million migrants arrived in Australia. Two million went home leaving a net gain of just under three million.[22]

This was not quite what Arthur Calwell wanted. Calwell, the Minister for Immigration in the Chifley Labor Government, was the architect of post-war immigration. Memories of the threat of a Japanese invasion, a conviction that all Asia was lustfully eyeing our open spaces, a disturbingly low birthrate in the Great Depression, a commitment to heavy industry as the centrepiece of post-war reconstruction and continuing chronic labour shortages convinced the government to adopt a policy of rapid population growth—2 percent per annum, half of it to be made up of immigrants.[23]

Calwell wanted British migrants for his annual 1 percent, and if he could not get them, northern Europeans would do. 'For every foreign migrant', he said, 'there will be ten people from the United Kingdom.'[24] There were not, as it turned out. There were shortages of ships and the British and Scandinavians were not as keen as he thought they might be. Instead, in the late 1940s he got 180 000 displaced persons from Poland, Latvia, Lithuania and Estonia, Hungary and Germany. To overcome the sensibilities of a population long accustomed to thinking of Australia as a white Anglo-Saxon/Irish country these were portrayed as Nordic. Many, Calwell later said, 'were red headed and blue eyed. There were also a number of natural platinum blondes of both sexes. The men were handsome and the women beautiful. It was not hard to sell immigration to the Australian people once the press published photographs of that group.'[25]

The long-term figures, from 1947 to 1985, show just how far post-war immigration diverged from the government's preferences. Only 37 percent of immigrants came from Britain and Ireland, and 9 percent from northern Europe. Some 19 percent came from southern and 13 percent from eastern Europe. About 11 percent came from Asia (in 1975 it was only 6 percent), 7 percent from Oceania (mainly New Zealand), and the rest from Africa and the Americas. The government's preferences are more clearly reflected in the figures for assisted migrants. The Australian government assisted 85 percent of the British, 77 percent of the German and 68 percent of the Dutch, but only 34 percent of the Greeks, 20 percent of the Italians and even fewer South-east Asians.[26]

In the final analysis governments wanted labour for the development of Australia and markets for Australian-made goods. 'Migrants make jobs', the Immigration Department proclaimed and the figures show just how crucial migrant labour has been to the Australian workforce. From 1947 to 1972 migrants filled 75 percent of all men's jobs created in Australia and 45 percent of all women's jobs. The change in the ethnic makeup of the workforce has outstripped the change in the demographic mix in the population.[27]

In fact migrant workers from different countries have gone into very different kinds of jobs. The first division was one which might have been expected. Men went disproportionately into heavy outdoor labouring work, heavy industry, and mining. Women went disproportionately into clothing, textile, boots and food processing factories. They were congregated in the lowest paid work, the work with the poorest conditions and the most sub-divided and meaningless work.

The segmentation of the post-war workforce began with the displaced persons who were forced to sign two-year agreements promising to work wherever they were sent. Migrant workers from Britain and northern and western Europe tended to go into jobs similar to those done by the Australian born, the skilled blue-collar work in industry, white-collar work in the service industries and the professions. Southern and eastern European and Asian migrant workers tended to go into the unskilled or at best semi-skilled, blue-collar, labouring jobs. This division has been such that some historians of migration argue that Australian-born workers and their migrant equivalents form a new labour aristocracy, separated from southern and eastern European migrants by the possession of skills, higher wages and job ladders in their industries, and that non-English speaking migrants have filled the jobs that no indigenous workers wanted.[28] In 1966, for example, 45 percent of women born in Italy, 56 percent of Greek women and 54 percent of women born in Yugoslavia worked as process workers, compared to just 9 percent of Australian born women.[29]

From the beginning of the programme migrant men were sent to work in industries thought to be crucial to Australia's development; to forestry camps, asbestos mines, railway camps, sugar fields and steel furnaces. They were sent to the Snowy River hydro scheme, where 60 percent of the workforce were migrants and to similar electricity projects throughout the Commonwealth. Their skills were ignored. For example, prior to coming to Australia, less than 10 percent of displaced persons were labourers. In Australia, doctors, architects, musicians, tradesmen and dentists alike were put to work with picks and shovels and migrants in the later programmes had similar difficulties as professional associations and unions refused to recognise their qualifications. This continued in the 1950s and beyond.

A 1973 survey of a number of non-English speaking workers showed that 66 percent of women and 52 percent of men were unhappy in their jobs and felt that they had 'no opportunity in life'.[30] This, and other surveys of migrant workers on process or assembly-line work, shows that they did not like the way their work was sub-divided. They would have preferred variety; to be moved around a factory doing different jobs, but they were too frightened of management to ask.[31] Nor did they like the systems of payment. Most work in clothing, textile and boot factories was paid either by the piece or under a bonus system, where a minimum output was set and workers were paid a bonus for what they produced over the minimum. Most women said the minimums were too fast. They felt they had to work too hard for their money, and that they were under constant surveillance and threat of the sack if they didn't achieve the basic rate. As one woman in a biscuit factory complained: 'The work is hard and monotonous and the bosses continually scream at you. Let a biscuit pass and they look at you as if you were from a mental institute. This is because the rate of work is too fast and women can't do it for long. This is why every week dozens leave.'[32]

Surveillance of their work, arbitrary timings of visits to toilets (at Ford workers had to 'book' in the morning for a visit to the toilet in the afternoon), cramped and rushed lunchtimes, no tea breaks and abuse led to fear, distrust and suspicion and sometimes to frustration, absenteeism and sabotage, as when workers in a light bulb factory deliberately smashed light bulbs out of sheer frustration.[33]

Of course they had little choice but to take this kind of work. Most migrant women worked not for pleasure, but for survival. The combined incomes of husband and wife frequently reached little more than the average wage of Australian-born male workers.[34] Management used this situation to demand hard work and discipline, but some had little regard for their workers anyway. Some managers in one survey thought migrant women worked hard but they tied sexist to ethnic stereotypes to depict their work as particularly suited to their nationality. One manager said:

> The women are suited to these jobs because they can sit at the machine all day doing the same thing. If they were more intelligent or better educated they would become bored or go around the bend. But this class of person is suited to the job. These women come from peasant type backgrounds.[35]

An illustration from a visit by Bill Ford, the industrial relations expert, to a car manufacturing plant shows how language difficulties increased the already considerable distance between management and workers.

> The first concerned the incentive bonus scheme operated by the management. Under this scheme, the worker received bonus payments for additional output above an established base level. It is regarded as successful. However, many of the migrants interviewed by the interpreters completely misunderstood the scheme. These people thought that foremen reduced their pay if they didn't work hard enough or were otherwise displeased with them. They had genuine fear of the foremen and it was fear, not incentive, that motivated them to work hard.[36]

The Yugoslav woman who was asked whether she thought management cared for its workers epitomised the workers' feelings. She bluntly replied, 'You must be joking'.[37]

While migrant workers made up the bulk of the unskilled workforce in the city, Aborigines made up a big proportion of it in the country. For most Aborigines technological, economic, political and social changes rendered obsolete many of the jobs that they had always done in Australia's rural industries. So when recession hit in the mid 1970s, Aborigines were ill-equipped for much more than an increasing descent into unemployment. Barry Morris called his important article on Aborigines and work in northern New South Wales 'From Under-employment to Unemployment', and that is a fair statement of the position.[38]

Government policies towards Aborigines after World War II were a part of that assimilationist programme which affected migrants as well. It saw the dismantling of the 'protective' legislation which governments had built up since the nineteenth century. As Paul Hasluck, Minister for Territories, put it in 1951: 'it is expected that all persons of Aboriginal blood or mixed blood in Australia will live like white Australians do'.[39] In terms of work, this meant that Aborigines could, in principle, henceforth work for whom, when and where they wanted, they could be hired by employers without the need for special permits and could earn wages that were on a par with those that white people could earn (in Queensland until the 1970s Aborigines still had controls set on their wages).[40] The facts, of course, were rather different.

Young Aborigines often look back in bitterness to the part their parents played in World War II. Many Aboriginal men fought alongside white soldiers, one thousand Aborigines worked with the army and airforce labour corps in the Northern Territory while Aborigines in or near cities or working in rural jobs were 'manpowered' into work essential for the War effort.[41] However, their contribution to the war effort brought few benefits to Aboriginal people. White Australians refused to recognise them as citizens until 1967, and the assimilationist policies of governments were still predicated on the belief that what was best for Aborigines was the destruction of their own culture. The only real benefit they won was an improvement in their position in the labour market to the point where, in Western Australia's Great Southern, they were earning 'unprecedented' wages in jobs such as general farm work, shearing and stock.[42] We have become accustomed to the fact that the northern pastoral industry was built on the back of Aboriginal labour. We must realise that southern agriculture, too, was heavily dependent on the labour of Aborigines.

Probably until the 1970s southern Aborigines were a rural people living close to places where their ancestors had lived: in Aboriginal settlements, on missions, on pastoral stations or on the fringes of cities and towns. They lived in a nether world, excluded and despised by white townsfolk and farmers and valued only for the labour that they sold and the goods that they brought with their wages. They worked mainly in the seasonal economy and formed a pool of unskilled labour, hired when needed, ignored when not. In New South Wales and Victoria, they actually monopolised seasonal work, like fruit picking, regarding it as their kind of work. Picking was a short-term job, lasting usually from January to March or April. To tide them over the winter months they took short-term labouring jobs where they could find them; building roads, laying pipes, or cutting timber. Where it was still possible others made money by hunting animals—possums for their pelts, rabbits and dingoes for the scalps. In some parts of the south-west of Western Australia up to 20 percent of Aborigines supported themselves by trapping. Yet others, such as those around government Aboriginal settlements like Wreck Bay in New South Wales, turned to the settlements for rations, garden produce and sharing. Others went on the dole.

On the margins of settlement and in the north Aborigines continued to work in the pastoral industry doing stock work and station work and domestic work in homes, but the process of closer settlement, which was turning southern grazing land into farms, meant clearing work—poisoning suckers, root picking, scrub bashing and stone picking. On cleared farms they worked with stock, harvesting grain, fencing, sinking dams, sewing bags and shearing.

Aboriginal men and women did all these jobs, but Aboriginal women also worked as domestics in private homes, or sometimes as nursing aides in rural hospitals.

Few Aborigines had permanent jobs. The rural economy did not provide full-time jobs and very few Aborigines possessed enough capital to buy farms. In New South Wales some Aborigines worked full-time in the timber industry, some more at Port Kembla steelworks, and in the later 1960s more Aborigines found work with local municipalities on their outdoor staff. In Victoria Aborigines in Gippsland worked full-time in saw milling, in the State Electricity Commission or on the railways, but this was unusual.[43]

The wages paid to southern Aborigines depended largely on whether their work was covered by an arbitration court or wages board award. Where it was, they generally were paid the same as white workers, but in Queensland things were different. Under the Aborigines and Torres Strait Islanders Act 'assisted aborigines' (some 20 500 out of a population of 60 000) living on government reserves and settlements had to work as directed by the manager and were paid wages set by the government. These were usually about one-third of the equivalent wages for whites.[44] Aborigines never got these wages themselves; they were paid into a trust fund administered by the Department of Aboriginal and Islander Affairs, only a small portion of which was returned to them, as pocket money. The Queensland government used a familiar analogy to explain why: 'The father or mother of a good family does the same as the Director of Native Affairs in protecting the earnings and spending of his wards'.[45] The policy basis was different but the effect was the same in the Northern Australian and New South Wales pastoral industry. In both regions pastoralists paid Aboriginal workers about half the level of white wages, and cut transport costs from these. Some were paid only in beef or flour and some in cheap wine. In New South Wales it was only in 1955, when the Department of Labour and Industry intervened, that award rates were paid.[46]

A great deal of work done by Aborigines, particularly in the south, was done not by individuals but by families, for Aborigines carried their kinship relations into the workplace. With few exceptions, Aborigines preferred to work near where they lived, close to family and kin and close to the land they were brought up on. Where they migrated for picking they went as a cluster of families, in which wives, husbands, grandparents, children and kin worked together. In clearing, adults did the heavy work, children picked up sticks, stoked fires and killed plants. Fathers were paid at the end of each week and paid that out to family members. So-called 'key men' often related by kin, contracted the work with farmers and paid their workers themselves.[47]

Most of this kind of work was done on contract or by the piece. In part this was the custom of these industries, but it seems that this kind of work suited Aborigines, whose attitude to work and work time was unique in Australia. (After all, imposing European ideas of work onto Aboriginal culture was what assimilation was all about.) Contract work was often more lucrative than day labour or payment by the hour, but more importantly, contract work allowed them to work at their own pace. They could more easily mix work and leisure, they could more easily knock off work when they felt inclined or work hard until the task was done. This is the essence of task work. Time is not the dominant way work is structured. Work is not dominated by the clock. South-west Australian Aborigines, with a touch of irony, called it 'Nyungar time' and valued its autonomy.[48]

Technological and structural changes in the late 1960s and 1970s combined to propel Aborigines into high levels of unemployment. Bulldozers and heavy farm machinery such as disc ploughs and root rakes made the hand labour of clearing largely redundant. There was also much greater competition for shearing work from New Zealand shearing teams, and stock work in the pastoral industry in New South Wales, for example, was increasingly done by the pastoralist himself on a motor bike. The domestic work done by Aboriginal girls declined, too, as homes became smaller and labour-saving devices more common.[49] And in the north the same process of 'disemployment' began on the pastoral stations in the 1960s. Aboriginal drovers were replaced by trucks as communications and roads improved. Helicopters and motor bikes replaced men on horses as the mainstay of mustering. Some alternative employment became available in mining and local government, but their dismissal from station life increased Aboriginal numbers in northern towns which did not have the work to absorb their new populations.[50]

In Gnowangerup in Western Australia unemployment among Aborigines reached 72 percent in 1972,[51] and this was not uncommon in such towns. Concomitantly, Aborigines began to move to the bigger towns and cities where work was more readily available, but this was part of a general drift to the cities by whites and blacks anyway.[52] There, increasingly forced to rely on social security, Aboriginal families as consumers kept many declining country towns afloat.

In 1981 Aboriginal incomes were only 55 percent of the average for Australia as a whole. Their unemployment rate was part of the reason for this. In 1971 when the Australia-wide rate was just 1.7 percent, it was 9 percent for Aborigines. In the midst of the recession, in 1981, when it was 5.9 percent for all Australians, it was a staggering 24.6 percent for Aborigines (in New South Wales,

Queensland and Western Australia it was over 30 percent).[53] The voice of a Wilcannia man sums up the despair felt by many Aborigines in an economy that no longer needed their labour.

> What've us blackfellows got going for us? ... I filled in for social but didn't get it through yet. I sent it in about six weeks ago. I went down to the shire this morning asked for a job. He said he's not putting no more men on. The Aboriginal Centre mob, they supposed to put us on work. What they giving us? Dollar an hour to clean up rubbish. That's only kids money. I'm a rouseabout. The shearing sheds, they full. Can't get a job. I'm thirty eight, got eight kids and without a woman now. Got to look after my mother every day. Seventeen years, she's blind. Look how she's living! what can we do? They ask, 'Where you blackfellers find the builders, what you going to do?' We'll fight for it. We'll build if you give us a job. Give us a job?[54]

Aborigines have been crucial to the Australian economy. Their labour underpinned the pastoral industry, they have picked the vegetables and fruit that filled the shops and stocked the factories and they cleared the land on which agriculture was founded. Yet their work is rarely recognised by white Australians. As one West Australian Nyungar observed:

> I don't think the old farmers would have told the younger people who did clear their land. The younger blokes have got it in their minds these days that Nyungars are bludgers, loafers, they didn't care that the Nyungars were the ones that cleared their land and that they were underpaid to do it. That's the reason why these days they think nothing of Nyungars, they never respected Nyungars. If they saw what he had to do in those times, they would think a lot different now.[55]

The unions and the un-unionised

If the health of a union movement can be judged by the size of its membership, then the Australian trade union movement after the war was very healthy indeed. Union membership reached its historic peak of 60 percent of workers in 1951 and it was still 57 per cent in 1982.[56] Of course this alone is not an adequate measure. The chronic factionalism between catholics and communists and groupers and ALP loyalists kept unions politically weak. The pervasive tendency of union leaders to bureaucratise their unions and separate themselves from their members left the movement unprepared to meet the challenges penal sanctions threw up to them in the 1960s and 1970s. And unions, dominated as they were by white, Australian-born men, were ill-equipped to organise and represent the new workforce—women, migrant and Aboriginal workers. The story of the new workforce's organisation in the long boom shows that they effectively had to rely on themselves.

While men's union membership rate hovered in the 60 percent range, women's participation rose slowly from 30 percent after the war to almost 40 percent throughout the 1950s and 1960s. In the 1970s, with the rapid unionisation of white-collar work, to which women were increasingly attracted, it rose still more.[57] By then women still made up fewer than a quarter of all union members,[58] but the overall figures conceal heavy concentrations of women in some unions. In 1977 thirty unions had a membership of 50 percent or more women. These were clothing workers, boot and shoe makers, clerks, sales assistants, air hostesses, and so on, those occupations dominated by women.[59]

For women unionists, there was no corresponding rate of employment in the unions themselves. The number of women officials fell right away the higher one looked up the union hierarchies. For instance, in the late 1970s only 5 percent of delegates to ACTU conferences were women while on the federal council of the peak white-collar union organisations, the Australian Council of Salaried and Professional Associations, there was one woman. On the other, the Council of Australian Government Employee Organisations (CAGEO) there were none. Women were much more likely, too, to be shop stewards than they were to be paid union officials.[60] Why? It was for much the same reasons that women had always been underrepresented in unions—a combination of their family responsibilities, the discriminatory attitudes of male union leaders, the often short-term nature of their employment and the failure of the unions to concern themselves with women's issues, like child care, sexual harassment, part-time work, and the discriminatory practices of governments which, in the name of protection, excluded women from certain kinds of work.

The flowering of women's consciousness in Australia in the 1970s was reflected in the creation of new, separate women's organisations within the trade union movement. In 1970 women unionists set up the Women's Action Committee to lobby the ACTU on a range of women's issues. In 1971, women white-collar workers set up a women's committee in CAGEO and a women's caucus in the ACTU. A National Conference of Women was held in 1972 and a Women's Alternative Trade Union Conference in 1973. The Working Women's Centre in Melbourne and the Women's Trade Union Commission in Sydney were both established in 1975. Then in 1977, the ACTU adopted its women's charter, at the same time abandoning its long commitment to the concept of the family wage. The charter itself promised great things for women workers—increased involvement in unions, equal pay for work of equal value, equal opportunity and affirmative action, improved child care and maternal and paternal leave, improved education in trade union training courses, and so on.[61] Although by the beginning of the 1980s there was still a long way to go, women had begun to alter the face of the union movement. Recently made trade union banners now symbolise the change. There is hardly one which does not have female workers represented on it.

The progress towards equal pay for men and women paralleled this improvement. Those women who had received higher pay during the war wanted their pay to stay high. Those on the usual 54 percent of male wages wanted their pay to increase. It did, after five years, when the Commonwealth government legislated to allow the arbitration court to fix a female basic wage, which it set at 75 percent of the male rate. It took another seventeen years for the Commonwealth Arbitration Commission to think seriously about equal pay. In 1968 the ACTU was invited to put a case for equal pay to the Commission in a new wage-fixing context. The old basic wage and margins system had been abolished and replaced by a total wage with a set minimum. The Commission accepted the ACTU case and granted equal pay for equal work. This was a great advance, but the ACTU produced figures in 1972 to show that only 18 percent of the 1.8 million women in the labour force were getting equal pay, because of the sex-segregated character of the workforce. Now under pressure from women unionists and the women's movement, the unions demanded equal pay for jobs of equal value. The Commission finally granted this in 1973, and then in 1974 the Labour government legislated to allow the Commission to abolish the male and female wage concepts and replace them with an adult wage.[62] The segregation remained, though, and women's wages are still on average only 75 percent of men's wages, because women are still congregated in low paying and part-time jobs, work less overtime and receive less extra-award pay like bonuses.

Historically unions have opposed the migration of workers of any kind to Australia. In the early nineteenth century the first craft unions campaigned against British migration on the grounds that it would loosen up the tight labour market. In the later nineteenth century the union movement attacked all non-British labour on similar grounds. Similar sentiments moved the unions in the 1940s although the close alliance between the Chifley government and the moderates in the movement meant that when Arthur Calwell tried to reassure unionists that migration would actually benefit them, he was at least listened to.[63] In fact it was the ability of governments of both stripes to deliver growth and full employment that comforted unionists. The government also assured them that migrants would work under the same awards as Australian-born workers. However, unions most liked the proposals to tie the displaced persons into two year indentures and to give them the dirtiest jobs.[64]

In those early years union attitudes towards their migrant members seemed to depend on their ideological line. The early ALP groupers and catholics fighting communists for control of several big unions used the east European refugees as front line troops, thinking (rightly) that they would be staunchly anti-communist. On the other hand, communist union leaders regarded their opponents as fascists and made sure they got the worst jobs in the factories and workplaces they controlled. Otherwise few unions made any attempt to look after migrant workers.[65] Closed shop agreements and payroll deductions meant that they got members with little effort. A few unions appointed non-English speaking organisers (in Victoria in the mid-1970s there were only nine migrant union officials out of a total of 300), and these knew that they were appointed only to make recruiting migrant workers easier. George Zangalis, a Victorian activist, said in 1975, 'In the 1950s I spent the best part of my time trying to sell the unions to the migrant workers, now I have changed my priorities, I try to sell the problem of migrant workers to the unions.'[66]

It was not the case that migrant workers were uninterested or opposed to unions *per se*. While women in one survey of migrant attitudes did not go to union meetings, vote in union elections or read union pamphlets, this and other surveys have shown that migrant workers were committed to unionism generally but to their own union only if that union earned their loyalty by protecting and pursuing their rights.[67] Said one migrant worker:

> Most migrants are disorganised ... they are farm labourers and people who haven't worked in factories before. They don't understand anything. But when they are organised, they will know what is going on, what is happening to them ... I joined the union so that I would know my rights, so I could protect them.[68]

In practice many unions did not do this, in fact most were slow to recognise migrants' fundamental language problem and they insistently printed material and conducted meetings in English. And, extraordinarily, many migrant workers thought that unions and management worked together to exploit them. At one Melbourne car plant Yugoslav workers staunchly refused to pay their dues because they thought their union and the company management were suspiciously close together, just like they had been in Yugoslavia.[69] Language problems, union uninterest, the unwillingness of officials to take up complaints, and the fact that pay rises were delivered irrespective of the union's character, meant that many migrant workers felt that unions served no useful purpose. When asked what she thought the role of unions was, one migrant worker replied crossly, 'To take $30 from us each year.'[70]

Migrant workers began to take matters into their own hands in the 1960s and 1970s. Several reports and surveys had expressed vividly their disillusionment with their unions and three Migrant Worker Conferences in 1973 and 1975 in Sydney and Melbourne had codified their discontent.[71] However, it was the big unofficial strikes at places like Mt Isa, GMH in Melbourne, and, most spectacularly, at Ford's assembly plant at Broadmeadows, Melbourne, that made unions sit up and notice their migrant members. The circumstance at Broadmeadows was a cold and authoritarian employer committed to centralised negotiations with the Vehicle Builders' Union, which was itself committed to arbitration and a top–down form of union organisation. Neither had any time for on-the-job organisation. In 1973 a strike broke out, essentially over time for relief, tea breaks and a pay rise. The dispute lasted for nine tense and sometimes violent weeks, till ultimately the union hierarchy was forced to support its members against its own judgement, and substantial concessions were won.

That strike and others were conducted by rank-and-file migrant workers. The strike was led by non-English-speaking shop stewards and it was as much against their own union hierarchy as against Ford. It exemplified a unity and militancy which surprised both Ford and the union—some shop stewards put it down to a new generation of migrant workers who cut their political teeth on urban working-class struggles in Europe. However, others noticed that the strikers were still divided on ethnic lines, holding their meetings separately in separate buildings. Yet this declined in the 1970s and a cross-ethnic unity developed, expressed in a militancy that Ford shop stewards claimed was stronger than that of Australian-born workers. This may be so, but Lever-Tracy and Quinlan, sociologists who have studied migrant workers, warn against this kind of assumption. Migrant worker militancy is too diverse for easy classification (GMH workers, for instance, are known to be non-militant); instead it depends, like any other militancy, on the circumstances, character and strategies of both management and union.[72]

The circumstances of Aboriginal workers and their workplace struggles were different in as much as the major barrier to organisation after the war was not the union movement but the state. Except for communist union officials, who actively supported Aboriginal rights and tried to break down exclusionary clauses in union rules, most unions before the war ignored the Aborigines and the brutality with which they were treated.[73] Despite this, the tactics of unionism inspired one group of workers to undertake one of Australia's longest and most famous strikes, the Pilbara Aboriginal workers' strike, which began on 1 May 1946, and which some of its participants claimed was still going on in 1990. Workers on 25 stations struck for higher pay, better living conditions and their right to appoint their own representatives. On some stations the battle was quickly won, on others it took years. On some Aborigines won all their demands. On others they won minor concessions. In any case most strikers refused to return to the stations, opting instead to abandon pastoral work altogether for self-managed communities like the Pindan mob's community at Strelley and others at Jigalong and Yandeyarra.[74]

Aborigines after the war were still controlled by repressive state government legislation, and the Labor government in Western Australia unhesitatingly used the law to attempt to crush the strike. Aborigines were intimidated by local police. Two of the strike leaders, Clancy McKenna and Dooley Bin Bin, were jailed for three months and another, Don McLeod, was fined heavily for breaching a section of the Native Administration Act, which read: 'Any person who entices or persuades a native to leave any lawful service without the consent of a Protector shall be guilty of an offence against this Act'.[75] Then McLeod was jailed under another section of the Act which prohibited 'unauthorized' people entering an Aboriginal reserve without the Department's consent while police continued to arrest, and the courts continued to fine and jail, the strikers up to the day of the strike's conclusion.[76]

The strike had been supported from the outset by some major southern unions, like the Sheet Metal Workers' Union, but the union with the most to gain from a successful strike, the AWU, decided to support the struggle for equal wages only as the strike reached its end.[77] Nevertheless, the strike had impressed the labour movement. Later in the 1950s several unions affiliated with the newly created Federal Council for Aboriginal Advancement and both lobbied hard to force the ACTU to adopt the equal-pay principle. This it did, finally, in 1963.

In 1965 the North Australian Workers' Union, pressured by the ACTU and Aboriginal lobby groups, applied to the arbitration court for Aborigines to be paid award wages. The union won the case, but the court, on the pastoralists' insistence, inserted a 'slow workers clause' in the award which allowed the pastoralists to pay their Aboriginal workers low wages for three years. The pastoralists argued before the court that Aborigines were inefficient and unreliable workers, although they freely admitted in other places that they had no peers as stock workers. The ACTU, in conference with the Federal government and pastoralists, agreed to the clause over the protests of Aboriginal workers, who began a new round of industrial action. But the issue faded in white minds as pastoralists began to evict Aborigines from their stations. John Watson, a Fitzroy River drover, recalled how it happened:

> When the equal wage decision was handed down by the courts twenty odd years ago, the Aboriginal people were forced off the stations. It had very far reaching effects, from one end of the Kimberley to the other. Hundreds of people were forced to leave the stations they'd grown up on, and to live under appalling conditions in town reserves. Those station managers just came out and said, 'We can't afford to pay you the basic wage, and we can't afford to keep feeding you. The Welfare mob have a lot of money for you to live on in the town. So, pack up your camp and start walking'.[78]

As Richard Broome wrote, Aborigines 'moved from no wages to small wages, to "equal" wages and then to unemployment'.[79] Unionism had been powerless to protect them.

10 Management, technology and the future

We live in a period of rapid change. Some observers call it the robotics, some the computer revolution, some the information revolution. Others call it post-industrialism and show how it has ended the world of work ushered in by the industrial revolution, where the logic was that of Henry Ford's assembly line. What, though, will be the long-term future of work? Will new technology and techniques of work open up opportunities for less work, more leisure and a better, more fulfilling way of life? Or will they open options for the few and close them for the many, who will become a 'caste' of permanently unemployed?

Although these are long-term prospects, Australia is also going through another significant moment of change. Until perhaps the mid-1980s, Australia was a primary producing country, prosperous from the export of wool, wheat and minerals. The downturn in the mid-1980s in the international produce markets persuaded the Hawke government to end Australia's relative isolation from the global economy. It has since reduced tariffs and deregulated the economy in a way which would have delighted those pre-Keynesian economists of the free market. The deregulation of investment, banking, much primary production, the dollar and trade have all opened our economy to the exigencies of the world economy in a way not before been seen in this century. Now the options for management and workers are much narrower than when secondary production, for instance, was designed for the small local market.

We are in the midst, too, of rapid long-term changes in the nature of the workforce. Employment in manufacturing fell away from 27.6 percent in 1965–6 to just 16.5 percent in 1982. Jobs in services, on the other hand, rose equally quickly, from 50.3 percent in 1901 to 67.2 percent in 1981, and both processes have continued since.[1] What are the prospects? Will we have jobs in twenty years' time? What does the revolution in technology mean for our world? A survey conducted for the Commission for the Future in 1987 found that Australians are generally fearful about our future, and we probably should be![2]

An active animal

Management began to insert itself between workers and owners of businesses in the nineteenth century. Businesses outgrew a personal relationship that is only possible when a workforce is small and the business of the business is small. Represented by people like Taylor, management grew in importance and influence in the years before World War II as companies and the way they were financed increased in size and complexity. Dispersed shareholdings spread ownership across more people and interests (although only a tiny minority of people in Australia held shares), and management became the link between the owners of capital and the workers in the workplace. Management exists to do capital's bidding and managers are frequently big shareholders in the businesses they run, although they do have their own interests to protect, as the extravagant salaries business executives pay themselves testifies. Like most people whose existence depends on a commitment to a course of action or an ideal, they are subject to the swings of contingency and the roundabouts of ideology. Australian managers organised themselves, in 1941, in the Australian Institute of Management, to give themselves a quasi-professional status, and imitating other professions began agitating for recognition by universities and other higher education institutions.[3] In the 1980s courses on economics, commerce and management were the biggest and fastest growing areas of academic study.[4] Graduates flocked to the lower levels of the burgeoning financial sector and management arm of business and to the new branch of business which services management, the management consultants. Nowadays these consultants do things for business which business once did for itself. One Perth group advertised its services in the Yellow Pages as follows:

> Recruitment and Selection, Team Building, Assessment and Diagnosis of Organisation Problems, Job Descriptions for Improving Performance, Performance Appraisal and Counselling, Organisation Communications—Analysis and Recommendations, Strategic Planning and Goal Setting, Workforce Attitude Surveys, Competency Assessment Grids, Project Management Training, Occupational Health and Safety, Feasibility Studies, Quality Management Programmes, Industry Research and Surveys, Creative Thinking and Lateral Thinking Workshops, Training Needs Analysis, Management/Supervisor Training Development, Employee Training Development, Custom Designed Training and Development.

It is an indication of the extent of this kind of work that advertisements for management consultants in the Perth Yellow Pages (for a small market) cover three pages.[5]

Frederick Winslow Taylor probably did more than anybody to popularise management as an occupation and a science in the USA. It took longer in Australia, although 'scientific management' boomed after World War II, as employers sought ways to discipline their workers in the context of full employment and ways to improve productivity to take advantage of the post-war mass markets. The Royal Melbourne Institute of Technology began running time-and-motion courses in 1951. In the 1950s an Australian Methods Engineer's Association was formed, and it is estimated that in 1959 there were about 1000 'recognised' methods engineers in Australia.[6] Their collective aim was, as one wrote, 'to bring the great bulk of industrial operations within the range of the largest possible number of people with normal sensory-motor equipment'.[7]

This phrase 'normal sensory equipment' could have been uttered by a time-and-motion expert. That it was not should alert us to another kind of development in management. It comes from an article in a journal called the *Bulletin of Industrial Psychology and Personnel Practice*, and ironically, although the quote expresses the very worst of Taylorism, the application of psychology to the workplace emerged as an alternative. It called itself the human relations school and was developed in the USA in the 1920s. Much of what has since developed in management has its origin there.

'If the psychologist is to help [industry] it must help it to make money'.[8] Industrial psychologists began to help industry make money by persuading management to set up personnel departments. By 1949, 47 percent of manufacturing companies with more than 50 workers had a personnel office or officer.[9] Industrial psychologists tended to fall into two groups. The first, who were close to the Taylorists, thought that workers were driven only by the prospect of material reward. Bonuses and incentive payments were their solution to the problem of productivity, a solution which suited the time-and-motion experts very well. The former set the reward and the latter set the rate of productivity above which the bonuses were paid. Olympic Tyres in Melbourne was one factory which introduced a bonus system. Workers were given a twice-yearly bonus based on their previous six months' earnings. Olympic also made shares available to workers, although it is not known how many took up the offer. *Rydges*, the management journal, was pleased: '... employees [now] feel that they have a stake in the organisation and give their best'.[10]

The alternative school took a broader look at the human character and drew a more complex picture of workers, thus launching the first substantial management attack on Taylorism. It argued that workers, far from being motivated by money, really wanted to belong, they wanted companionship and friendship with their bosses, they wanted to feel that they were worthwhile and that their contribution to the company mattered. Management's task, then, was to understand and make use of this essentially sociable worker. Its job was to blandish and cajole its all too human workforce into adopting management's aims as its own and adapting the workers to their work. The unadaptable and the unconscientious could then be weeded out, for they were pathological. Indeed, Elton Mayo, the Australian-born founder of one school of industrial psychology, regarded industrial unrest in the same way: 'Industrial unrest is not caused by mere dissatisfaction with wages and working conditions but by the fact that a conscious dissatisfaction serves to 'light up' as it were the hidden fires of mental uncontrol'.[11]

In both of these schools, the psychologists took the work as given and the workers as variable, but it was from these ideas that the possibility of real changes to work began to enter the minds of managers. They tended to come from Europe, not from the USA, where management was still committed to brutalising its workforce. A journalist in *Rydges* wrote:

> Man is an active animal who likes to work provided the work gives him the opportunity of self-realisation, a flowering of the intellect, an enrichment of knowledge, recognition and appreciation for his ideas and inventions in the context of a collective effort and co-operation.[12]

This clearly has links to the more generous school of psychology, but the implications of it after the war were, in some ways, quite different. Now workers might be encouraged to take part in the actual running of the company and so a variety of worker-participation schemes were promoted by enthusiasts and adopted by some companies such as Rexona, Sidchrome and Philips (Australia).[13] Of course worker participation meant different things to different people, important innovations like worker directors, co-partnerships and co-ownerships, collective bargaining, profit sharing, informal consultation and, most peripherally, suggestion boxes. In the 1980s 'Common Interest Programmes' tied participation to the old and trusted cash incentive payments.[14] In reality, however, worker participation did not necessarily mean that the organisation of work itself might change.

The programmes emanating from northern Europe in the 1960s and 1970s have shown Australian managers and workers that there *are* ways of reorganising the work process itself which can return to workers the satisfactions that, for decades, managers have been trying to destroy. Work groups, responsible autonomy and 'multi-skilling', are the new management programmes. Autonomous work groups, independent production groups, job enlargement and enrichment programmes, quality control circles and others began to inch their way into Australian manufacturing in the 1960s and 1970s. Indeed, the introduction of quality control circles represented an historic shift in the sources managers looked to for their ideas. They turned their backs on the USA and Europe and looked instead to Japan.[15]

The historic 1987 national wage case really gave promise to revolutionise the world of work in Australia. The Arbitration Commission granted two pay rises to Australian workers but tied the second to new principles of restructuring and productivity. It wanted to abolish restrictive work and management practices, to introduce new job classifications to permit multi-skilling and new career structures for all workers, and reduce those demarcations which ensured that workers stayed in the jobs for which they had trained. Why has there been such a sudden change? The Arbitration Commission itself gave several reasons when referring to the submissions it received:

> There were no essential differences between the parties and the interveners on the nature and magnitude of our economic difficulties nor on the objectives of economic policy and its direction. All emphasised the importance of maintaining international competitiveness, for continued wage restraint, for a revival in private investment, for a restructuring of the economy to promote manufacturing exports, and for increased efficiency and productivity.[16]

However, it is also clear that technological advance has made workplace reform imperative. New technologies have made many of the old job demarcations redundant and have demanded that workers develop a range of new skills to operate them. Australia is not only in a post-Fordist age, it is also in the grip of a profound technological revolution, and that by itself is sufficient to cause a sea-change in the way we work.

The replacement of body and mind by a machine

Anybody who shops at a supermarket can see the impact computers have had on work. Checkout operators no longer search for a price on each item the customer brings them, ring it up by hand, press the addition button, then calculate in their heads what change the customer should receive. Now, a product code is part of the item's label, the checkout operator runs it over a laser scanner and the price registers on the cash register. The register displays the item's price, calculates the change the customers receive and gives them a receipt. It does not seem noticeably faster than the previous way but the big supermarket chains claim that it cuts 33 percent off the time it takes to get a customer through the checkout, and, just as importantly, makes errors impossible.[17] It represents the final stage in a process of technological change which has revolutionised supermarket work. The product coding of items has abolished the time-consuming job of labelling, the cash register is connected to an inventory control system which records what the shop has in stock and there is no need now for complicated paper or visual calculations of what is needed. The supermarket now has a stock ordering system, connected through the chain's computers both to head office and to warehouses, where computers now organise the distribution of new goods and automated machines are just as likely to load them. Moreover, back at the checkout, most supermarkets now have electronic fund transfer facilities, where the cost can be billed straight to your bank account.[18]

It would be rash to suggest that the fully automated supermarket is the final stage to which computerisation can go, but where we are now seems astonishing when it is considered that the first automated machine appeared in Australia only after World War II. Automation is not mechanisation, for that simply extends by mechanical means the work that humans did. An automated machine is one that runs itself, or as one early manufacturing journal put it, it effects 'the replacement of . . . body and mind by a machine':

> When an engineer designs an automation or a robot to replace say a skilled machinist, he first examines carefully what the machinist's mind and hands do. When the machinist moves the tool up to the job he measures the distance between the tool tip and the job with his eye and his brain then directs his hands moving the tool so that this distance is reduced. He is acting as a closed loop system of information and muscular effort, and will continue to do so until that operation has been completed. There is also some reference information in his system to tell him when the position of the tool is good enough. The reference is probably a mark on the job and is fed into the loop as he sees it.
>
> Robots that replace a man doing a particular job are designed in principle in the same way. They measure the difference between their performance and the reference to which they are set and work until the difference has disappeared. Their actual operation may differ greatly from that of a man. They will probably be quicker and more accurate.[19]

The first automated machines were installed in Australian factories in the late 1940s, in printers where automatic guillotines cut paper, in car factories where transfer machines turned metal castings into engine blocks in 343 automated operations, and in newspapers where punched tapes were run through teletype setters on linotype machines. After a Tasmanian canning factory introduced fourteen automatic cooking retorts, its manager boasted that three men replaced the ten who operated the normal retorts, that spoilage had been eliminated and that the whole system could be overseen on an indicator screen in the manager's office.[20]

Automated equipment spread quickly through all kinds of manufacturing, but was quickly superseded by computerisation. The first modern computers were really electro-mechanical devices, slow, big and cumbersome. They date from World War II, and how quickly they have changed! The silicon chip made the difference. While their speed and reliability were going up, their size and cost were going down. Their obvious cost advantages made them attractive to engineers, technicians and employers and their sophistication and versatility made them applicable to a huge variety of functions and hence to a huge variety of jobs.

Numerical control of machine tools exemplifies the changing nature of automation. The lathe, for example, had long been the centrepiece of the engineer's tool kit. Hand driven, it was the tool on which fitters and turners exercised their skills and judgement in working a piece of metal into the desired shape. Numerical control of lathes was developed by the US Army in the 1940s. Instructions were punched onto a tape which was then run through electronic devices to actually run the machine. The machine then did the movements it was told to do by the pre-programmed tape and the former operators had only to set up the job, press the 'go' button, and disconnect the job when it was completed. The lathe itself did all the work to a plan drawn up by the people who made the tape, the engineers in the factory's design department. Computers were applied to the process in the 1960s, building on and eventually replacing, the punched card. They also gave manufacturers much more flexibility in what they could ask their machines to do, in quicker programming or reprogramming, as, for instance in sending different instructions when a new order might demand different specifications for a finished product. Microprocessors have taken the process even further. They now allow machines to memorise instructions.[21]

The computerisation of machine tools now permits manufacturers to link them together in integrated sets performing more of the productive process. In some overseas factories computer numerical controlled machines are used with robots which do routine jobs such as welding and painting and are linked to automatic delivery vehicles which deliver raw material and half-finished parts to the machines. Indeed, when computer-aided design (where design is done on personal computers) is linked into the computer-aided manufacture, and overall planning by computer is added on, then, as John Mathews has observed, we have the 'factory of the future'.[22] Ford at Broadmeadows has done this with the production of car doors. Only one operator is needed to change the tooling from one kind of door to the next and the 'flexible manufacturing system' does the rest, making 100 doors per hour. So un-human has the process become that the system shuts down if anybody enters the line.[23] Of course there are still only a few factories like this in Australia. Most manufacturing here is still done in small factories, producing goods either on assembly lines or in batches for the small local market.

Automation and the prospect of the workerless factory revived an argument that began with the mechanisation of production in Australia in the 1860s—a debate about the consequences of new technology. A Royal Commission into changing technology in New South Wales in the late 1950s began the current round of enquiries, but the growing economy and full employment ensured that the debate was rather subdued until the 1970s. From then until the last few years the effects of new technology became the focus of a debate about the future direction of Australia and the future of work itself.

Employers have been the most enthusiastic supporters of the development and deployment of new technology. They have always presented it as a boon to Australia, to workers, and to consumers. At the same time they argued that neither they nor Australia had any choice but to adopt new technologies if they, or Australia, were to survive in the competitive world. They also argued that with increasing productivity workers' wages would rise and their hours of work would shorten. Leisure would displace work as the centre of people's lives and (for some apologists) education and cultural attainments would become the measure of people's status. Increasing wages would lead to increased demand, especially for leisure and recreation, which would boost their industries and so solve whatever problems of unemployment might arise.[24]

Employers did not agree with the opposing view that new technology created unemployment, nor did they agree that it de-skilled workers. Instead, they argued, it liberated workers from boring and routine jobs, and opened up a whole new range of work for semi-skilled machine operators, technicians and design engineers. This point, they considered, refuted another argument the critics presented, that by introducing new technology a split would develop between the machine operators and the new technicians, destroying internal labour markets.

The proponents presented another argument, too, to support

their case. They contended that new technology, by reducing workers' contact with moving parts, removed them from danger, and that by removing them from the workplace altogether it removed them from picking up occupational diseases. They pointed to the clean, sanitised atmosphere of the fully-automated chemical plant and petrol refinery to prove their point.[25] On the other hand, the critics of new technology pointed to the link between word processors and repetitive strain injury. They also raised another very obvious point, that women were more likely to suffer ill-effects from new technology, because women were more often employed in those industries which were most automated, such as small manufacturing and office work.[26]

Despite the attempt by some employers to depict them as modern-day Luddites, trade unions have not argued that new technology be abandoned. Rather, they tried to assert some control over it by insisting on a fully-fledged apprenticeship system to limit the effect it had on their work. It was more common, however, for them to accept it as 'progress' and claim the benefits of improved productivity in higher wages and shorter working hours. They regarded the question of new technology as the bosses' business and they were encouraged in this by the judges in the arbitration systems, who resolutely defended what they regarded as 'management's prerogative'. With the exception, then, of unions like the Waterside Workers' Federation, which lost over half its numbers when containers were introduced onto the wharves, most unions ignored the problems of new technology.[27]

This changed in the 1970s recession. The ACTU and big unions who had begun to see the impact of technology on jobs called on employers to involve unions in planning the introduction of new technology, to give more protection to workers in danger of losing their jobs and to give better redundancy deals to those who did. The first union to take industrial action over the introduction of new technology was the Australian Telecommunications Employees' Association (ATEA) in the celebrated Telecom strike of 1978. This was a very complex dispute, but the gist of it was that Telecom proposed to introduce new telecommunications systems into new exchange maintenance centres, so bypassing local telephone exchanges. The new systems would cause some job loss, Telecom admitted, but their major effect would have been to upgrade the skills of some technicians while degrading the skills of the rest. One former union official remembered:

> What sparked our awareness was not so much that technology as such would put us out of work but that it would reduce the functions of skilled technical workers to mundane tasks, repetitive, semi-skilled and non-skilled tasks. That's what

stung our people more than anything else. Our people do take pride in what they do; this is true whether skilled or not skilled. Communications workers like to think communications are the lifeblood of the community. They get their job satisfaction from this and out of the fact they've got skills not readily available in the community. They now had grave doubts about that.[28]

A very bitter strike ensued which lasted for several weeks, but its settlement was based on some new developments in the history of work in Australia. While Telecom was able to install its exchange maintenance centres, ATEA won the right to establish five 'exchange service centres'. After a two-year trial the success of the two systems would be judged on various criteria, including job satisfaction and career prospects. Telecom agreed, as well, to full consultation on every major piece of new equipment it wanted to install. Again these would be judged on similar criteria, including the maintenance of technical standards. The final result of the two-year trial was a compromise between the two.[29]

Since that dispute some unions have tried to have provisions for consultation inserted into industrial awards and in 1984 this happened in the Termination, Change and Redundancy Award handed down by the Commonwealth Industrial Commission in a metal industry case. Its value was limited, however, because it imposed the obligation to consult only after employers had made the decision to invest.[30] Nevertheless, it was a big step forward for workers, although the 1980 Myers Report into Technological Change found that employees were consulted in advance in less than 5 percent of cases where new technology was introduced. New and improved provisions of retrenchment agreements and agreements over continuing employment and staffing levels were also part of the award and these, too, meant real progress.

The implication of this award, and it was one not lost on the unions, was that consultation implied a much greater say for workers in that hitherto sacrosanct area—management prerogative. Since it sent its mission to Europe and it produced the report *Australia Reconstructed*, the ACTU tends to see new technology not just in terms of consultation, but in terms of a new range of options with a heavy emphasis on retraining, new skills formation and award restructuring; and it sees in all of these increased participation of workers in the management of their companies.[31] The Hawke government has enthusiastically adopted some aspects of this agenda. It particularly supports the declining interest of the ACTU in consultation over new technology because it believes that 'high tech' production is the country's way out of its foreign trade and overseas debt problems. Its own agenda is restructuring industry, amalgamating unions and restructuring those arbitration court awards which it says stands in the way of higher productivity.³² This, of course, has profound implications for workers, and indeed for the whole world of work, for it promises to reverse the dominant paradigm within which people have worked since the industrial revolution.

The electronic cottage

The future of work in the short term in Australia will be shaped by its economic context. The trade crisis in the mid-1980s persuaded the Hawke government that we could no longer rely on the export of wool, wheat and minerals for national solvency. Hence its priorities shifted to a general assault on all those practices which rendered work in Australia vulnerable to the new world it planned to open up for us. Since the mid-1980s Australia has been pushed, falteringly, into the global economy, where international movements of trade and investment, and of labour, are forcing an historic decline in the power of the nation state. This has involved an attack, in the name of micro-economic reform and award restructuring, on a whole world of behaviours and practices which the government thinks are standing in the way of Australia's ability to compete successfully in the world economy.

The implications of this for work and workers are profound. The new world of work is a 'post-Fordist' one in which the decades of sub-division, de-skilling, and the creation of mindless, routine jobs are being reversed. A new skilled, highly educated and trained workforce is needed to adapt to and master new technologies. A new flexibility is essential for Australian industry to find a place in the new international division of labour. The changes are labelled multi-skilling, up-skilling or broad-banding, but they promise for workers the chance to re-establish meaning and fulfilment at work and to regain the pleasure of skill through the reintegration of the conception and execution of tasks. Clearly defined job ladders are part of the new world of work as the old and rigid divisions between the skilled and the unskilled are bridged by continuous training. Workers, too, will become much more involved in the management of the workplace. Autonomous work groups engaging in batch production will replace the moving assembly line as employers understand both the latter's inflexibility and the barrier to increased productivity that it represents. Worker participation schemes and industrial democracy will mean that the old authoritarian workplace structures will break down. An expanded role for quality control circles will ensure that Australian goods will be able to compete not just in terms of prices but in terms of quality as well.³³

Doubtless, this is what the reformers of the Australian economy would like to see, and those interested in reforming the workplace could hardly disagree. However, the model, and it is still just a model, is based on the restructuring of work in the metals industry. Employment in metals manufacturing is declining, though, just as it is across the whole of manufacturing. Most workers are in jobs where multi-skilling is much less practicable, either through the nature of the work itself or because of a lack of imagination among management and unions. In workplaces like these, where productivity increases have to be gained through award restructuring, they will be won at the expense of working conditions. This has already happened in jobs as different as the shop assistant's and the university academic's. The former recently traded away weekend work and the latter an increased ratio of short-term contracts to tenured positions, both for pay rises of a few percent.[34] Some jobs do not easily fit into the categories which the reformers are proposing.

Also, it remains to be seen whether employers will opt for a labour process which does turn its back on the Fordist paradigm. Some employers are bold and imaginative, but most are not, and, like all of us, find it difficult to see such long-term solutions as practicable in the context of the short-term problems every employer has to face. Others will take the old-fashioned route to increasing productivity, which means, where new technology permits it, getting rid of their skilled workforce altogether. As one manager recently observed:

> More or less anyone can come in off the street now and do the setting and heading. They just have to slot in the requisite tooling and press the button. The system is much less dependent on specialist or operator expertise than formerly. Most of the subjective aspects of the job have been lost and isolated to the office instead . . . The operators aren't required to exercise judgement anymore.[35]

Is it possible for every job to be made fulfilling? Perhaps not in the organisation of the job itself, although every workplace has a range of tasks that could be spread around. But perhaps it could be, in the reorganisations of the pattern of authority in the workplace. Industrial democracy has many meanings, but it is a crucial concept for the existing worker organisations, the trade unions. It involves a greater role for workers in the running of their employer's organisation, and some unions (and bosses) see it as an alternative to unionism. Employers hope it will increase their workers' commitment to management objectives; some unions see it as a deliberate policy by management to destroy the influence of the union. There is a small number of firms which have introduced new workplace structures, and the future of the unions in these places depends on their involvement in these.

However, there is a far greater threat to the future of unions than this, and it lies in the re-making of the Australian workforce itself. In the early 1960s, as we have seen, trade unions represented nearly 60 percent of the workforce, today it is under 40 percent. Union membership in all sectors has been declining. Even in manufacturing the decline has been greater than the rate of job loss. Unions are just not attracting enough members in the expanding service sector to retain their powerful position in Australian society.[36]

What happens in the short term will largely depend on the unions themselves. Many workers think unions are irrelevant and remote and there has been a growing tendency for workplace negotiations to be conducted, not on the shop floor, but at the level of the peak bodies, the ACTU, the government and the employers' organisations. There is a long-standing critique of Australian unions which suggests that they have pursued bureaucratic decision making at the expense of the real involvement of their members and that the arbitration system, where workplace conflict has been institutionalised, has been one major cause of this. It is in this context that workers are becoming cynical about the Accord between the ACTU and the Hawke government, which has delivered declining real wages. Other high level policies like union amalgamation, which its proponents say will improve productivity and efficiency, especially at the individual business level, are also regarded with mixed feeling by workers.

The trend in Australian industrial relations seems to be away from centralised wage fixing to what is called enterprise bargaining. Should this mean the abolition of a minimum wage, then Australia can expect to see a growing inequality in wages and conditions between the well-placed craft workforce and the semi- and unskilled workers. The return of the trend towards the creation of a small cadre of highly trained technicians and an expendable, intermittent workforce in manufacturing will also make for a newly divided workforce. This will be exacerbated, too, by the restructuring of some industries, where a central core of workers do a central core of tasks and the husk of work is hired off to contractors and sub-contractors whose operations are much more intermittent. More employers now strike bargains, too, with non-unionised workers or with workers re-designated as sub-contractors. Plainly, some workers will be more vulnerable than others.

None, though, are or will be as vulnerable as the unemployed. At present the unemployment rate stands at between seven and eight percent of the workforce and is rising because government policies are deliberately slowing economic activity. It will stay at this kind of level for several reasons. One is the fact that many manufacturing companies are shifting their operations to take advantage of low-paid workers in South-east Asia. Another is the belief that a six to eight percent rate now represents full employment. If this is the case, then there will be renewed efforts to categorise the unemployed as ungenuine and to shift the responsibility for their situation on to themselves. Governments always do this when they think unemployment is intractable or when they are trying to cut social welfare spending and the Hawke government is no different. One path to reducing unemployment is retraining, although no amount of retraining will help workers if there are no jobs for them to go to. Nevertheless, governments are spending more money on re-training, albeit in an *ad hoc* and ambivalent way, working on the reasonable principle that the best way to end the poverty which unemployment causes is for people to find jobs.

The foregoing has shown just how problematic the short-term future of work is in Australia. Its long-term future is really a matter of guess work, although, there are, among the prophets who consider this question, some common answers. Most seem to agree that new technology is at the core of the problem. Some argue that less and less work will be necessary as dull and routine operations are done by machines run by a caste of highly trained specialists. Andre Gorz and Barry Jones both posit the stark alternatives— massive unemployment or a sharing out of available work. If the former is the case, then there will be even greater extremes of wealth and poverty and social dislocation. If it is the latter, then we shall all work perhaps twenty hours a week and be happy doing it.[37]

However, this will make it necessary for workers to find an alternative to the sense of identity that our work gives us. We shall have to re-create ourselves as leisured people or at least as people doing alternative autonomous and localised work. For Jones the answer lies in 'developing new forms of participation and recognition'.[38] For Gorz it is in new forms of non-work, where people would define themselves.[39]

Alvin Toffler, another of the post-industrial prophets, does not look ahead to the alternatives that Gorz and Jones foresee, with their mixture of optimism and pessimism. Instead he sees a return to what we call the proto-industrial stage of economic change. Technological change in the information sector, particularly in computers and satellite communications, will make the centralised workplace redundant, except as the location for machines to do routine work. People will work in and from their homes, in what he calls, with his well-known penchant for the arresting phrase, 'the electronic cottage':

The Third Wave brings with it a genuinely new way of life based on diversified, renewable energy resources; on methods of production that make most factory assembly lines obsolete; on new, non-nuclear families; on a novel institution that might be called the 'electronic cottage'; and on radically changed schools and corporations of the future.[40]

And, in the home, Toffler continues, the pre-industrial integration of paid and unpaid work will be revived.

If this, or the worlds Gorz and Jones prophesy, is to happen, then it will be a long way into the future. There is some work being done at home in the way Toffler imagines it, but only a tiny proportion of the workforce is doing it.[41] Similarly, Australian workers have been imprisoned in or near the 40-hour-week for many years and this shows no signs of falling further. This leaves us with the existing workplace intact, a fact which some of the prophets have come to accept. Jones' argument here still concerns the impact of technology. He criticises the view that humans can do no more than adjust to technological change and shows that it has been, and must continue to be, a process where values dictate what, how and when new technology is introduced. The quest for control, or the profit motive, which have been the values hitherto, must be replaced by humanist values. However, Jones gives little practical advice on how this can be done. John Mathews does, and shows how unions can intervene at the point where new technology invades the labour process, in what he calls the 'democratization of technology'.[42]

What of work in the home? Will work in the 'electronic cottage' be divided by sex? One recent survey of the several hundred 'electronic cottages' that do exist in Australia has shown a pronounced division between male computer programmers and female word processors.[43] And it is possible to make an educated guess that the division of labour in housework and child care will not change. But perhaps that is being too pessimistic. A survey, conducted by the Australian Bureau of Statistics, has shown that things may be changing. Early reports of 1000 households in Sydney show that married women not in the labour force worked an average of just under 48 hours a week in the home, while their 'male counterparts' did just under 26 hours. On the other hand, the employed wife did 35 hours per week and her husband 16½. The reports say little about who did precisely what kind of work (whether, for instance, women worked inside and men outside the house) nevertheless, the figures do suggest that women and men still follow that traditional sexual division of labour in the home. [44]

The question of home work is one question which should be posed when we consider the future of work, but there are others:

How can work be made more interesting, fulfilling and meaningful? How can those ideologies which have prescribed different categories of work to different categories of people be overcome? How can the democracy which we all take for granted outside be transferred into the workplace? How can new technologies which have, hitherto, been put to private, selfish and unequal uses, be put to socially responsible uses so that everyone benefits equally from them? The post-industrial prophets tell us that the age of Fordism is dead, but work can only become fulfilling for all of us if the logic which has underpinned it for 200 years of Australian history is also laid to rest.

Endnotes

1 Before and after the invasion

1. J.P. White and D.J. Mulvaney, 'How Many People', in D. J. Mulvaney and J.P. White (eds) *Australians To 1788*, 1987
2. A.P. Elkin, *The Australian Aborigine*, 1968, pp. 74–6
3. ibid, pp. 84–90
4. K. Maddock, *The Australian Aborigines: A Portrait of Their Society*, 1982, pp. 51–3
5. A. Hamilton, 'Aboriginal Women: The Means of Production', in J. Mercer, *The Other Half: Women in Australian Society*, 1985, p. 171
6. D. Bell, *Daughters of the Dreaming*, 1983, pp. 52–4
7. F.G.G. Rose, *The Traditional Mode of Production of the Australian Aborigines*, 1987, pp. 74–80
8. G. Blainey, *Triumph of the Nomads: A History of Ancient Australia*, 1978, pp. 151–2
9. D. Thomson, *Economic Structures and the Ceremonial Exchange Cycle in Arnhem Land*, 1949, pp. 42–3. For an extended analysis of this see J. Bern, 'Ideology and Domination: Towards a reconstruction of Aboriginal social formation', *Oceania*, vol. 50, no. 2, December 1979
10. Rose, op. cit., p. 118
11. B. Malinowski, *The Family among Australian Aborigines: A Sociological Study*, 1913, pp. 283–4
12. ibid, for Malinowski's own views
13. Bell, op. cit., Chapter 5 discusses recent developments in anthropology which bear on this question
14. Elkin, op. cit., p. 35
15. Blainey, op. cit., pp. 185–9. W.C. Ferguson, 'Mokare's Domain' in Mulvaney and White, op. cit., pp. 134–7
16. H. Lourandos, 'Change or Stability?: Hydraulics, Hunter Gatherers and Population in Temperate Australia', *World Archaeology*, vol. 3, no. 11, 1980
17. For example in Oyster Harbour, Albany, Western Australia
18. For discussion of the development of Aboriginal technology see J.P. White and R. Lambert, 'Creation and Discovery', pp. 18–20; S. Hallam, 'Changing Landscapes and Societies—15,000 to 6000 years ago', pp. 66–68, and D.J. Mulvaney, 'The End of the Beginning: 6000 years ago to 1788', pp. 81–86, in Mulvaney and White, op. cit.
19. Quoted in J. Flood, *Archaeology of the Dreamtime: The Story of Prehistoric Australia and its People*, 1989, p. 221

20 See the many examples in S.J. Hallam, *Fire and Hearth: a study of Aboriginal usage and European usurpation in south-western Australia*, 1975, Chapters 3 and 4
21 R. Jones, 'Fire-stick Farming', *Australian Natural History*, no. 16, 1969
22 T. Dingle, *Aboriginal Economy: Patterns of Existence*, 1988, pp. 18–19
23 I. McBryde, 'Goods from Another Country: Exchange Networks and the People of the Lake Eyre Basin', in Mulvaney and White, op. cit.
24 J. Flood, 'Moth Hunters of the South Eastern Highlands', in Mulvaney and White, op. cit.
25 Quoted in T. Dingle, *The Victorians: Settling*, 1984, p. 6
26 M. Sahlins, *Stone Age Economics*, 1972, Chapter 6
27 McBryde, op. cit., p. 258
28 Perhaps the most accessible short account of the complexity of Aboriginal religion is in Maddock, Chapter 5 'The World Creative Powers' and Chapter 6 'The Rites of Life'
29 ibid, pp. 123–4
30 ibid, p. 33
31 McBryde, op. cit., p. 267
32 Flood, *Archaeology of the Dreamtime*, pp. 230–2
33 Quoted in S. Williams, 'Reactions on Cook's Voyage', in I. and T. Donaldson (eds), *Seeing the First Australians*, 1985, p. 35
34 See B. Smith, *European Vision and the South Pacific 1768–1850*, 1985, pp.176–7
35 Flood, *Archaeology of the Dreamtime*, Chapter 17, puts the arguments for and against this position
36 A. Frost, 'New South Wales as *terra nullius*: the British denial of Aboriginal land rights', *Historical Studies*, vol. 19, no. 77, October, 1981
37 ibid
38 Quoted in ibid, p. 518
39 Clarke, *A Short History of Australia*, Chicago: Mentor, 1963, p.18
40 Quoted in C.D. Rowley, *The Destruction of Aboriginal Society: Aboriginal Policy and Practice*, vol. 1, 1970, p. 37
41 Quoted in J. Miller, *Koori: A Will to Win. The Heroic Resistance, Survival and Triumph of Black Australia*, 1985, p. 25
42 See the answers to the enquiries concerning the employment of Aborigines on New South Wales pastoral properties in an 1841 report on immigration, quoted in C. Fox and M. Lake, *Australians at Work: commentaries and sources*, 1990, pp. 63–5
43 ibid
44 Quoted in H. Reynolds, *Aborigines and Settlers: The Australian Experience 1788–1934*, 1979, p. 109
45 Fox and Lake, op. cit.
46 See the 1869 report of the Central Board Appointed to Watch over the Interests of Aborigines in Victoria, quoted in Fox and Lake, op. cit., pp. 69–70
47 H. Reynolds, *The Other Side of the Frontier: Aboriginal resistance to the European Invasion of Australia*, 1982, pp. 140–5
48 ibid, p. 24–5.

49 M. Fels, *Good Men and True: the Aboriginal police of the Port Phillip district. 1837–1853*, 1988
50 M.F. Christie, *Aborigines in Colonial Victoria, 1835–86*, 1979, p. 89

2 The felonry and the free

1 R.W. Connell and T.M. Irving, *Class Structure in Australian History: Documents, Narrative and Argument*, 1980, p. 69
2 Quoted in D.R. Hainsworth (ed.), *Builders and Adventurers: The Traders and the Emergence of the Colony 1788–1821*, 1968, p. 13
3 P. Cunningham, *Two Years in New South Wales*, London: Henry Colburn, 1827, vol. 2, p. 67
4 Quoted in K. Buckley and T. Wheelright, *No Paradise for Workers: Capitalism and the Common People 1788–1914*, 1980, p. 34
5 L.L. Robson, *The Convict Settlers of Australia*, Melbourne: MUP, 1976, p. 3. This number does not include 9688 men sent to Western Australia between 1850 and 1868 and several thousand others sent direct to the places of secondary punishment.
6 ibid, contains a systematic analysis of convict crimes and records.
7 See for example Robson, A.G.L. Shaw, *Convicts and the Colonies*, London, Faber, 1966; and M.B. and C.B. Shedvin, 'The Nomadic Tribes of Early Britains: A Prelude to Botany Bay', *Historical Studies*, vol. 18, no. 71, 1978
8 S. Nicholas (ed.), *Convict Workers: Re-interpreting Australia's past*, 1988, contains this last restatement
9 See the tables in S. Nicholas and P.R. Shergold, 'Convicts as Workers' on pp. 64, 66 and 67 in ibid.
10 S. Nicholas and P. Shergold, 'A Labour Aristocracy in Chains' in ibid
11 S. Blair, 'The Felony and the Free: Division in Colonial Society in the Penal Era', *Labour History*, no. 45, November 1983
12 ibid, pp. 5 and 12
13 R. Hughes, *The Fatal Shore: A History of the Transportation of Convicts to Australia 1787–1868*, 1987, p. 298
14 See Robson, op. cit., Chapter 4, and D. Oxley, 'Female Convicts' in Shergold (ed.) op. cit. pp. 85–6 for some contemporary description
15 Hughes, op. cit., p. 244. The percentage figure is given by Robson op. cit., p. 76, but see J. Williams 'Irish Female Convicts in Tasmania', *Labour History*, no. 44, May 1983, who shows 13% of convict women transported to Tasmania from Ireland's cities described themselves as being 'on the town'.
16 Oxley, op. cit., p. 92
17 J. Burnett (ed.), *Useful Toil: Autobiographies of working people from the 1820s to the 1920s*, London: Allen Lane, 1984, Chapter 2. For a closer analysis of convict women workers in Tasmania, see Williams, op. cit.
18 J. Hirst, *Convict Society and its Enemies*, 1983, esp. Chapter 2 'Masters and Servants'
19 S. Nicholas, 'The Organisation of Public Work', in Nicholas, op. cit.
20 Hirst, op. cit., pp. 42–4

21 Quoted in K. Alford, *Production or Reproduction? An economic history of women in Australia, 1788–1850*, 1984, p. 78
22 Hughes, op. cit., p. 255
23 Alford, op. cit., p. 23
24 Quoted in ibid, p. 80
25 For a recent statement of this argument see M. Dunn, 'Early Australia: Wage labour or slave society', in E.L. Wheelright and K. Buckley, *Essays in the Political Economy of Australian Capitalism, Volume One*, 1975. For the major critique of contemporary and recent arguments see Hirst, op. cit., Chapters 1 and 3
26 Hughes, op. cit., p. 330
27 Hirst, op. cit., p. 110
28 A. Atkinson, 'Four Patterns of Convict Protest', *Labour History*, no. 37, November 1979
29 Quoted in K. Buckley and T. Wheelright, *No Paradise for Workers.*, p. 54
30 See R. Ward, *The Australian Legend*, Melbourne, 1977, Chapter 2, for example. See H. McQueen, *A New Brittannia*, Ringwood: Penguin, 1970 for the major rebuttal
31 Quoted in M. Sullivan, *Men and Women of Port Phillip*, 1985, p. 100
32 See the evidence of John McKay, 'Additional Memoranda on Indian Immigration: on the Introduction of Indian Labourers,' *New South Wales Voter and Proceedings*, 1837
33 For the Macarthurs see A. Atkinson, 'Master and Servant at Camden Park', *Push from the Bush*, no. 6, May 1980, pp. 58
34 D. Simon, 'Master and Servant' in J. Saville, *Democracy and the Labour Movement: Essays in Honour of Dona Torr*, London: Lawrence and Wishart, 1954
35 This paragraph largely comes from A. Brooks, 'A Man is as Good as his Master', in V. Burgmann and J. Lee (eds), *Making a Life: A People's History of Australia since 1788*, 1988; A. Merritt, 'The Historical Role of Law in the Regulation of Employment', *Australian Journal of Law and Society*, vol. 1, 1982; J. Cashen, 'Master and Servant in Early South Australia', *Push from the Bush*, no. 6, May 1980; F. Crowley, 'Master and Servant in Western Australia 1829–1857', *Journal of the Royal Western Australian Historical Society*, no. 4, May 1953; and M. Sullivan, *Men and Women of Port Phillip*
36 A. Brooks, op. cit.
37 M. Clarke, *A Short History of Australia*, 1963, p. 90
38 A. Brooks, op. cit.
39 Quoted in Sullivan, op. cit., p. 194. See also pp. 192–4 for the general picture
40 Ward, op. Cit., Chapter 4
41 N. Townshend, 'A Strange Wild Set? Cedar Cutters on the McLeay, Nambucca and Ballinga Rivers, 1838 to 1848', *Labour History*, no. 55, November 1988; F. Broeze, 'The Seamen of Australia', *Push from the Bush*, no. 10, September 1981; D. Hainsworth, 'Iron Men in Wooden Ships: The Sydney Sealers, 1800–1820', *Labour History*, no. 13, 1967; B. Little, 'The Sealing and Whaling Industry in Australia before 1850',

Australian Economic History Review, vol. 9, 1969; Ward, op. cit., esp. Chapters 4 and 7
42 E. Richards, 'A Voice from Below', Benjamin Boyce in South Australia, 1839–1846, *Labour History*, no. 27, November 1974
43 For a sympathetic account of shepherds see T. Dingle, *The Victorians: Settling*, 1984, pp. 31–3
44 The information in these two paragraphs is drawn from G.P. Walsh, 'Factories and Factory Workers in New South Wales 1788–1900', *Labour History*, no. 21 November 1971; M. Aveling and A. Atkinson (eds), *Australians 1838*, 1987, Chapter 4 'Work'; and P. Robinson, *The Hatch and Brood of Time: A study of the first generation of native born white Australians, 1788–1828*, 1985, Chapters 8–10
45 Alford, op. cit., Chapter 7, and Robinson, op. cit., p. 155
46 For a description of some of the larger staffs see B. Dyster, *Servant and Master: Building and Running the Grand Houses of Sydney*, Sydney: New South Wales University Press, 1989
47 Alford, op. cit., p. 217
48 ibid, pp. 189–90
49 Quoted in ibid, p. 190

3 Working in the country

1 Quoted in J. Merritt, *The Making of the A.W.U.*, 1987, p. 40
2 The sources for this paragraph are G. Davison, J.W. McCarty, A. McLeary (eds), *Australians 1888*, 1987, pp. 40–113; B. Kingston, *The Oxford History of Australia Volume Three*, 1860–1900 Glad Confident Morning, 1989, p. 9; W. Vamplew, *Australians. Historical Statistics*, Sydney, 1987, pp. 72, 78, 88
3 Interview with Charles Fahey, Radio 3CR History Show, 1986. Tape in the possession of the author
4 M. Kiddle, *Men of Yesterday: A social history of the Western District of Victoria 1824–1890*, 1967, pp. 183–4
5 For a general picture of the period see T.A. Coghlan, *Labour and Industry in Australia: From the First Settlement in 1788 to the Establishment of the Commonwealth in 1901*, vol. 2, Part 5, Chapter 5, passim.
6 ibid, p. 285
7 R. Ward, *The Australian Legend*, p. 10
8 ibid, pp. 243–5
9 J. Walker, *Jondaryan Station: The Relationship between Pastoral Capitalism and Pastoral Labour 1840–1870*, 1985, p. 81
10 Kiddle, op. cit., p. 285
11 ibid, p.287
12 ibid, p. 285–6
13 ibid, pp. 408–9; Merritt, op. cit., pp. 41–2
14 Merritt, op. cit., p. 43
15 Quoted in L. Kelly, 'Knights of the Blade: Shearers in 1888', *Australia 1888*, no. 8, September 1981, p. 52
16 Merritt, op. cit., pp. 38 and 42
17 W. Evans (ed.), *Diary of a Welsh Swagman 1869–1894*, 1977

18 ibid, p. 70
19 M. Lake, 'Socialism and Manhood: The Case of William Lane', *Labour History*, no. 50, May 1986, p. 57
20 Quoted in ibid, p. 61
21 Buckley and Wheelright, op. cit., p. 130
22 T. Irving, '1850–1870' and G.L. Buxton, '1870–1890' in F.K. Crowley (ed.), *A New History of Australia*, Melbourne: William Heinemann, 1980
23 S. Macintyre, *Winners and Losers: The pursuit of social justice in Australian History*, 1985, pp. 32–3
24 ibid, p. 38
25 T. Dingle, *The Victorians: Settling*, pp. 58–60
26 Buckley and Wheelright, op. cit., p. 124; Macintyre, op. cit., pp. 36–7; H. McQueen, *A New Brittannia*, p. 158
27 G.L. Buxton, *The Riverina 1861–1891. An Australian Regional Study*, 1967; D.W. Meinig, *On the Margins of the Good Earth: The South Australian Wheat Frontier 1869–1884*, Adelaide: Rigby Limited, 1970; D.B. Waterson, *Squatter, Selector and Storekeeper: A History of the Darling Downs 1859–1893*, 1968
28 P. Grimshaw, *et al.*, 'Families and selection in colonial Horsham', in P. Grimshaw, C. McConville and E. McEwen (eds), *Families in Colonial Australia*, 1985, pp. 129–30
29 Buxton, '1870–1890', p. 174 and 'The Riverina', pp. 197–8
30 M. Lake, 'Building Themselves Up with Aspros: Pioneer Women Re-Assessed', *Hecate,* vol. 7, no. 20, 1981; Grimshaw, *et al.*, op. cit., p. 133
31 For the Wimmera see ibid, pp. 126–9. For the Darling Downs see Waterson, op. cit., p. 150
32 E. Williams and M. Williams, 'Rural South Australia in the Nineteenth Century', in E. Richards (ed.), *The Flinders History of South Australia: Social History,* Netley: Wakefield Press, 1986, p. 541
33 Buxton, *The Riverina*, p. 199
34 Davison (ed.) *et. al., Australians 1888,* p. 273; Cannon, *Life in the Country: Australia in the Victorian Age,* vol. 2, 1973, p. 155
35 Davison *et al.*, op. cit., p. 302
36 ibid
37 Cannon, *Life in the Country*, p. 162
38 R. Frances, 'Never done but always done down', in V. Burgmann and J. Lee (eds), *Making a Life: A Peoples History of Australia since 1788,* 1988
39 W.K. Hancock, *Discovering Monaro: A Study of Man's Impact on His Environment,* Cambridge: Cambridge University Press, 1970, pp. 120–1
40 Quoted in Cannon, *Life in the Country*, p. 159
41 R. Evans, 'Kings' in Brass Crescents: Defining Aboriginal Labour Patterns in Colonial Queensland' in K. Saunders, *Indentured Labour in the British Empire 1834–1920,* Canberra: Croom Helm, 1983, p. 189
42 There is now a substantial literature on the frontier in Australia. See particularly C.D. Rowley, *The Destruction of Aboriginal Society,*

    Ringwood: Penguin Books, 1980; and H. Reynolds, *The Other Side of the Frontier,* Ringwood: Penguin Books, 1982
43 Evans, op. cit.
44 D. May, 'Aboriginal Labour in the North Queensland Cattle Industry 1897–1968', Phd thesis, James Cook University, 1986, is excellent on this complex process
45 G. Davison et al., *Australians 1888,* pp.126–9
46 C. Anderson, 'Aborigines and Tin Mining in North Queensland: A Case Study in the Anthropology of Contact History', *Mankind,* vol.13, no.6, April, 1983
47 B. Shepherd, 'A History of the Pearling Industry off the North West Coast of Australia from its origins until 1916', MA thesis, University of Western Australia, 1975, p.86
48 G. Cowlishow, *Black, White or Brindle. Race in rural Australia,* Melbourne: Cambridge: CUP, 1988, pp.70–74
49 A. Haebich, *For Their Own Good. Aborigines and Government in the South West of Western Australia 1900–1940,* Perth: UWA Press, 1988, Chapter 1
50 R. Broome, *Aboriginal Australians: Black Response to White Dominance 1788–1980,* 1982, Chapter 7; Christie, op. cit., Chapter 8
51 Yen Ching Hwang, *Coolies and Mandarins: China's Protection of Overseas Chinese during the Late Ching Period 1851–1911,* Singapore: Singapore University Press, 1985, pp. 33–6
52 P. Corris, *Passage, Port and Plantation: A History of Solomon Islands Labour Migration 1870–1914,* 1973, pp. 21–2 and 53–5
53 Yen Ching Hwang, op. cit., pp. 32–72
54 Corris, op. cit., Chapter 4; C. Moore, *Kanaka: A History of Melanesian Mackay,* 1985, pp. 52–3
55 C.A. Price, *The Great White Walls are Built: Restrictive Immigration to North America and Australia 1831–1888,* 1974, p. 42
56 A. Markus, *Fear and Hatred: Purifying Australia and California, 1850–1901,* 1979, p. 183; A. Powell, *Far Country: A Short History of the Northern Territory,* Melbourne: MUP, 1982, pp. 97–98
57 D. Sissons, 'Karayuki-San: Japanese Prostitutes in Australia 1887–1916', 1 and 2, *Historical Studies,* vol. 17, no. 68, April 1977, and vol. 17, no. 69, October 1977
58 A.T. Yarwood and M.J. Knowling, *Race Relations in Australia: A History,* 1982, p. 237
59 ibid, p. 208
60 R. Fitzgerald, *From the Dreaming to 1915: A History of Queensland,* St Lucia, University of Queensland Press, 1982, pp. 180–91; G. Burrows and C. Morton, *The Canecutters,* Melbourne, MUP, 1986, Chapter 2
61 C. Moore, op. cit., pp. 156–9 and 163–4
62 ibid, Chapter 5; Corris, op. cit., Chapter 5
63 Moore, op. cit., p. 252
64 C.Y. Choi, *Chinese Migration and Settlement in Australia,* 1975, pp. 18–19, 28–32, 34–35; R. Fitzgerald, op. cit., p. 225; Powell, op. cit., pp. 97–8
65 D. Horsefall, *March to Big Gold Mountain,* Ascot Vale: Red Rooster

Press, 1985, pp. 5–8, 31 and 35; see also Choi, op. cit.
66 Choi, op. cit., p. 14
67 Blainey, *The Rush that Never Ended,* p. 88
68 Horsefall, op. cit., p. 33
69 Quoted in Yarwood and Knowling, op. cit., p. 70
70 The history of this legislation can be found in Yarwood and Knowling, op. cit. and Markus, 'Fear and Hatred'

4 Working in the city

1 J.C. Caldwell, 'Population' in W. Vamplew (ed.), *Australians: Historical Statistics,* p. 41
2 ibid. p. 287
3 J. Lee & C. Fahey, 'A Boom for Whom? Some developments in the Australian labour market, 1870–1891', *Labour History,* no. 50, May 1986
4 This paragraph is compiled from ibid, J.C. Caldwell; op. cit., S. Fitzgerald, *Rising Damp: Sydney 1870–90,* 1987, Chapter 5; G. Davison, *The Rise and Fall of Marvellous Melbourne,* 1978, Chapter 2
5 A. Smith, *The Wealth of Nations,* New York: 1937, pp. 4–5
6 ibid, p. 7
7 C. Babbage, *On the Economy of Machinery and Manufacturers,* London: 1832; reprint ed. New York 1963, p. 184
8 G. Davison, 'Festivals of Nationhood: The International Exhibitions', in S.L. Goldberg and F.B. Smith, *Australian Cultural History,* Melbourne, CUP, 1988
9 A. Ure, *The Philosophy of Manufactures,* 1835, reprinted 1967, p. 23
10 Davison, *Marvellous Melbourne,* pp. 67–8
11 E.P. Thompson, 'Time, Work Discipline and Industrial Capitalism', *Past and Present,* 38, 1976
12 Minutes of evidence taken before the Select Committee on the Employment of Children, *N.S.W. Legislative Assembly, Votes and Proceedings,* 1875–6. See the evidence of James Cook, brickmaker, and D. Dixon, tobacco manufacturer
13 S. Fitzgerald, op. cit., p. 150
14 Quoted in R. Frances, 'The Clothing and Boot Industries 1880–1939', in E. Willis (ed.), *Technology and the Labour Process: Australasian Case Studies,* 1988, p. 98
15 ibid
16 George Gray to 'Dear Sister', 8 March 1885, Letters to George Gray, La Trobe Library Manuscript Collection, M/S H., 15969
17 *Weekly Times,* 4 March 1876, Page 2
18 Quoted in L. Lynch, 'T.S. Mort, His Dock and Balmain Labour', in M. Kelly (ed.), *Nineteenth Century Sydney, Essays in Urban History,* Sydney: SUP, 1978, p. 89
19 L. Sgt. T. Stephenson to Mr Ashley, Foy and Gibson Textile Mills 6, 12–1917. Foy and Gibson Collection, Melbourne University Archives
20 Quoted in J. Lee, 'The Marks of Want and Care', in V. Burgmann and J. Lee, *Making a Life,* pp. 198–9

21 Evidence of Mr Droop. Report of the Board appointed to Enquire into the Management of the Williamstown Workshops, *Victorian Parliamentary Papers*, 1869, vol. 4
22 *The Tocsin*, 23 August 1900, p. 8
23 R. Markey, 'The Aristocracy of Labour and Production Reorganisation in NSW c1880–1900', *Australian Economic History Review*, 28 March 1985, p. 47
24 M. Bray and M. Rimmer, *Delivering the Goods: A History of the Transport Workers' Union in New South Wales 1888–1986*, 1987, p. 11
25 M. Cannon, *Life in the Cities*, 3, 1975, Chapter 17
26 Markey, 'The Aristocracy of Labour', p. 47
27 H. Braverman, *Labour and Monopoly Capital: The Degradation of Work in the Twentieth Century*, 1974, pp. 133–6 and Chapter 20
28 B. Ellem, *In Women's Hands? A History of Clothing Trades Unionism in Australia*, 1989, p. 17
29 R. Frances, 'No More Amazons: Gender and Work Process in the Victorian Clothing Trades, 1890–1939', *Labour History*, no. 50, May 1986 Markey, 'The Aristocracy of Labour', p. 48. T. Sheridan, *Mindful Militants: The Amalgamated Engineering Union in Australia 1920–1972*, 1975, p. 13
30 Frances, 'The Clothing and Boot Industries', pp. 97–102
31 Frances, 'No More Amazons', p. 101
32 See for example Markey, 'The Aristocracy of Labour', pp. 54–55, and E. Butler-Bowden, 'Class Confrontation–Class Collaboration: the construction of skill and the re-establishment of apprenticeship in the painting and electrical trades in Victoria', BA Hons, University of Melbourne, 1986
33 Davison, *Marvellous Melbourne*, p. 60
34 I thank Raelene Frances for this point
35 E.H. Buchanan, Minutes of Evidence. Royal Commission into the Decline of Apprenticeships of Boys to Skilled Trades, *N.S.W. Joint Volume of Papers*, 1911–12, vol. 2
36 Sheridan, op. cit., Chapter 1
37 Davison, *Marvellous Melbourne*, p. 48
38 C. Fisher, 'Technological Change and the Unions: The Case of the Marine Engineers Before 1890', *Labour History*, no. 41, November 1981
39 The best analyses of this are (for Melbourne) Lee and Fahey, op. cit. and (for Sydney) Fitzgerald, op. cit., Chapter 7
40 Quoted in G. Davison *et. al.* (eds), *Australians 1888*, p. 202
41 Fitzgerald, op. cit., pp. 210–11
42 R. Morris, 'The N.S.W. Ship Painters and Dockers Union, 1900–1914: A Small Union and the Institutionalisation of Industrial Relations', *Labour History*, no. 43, November 1982
43 G. Davison *et al.* (eds), *Australians 1888*, p. 208
44 Lee and Fahey, op. cit., p. 10
45 Bray and Rimmer, op. cit., pp. 9–10
46 Fitzgerald, op. cit., pp. 203–4
47 Lee and Fahey, passim

48 ibid, p. 25
49 Fred Riley to H. Green, Secretary to the Royal Commission on National Insurance, 17 October 1924, in Fred Riley Papers M/S 759/1/597, Canberra: Australian National Library
50 ibid
51 G. Davison et al. (eds), *Australians 1888*, p. 204
52 A. O'Brien, *Poverty's Prison: The Poor in New South Wales 1880–1918*, 1988, p. 20
53 ibid, p. 181
54 W.A. Sinclair, 'Women at work in Melbourne and Adelaide since 1871', *The Economic Record*, 57, December 1981, pp. 345–6
55 ibid, p. 349
56 ibid
57 An Old Housekeeper, *Men and How to Manage Them, A Book for Australian Wives and Mothers*, Melbourne: 1885
58 E. Ryan and A. Conlon, *Gentle Invaders: Australian Women at Work 1788–1974*, 1975, p. 31
59 M. Barbalet, *Far from a Low Gutter Girl: The forgotten world of state wards: South Australia 1887–1940*, 1983, p. 47
60 Quoted in M. McMurchy, M. Oliver and J. Thornley (eds), *For Love or Money: A pictorial history of women and work in Australia*, Ringwood: Penguin, 1983, p. 44
61 The best description of nineteenth-century housework is in B. Kingston, *My Wife, My Daughter and Poor Mary Ann: Women and Work in Australia*, 1977, Chapter 3
62 Barbalet, op. cit., pp. 31–2
63 Given the importance of domestic service in the nineteenth century it is surprising that there are so few analyses of it. This paragraph comes from Barbalet, Chapter 2 and Kingston *My Wife, My Daughter and Poor Mary Ann*, Chapter 3
64 R.E.N. Twopeny, *Town Life in Australia*, 1883, facsimile ed. 1973, p. 52
65 Richard Bennett, Manager National Labour Bureau of Victoria, June 9 1875, in Minutes of the Meetings of the Committee of the National Labour Exchange, Victorian Public Records Office Series 3454, Item 1
66 See, for example, The Shops, Factories and Workshops Commission, Minutes of Evidence, *Queensland Votes and Proceedings of the Legislative Assembly*, 1891, vol. 2
67 Kingston, *My Wife, My Daughter and Poor Mary Ann*, p. 60 Sinclair, op. cit., p. 349
68 The best description of the realities of factory work for girls can be found in Cannon, *Life in the Cities*, Chapter 17
69 See the illustrations in Kingston, *My Wife, My Daughter and Poor Mary Ann*
70 G. Davison et al. (eds), *Australians 1888*, p. 319
71 Report of the Chief Inspector of Factories on the Sweating System, *Victorian Parliamentary Papers*, 1890, vol. 3
72 ibid

5 Work and the middle class

1. 'The Chemist and Druggist of Australia', vol. 9, no. 3, 1894, pp. 63–4, and no. 5, 1894, pp. 106–7
2. On Australia and the cost of education see Davison, *Marvellous Melbourne*, pp. 95–8. On the medical profession in Britain see W.J. Reader, *Professional Men: The Rise of the Professional Classes in Nineteenth Century England*, Weidenfeld and Nicholson, 1966. The 'rough and bloody' quote is on p. 33
3. Quoted in B.E. Lloyd and M.R. Rees (eds), *Labour Market Roles of Professional Engineers*, Canberra, 1986, p. 18
4. Davison, *Marvellous Melbourne*, Chapter 4
5. J.M. Freeland, *The Making of a Profession: A History of the Growth and Work of the Architectural Institute of Australia*, 1971, p. 7
6. T.S. Pensabene, *The rise of the medical practitioner in Victoria*, Health Research Project, Research Monograph no. 2, p. 7
7. The material in this paragraph comes from N.J. Marshall, *A Jubilee History 1928–1978: The Institute of Chartered Accountants in Australia, Victorian Branch*, 1978; J.M. Bennett, op. cit.; R. Johnston, *History of the Queensland Bar*, 1978; R.A. Buchanan, 'Engineers in Australia, 1788–1890. A Preliminary Analysis', *Transactions of the Institute of Engineers Australia*, vol. GE 6, no. 1, 1982 and Freeland, op. cit.
8. J. Robertson, 'The Professionalisation of Dentistry in Victoria 1884–1905', BA Hons, University of Melbourne, 1985
9. R. Price, 'The Engineering Library, University of Melbourne, A Brief History', *Australian Academic and Research Libraries*, vol. 17, no. 2, 1986, p. 84; Lloyd and Rees, op. cit.; and Buchanan, op. cit.
10. Bennett, op. cit., Chapter 6 and p. 213
11. ibid, p. 109
12. Johnston, 'History of the Queensland Bar', p. 12
13. Freeland, op. cit., pp. 204–24
14. Pensabene, op. cit., p. 66, Melbourne University opened in 1855 and the medical school began in 1862
15. ibid, Chapter 7. See also M. Lewis and R. McLeod, 'Medical Politics and the Professionalisation of Medicine in New South Wales, 1850–1901', *Journal of Australian Studies*, no. 22, May 1988
16. E. Willis, *Medical Dominance: The division of labour in Australian health care*, 1983, Chapter 4
17. Davison, *Marvellous Melbourne*, p. 25
18. Quoted in J. Hill, *From Subservience to Strike: Industrial Relations in the Banking Industry*, 1982, p. 8
19. National Bank of Australia Ltd., Chief Manager's Office, Melbourne: 1929, in Bank Officials Association 'Re Trading Banks', ABEU Collection, ANU, ABL A2/67/B
20. Regulations and Instructions for the Guidance of Officers of the Bank of Adelaide, Circa 1925, in ABEU, 'Federal Office-Branches', ANU.ABL.AZ.67A
21. See, for example, Hill, op. cit.; G. Griffin, *White Collar Militancy: The Australian Banking and Insurance Unions*, 1985, pp. XI and 36

22 Davison, et al. (eds), *Australians 1888*, p. 235
23 See for example the 1882 cartoon in Davison, *Marvellous Melbourne*, p. 32
24 Hill, op. cit., p. 7
25 Davison, *Marvellous Melbourne*, p. 28; Cannon, *Life in the Cities*, p. 206
26 Hill, op. cit., p. 7; Davison, *Marvellous Melbourne*, p. 96
27 Quoted in Davison, *Marvellous Melbourne*, p. 33
28 ibid, pp. 29–30. See also G. Anderson, *Victorian Clerks*, Manchester: Manchester University Press, 1976, esp. Chapter 4
29 B. Juddery, *White Collar Power: A History of the ACOA*, Sydney: Allen and Unwin, 1980, p. 29
30 K. Knight, 'Patronage and the 1894 Royal Commission of Inquiry into the New South Wales Public Service', *Australian Journal of Politics and History*, no. 7, 1961, p. 180
31 P. Loveday and A.W. Martin, 'Colonial Politics before 1890', in P. Loveday, A.W. Martin and R.S. Parker, *The emergence of the Australian party system*, Sydney: Hale and Iremonger, 1977
32 ibid, pp. 342–4
33 Davison, *Marvellous Melbourne*, pp. 115–6; and Knight, op. cit., pp. 174–5
34 Quoted in Knight, op. cit., p. 172
35 Davison, *Marvellous Melbourne*, p. 119; Knight, op. cit., p. 166; and G. Whitehouse and K. Wiltshire, *The History of the Queensland Professional Officers Association*, Brisbane: Boolarong Publications, 1987, p. 6
36 Juddery, op. cit., pp. 7–9
37 E.J. Rotella, *From Home to Office: U.S. women at work*, 1981, p. 69
38 Quoted in ibid p. 68
39 G. Reekie, 'Female Office Workers in Western Australia, 1895–1920: The Process of Feminisation and Patterns of Consciousness', *The Work Place: Time Remembered*, no. 5, 1982, p. 6; and K. Fitzsimmons, 'The Involvement of Women in the Commercial Sector 1850–1891', *Second Women and Labour Conference Papers*, 1980, p. 11
40 See the debate in G.S. Lowe, *Women in the Administrative Revolution. The Feminisation of Clerical Work*, 1987, Chapters 1 and 2; and C. Srole, 'A Blessing to Mankind, and especially to Womankind: The Typewriter and the Feminization of Clerical Work, Boston, 1860–1920', in B.D. Wright (ed.), *Women, Work and Technology*, Ann Arbour: University of Michigan Press, Ann Arbour, 1987
41 Davison, *Marvellous Melbourne*, p. 29
42 Reekie, 'Female Office Workers', p. 12
43 Evidence of Robert Henry Broad to Industrial Commission of NSW Bank Officers Case, 1928, Australian Bank Employees Union Records, ANU ABL File A2/37/9
44 Judgement of Full Bench delivered by Piddington, J., President of the NSW Arbitration Commission, ibid
45 A.V. Langker, General Secretary of the Public Service Board to Muriel Heaguey, 5 August 1955, quoted in Fox and Lake, op. cit., pp. 160–1

46 Charles Henderson to Richard Jeans, General Manager Australasian Bank, London, 30 June 1915, quoted in Fox and Lake, op. cit., p. 155
47 Ryan and Conlon, op. cit., p. 101
48 Reekie, 'Female Office Workers', p. 18
49 ibid, p. 10
50 Srole, op. cit., p. 90; and Kingston, *My Wife, My Daughter and Poor Mary Ann*, pp. 92–3
51 'An Old Housekeeper', op. cit.
52 C. Hall, 'The Early Formation of Victorian Domestic Ideology', in S. Burman (ed.), *Fit Work For Women,* London: Croom Helm, 1979
53 Kingston, *The Oxford History of Australia* esp. pp. 76–7, describes the place of women and the family in late nineteenth-century Australian puritanism. See also C. Bacchi, 'The Woman Question', in E. Richards (ed.), *The Flinders History of South Australia*
54 Kingston, *My Wife, My Daughter and Poor Mary Ann*, pp. 47–8
55 J. Gothard, 'Radically Unsound and Mischievous', Female migration to Tasmania, 1856–1863', *Historical Studies,* vol. 23, no. 93, October 1989
56 Quoted in R.E.N. Twopeny, *Town Life in Australia*, pp. 60–1. See also P. Russell, 'Mrs Coles Servants: A study in domestic politics', *Lilith* 4, 1988, for an early period
57 J. Godden, 'The Work for Them and the Glory for Us: Sydney Women's Philanthropy, 1880–1900', in R. Kennedy (ed.), *Australian Welfare History: critical essays,* Melbourne, MacMillan, 1982; and R. Kennedy, *Charity Warfare. The Charity Organisation Society in Colonial Melbourne,* Melbourne, Hyland House, 1985, esp. Chapter 4
58 Quoted in Gothard, op. cit., p. 397
59 Kingston, 'The Oxford History of Australia', p. 206–7. See also A. Mackinnon, 'The Advanced School for Girls (1879–1908): A Case Study in the History of Women's Education', *Second Women and Labour Conference,* vol. 2, 1980, pp. 206–7.
60 Quoted in Kingston, *My Wife, My Daughter and Poor Mary Ann*, p. 82
61 M. Kenely, 'Handmaidens of Medicine: Working Conditions for Nurses in Late Nineteenth Century Victoria', *Journal of Australian Studies,* no. 22, May 1988; and Kingston, *My Wife, My Daughter and Poor Mary Ann,* pp. 81–91; and McMurchy *et al.,* 'For Love or Money', p. 38
62 A.J. Hammerton, *Emigrant Gentlewomen: Genteel Poverty and Female Emigration, 1830–1914,* Canberra, ANU Press, 1979; and C.G. Chambers, 'Educated and White Collar Women in the 1880s', in E. Windschuttle, 'Women, Class and History'
63 N. Williamson, 'The Employment of Female Teachers in the Small Bush Schools of New South Wales, 1880–1890: A Case of Stay Bushed or Stay Home', *Labour History,* no. 43, November 1982; and S. Kennedy, 'Useful and Expendable: Women Teachers in Western Australia in the 1920s and 1930s', *Labour History,* no. 44, May 1983
64 Quoted in A.J. Truscott, 'Primary Teachers: Experiences in Rural Victoria, 1888', *Australia, 1888*, no. 8, September 1981, p. 33
65 Williamson, op. cit., p. 1

6 Control and protection: unions, the state and women workers

1. M. Quinlan, 'Early Trade Union Organisation in Australia: Three Australian Colonies 1829–1850', *Labour and Industry*, vol. 1, no. 1, October 1987
2. ibid. See also L. Hume, 'Working-Class Movements in Sydney and Melbourne before the Gold Rushes', *Historical Studies*, vol. 9, no. 34, 1960
3. Quoted in H. Hughes, 'The Eight Hours Day and the Development of the Labour Movement in the 1850s', *Historical Studies*, vol. 9, no. 35, Nov. 1960, p. 399
4. R. Gollan, *Radical and Working Class Politics: A Study of Eastern Australia, 1850–1910*, 1976, pp. 71–3
5. ibid, see p. 71. The best survey of wages and hours of work in the nineteenth century is E. Fry, 'The Condition of the Urban Wage Earning Class in Australia in the 1880s', PhD Thesis, Australian National University, 1956
6. R. Markey, 'New Unionism in Australia, 1880–1900', *Labour History*, no. 48, May 1985, pp. 21–8. See also A. Curthoys, 'Conflict and Consensus: The Seamen's State of 1878', and A. Markus, 'Talka Longa Mouth: Aborigines and the Labour Movement 1890–1970', in A. Curthoys *et al.*, 'Who Are Our Enemies?', for union attitudes towards the Chinese and Aborigines. The shearer's statement is from Ward, 'The Australian Legend', p. 186; M. Rimmer and P. Sheldon, 'Union Control Against Management Power: Labourers' Unions in New South Wales Before the 1890 Maritime Strike', *Historical Studies*, no. 23, no. 92, April 1989. On the colonial bodies see Gollan, op. cit., Chapters 4 and 5
7. Macintyre, *Winners and Losers*, Chapter 4
8. P.G. McCarthy, 'Labour and the Living Wage, 1890–1910', *Australian Journal of Politics and History*, no. 13, 1967, pp. 116–7 and esp. p. 124
9. P.G. McCarthy, 'Victorian Wages Boards: Their Origin and the Doctrine of the Living Wage', *Journal of Industrial Relations*, vol. 10, no. 2, 1968
10. I. Davey, 'Growing up in a working class community: school and work in Hindmarsh', in P. Grimshaw, C. McConville and E. McEwen (eds), *Families in Colonial Australia;* and A. Barcan, *A Short History of Education in New South Wales,* Sydney: Martindale Press, 1965, p. 151
11. O'Brien, op. cit., pp. 165–6 and 180–1
12. Broome, *Aboriginal Australians* has the best short discussion of protection, see p. 97; Rowley, 'The Destruction of Aboriginal Society' has a more detailed analysis
13. P. Biskup, *Not Slaves Not Citizens: The Aboriginal Problem in Western Australia 1898–1954,* St Lucia, UOP, 1973, pp.35–7
14. R. Fitzgerald, op. cit., pp. 238–252; Moore, op. cit., p.129
15. D. Hunt, 'Exclusivism and Unionism. Europeans in the Queensland Sugar Industry 1900–1910', in A. Curthoys and A. Markus (eds), *Who Are Our Enemies?* pp. 82–3

16 ibid p.83
17 J.S. Bach, 'Pearl Shelling Industry and the White Australian Policy', *Historical Studies,* vol. 10, no. 38, April 1962
18 Macintyre, *Winners and Losers* has the best discussion of the Victorian Acts, see p. 43-8. Given the obvious importance of the Factory Acts in Australian history there is very little analyses of them. Generally, see Gollan, op. cit., pp. 158-9
19 Macintyre, *Winners and Losers*
20 A.M. Lynzaat, 'Respectability and the Outworker: Victorian Factory Acts 1885-1903', in J. Mackinolty and H. Radi (eds), *In Pursuit of Justice: Australian Women and the Law 1788-1979,* Sydney: Hale and Iremonger, 1979
21 Macintyre, *Winners and Losers*; and Kingston, *My Wife, My Daughter and Poor Mary Ann,* p. 63. For the restrictions on the Chinese in Western Australia see A. Atkinson, 'Perth's Chinese Laundry Workers and the Effect of the Factories Act of 1904', in L. Layman (ed.), *'The Workplace' Time Remembered,* Special Issue, no. 5, 1982
22 *The Australian Leather Journal and Boot and Shoe Recorders,* vol. 2, September 15, 1899, p. 605
23 Gollan, op. cit., p. 159
24 H.B. Higgins, 'A New Province for Law and Order', no. 1, *Harvard Law Review,* no. 29, 1915/5; no. 2, *Harvard Law Review,* no. 32, 1918/9
25 McCarthy, 'Victorian Wage Boards', traces the development of the system
26 K.F. Walker, *Industrial Relations in Australia,* Cambridge, Massachusetts, Harvard University Press, 1956, pp. 19-22
27 ibid pp. 22-31 for the states and 17-19 for the Commonwealth
28 Gollan, op. cit., p. 163
29 Quoted in ibid, p. 165
30 For a short sketch of Higgins and an account of the Judgement, see P.G. Macarthy, 'Justice Higgins and the Harvester Judgement', in J. Roe (ed.), *Social Policy in Australia: Some Perspectives, 1901-1975,* Stanmore: Cassell Australia, 1976. For a longer account see J. Rickard, *H.B. Higgins, the Rebel as Judge,* Sydney: George Allen and Unwin, 1984. For a short description of Mackay, see the Australian Dictionary of Biography, Melbourne, MUP, 1988, vol. 10, 1891-1939, pp. 291-4
31 J. Kitay and C. Littler, 'The State and the Labour Process in Australia', Paper delivered to the Australian–Canadian Labour History Conference, Sydney University, December 1988, Section 3, pp. 5-6
32 ibid, pp. 11-12
33 ibid, pp. 9-11
34 This table combines tables found in ibid p. 7 and S. Macintyre, *The Labour Experiment,* Melbourne: McPhee-Gribble Publishers, 1989, p. 34
35 E. Ryan, *Two Thirds of a Man: Women and Arbitration in New South Wales, 1902-8,* 1984, pp. 28-38, 37 and 91
36 R. Brooks, 'The Melbourne Tailoresses' Strike 1882-1883: An Assessment', *Labour History,* no. 44, May 1983, p. 37; M. McMurchy *et al., op. cit.,* pp. 39-40

37 Ryan, op. cit., p. 28, Ryan and Conlon, op. cit., p. 58; McMurchy, op. cit., p. 39–40 for the references to the AWU
38 McMurchy *et al.*, op. cit., p. 48
39 Quoted in Brooks, op. cit., p. 36
40 Ellem, op. cit., p. 66; R. Brooks, op. cit., p. 37
41 Quoted in R. Brooks, op. cit., p. 36
42 Lee, 'Victoria's Wage Boards in Action', p. 367. See also Frances, 'No More Amazons', p. 98
43 Frances, 'The Clothing and Boot Industries', pp. 97–102, shows how the process worked in the Victorian boot trade
44 *The Australian Typographical Journal,* January 1890, p. 1098
45 Quoted in Ryan and Conlon, op. cit., p. 91
46 Quoted in ibid, p. 98
47 L. Bennett, 'Job classification and women workers: Institutional practices, technological change and the conciliation and arbitration system 1907–72', *Labour History,* vol. 51, November 1986
48 Frances, 'No More Amazons', p. 99
49 Frances, 'Clothing and Boot Industries', p. 107
50 Raelene Frances argues this case in 'Marginal Matters: Gender, Skill and the Commonwealth Arbitration Court—A Case Study of the Printing Industry, 1925–1937', paper presented to the Law, History, Theory Conference, La Trobe University, May 1988. (I thank her for permission to use this paper.)
51 South Australia, Blue Book, *South Australia Parliamentary Proceedings,* vol. 1, 1900
52 C. McCusky, 'Women in the Victorian Post Office', in Bevege, James, Shute (eds), op. cit., p. 61

7 Managing the workplace

1 R.E. Callanan, *Education and the Cult of Efficiency: A Study of the Social Forces that have Shaped the Administration of the Public Schools,* Chicago: The University of Chicago Press, 1964, Chs. 1–3
2 T. Rowse, *Australian Liberalism and National Character,* Melbourne: Kibble Books, Melbourne, 1978, pp. 61–73
3 C. Wright, 'The Formative Years of Management Control at the Newcastle Steelworks, 1913–1924', *Labour History,* no. 44, November, 1988, pp. 56–8
4 ibid, passim
5 ibid, pp. 65, 67, 69
6 The fullest account of Taylorism is in H. Braverman, *Labour and Monopoly Capital: The Degradation of Work in the Twentieth Century,* 1974, Chapter 4
7 C. Littler, *The Development of the Labour Process in Capitalist Societies,* Gower: Aldershot, 1986, pp. 179–81
8 K. Buckley, *The Amalgamated Engineers in Australia, 1852–1920,* 1970, p. 237. Much other information for this section comes from R. Dunford, 'Scientific Management in Australia: A Discussion Paper', *Labour and Industry,* vol. 1, no. 3, October 1988
9 See for example *Rydge's,* 1 July 1937, pp. 53809 and 638; and 1 September 1937, p. 720. For an account of scientific management after

World War II and Muscio's article see P. Cochrane, 'Company Time: Management, Ideology and the Labour Process 1940–1960', *Labour History,* no. 48, May 1985, p. 57
10. D. Saunders, 'Hiking in the Factory', *Rydge's* 1 January 1934, p. 43
11. *Australian Manufacturer,* 28 October 1916, p. 22
12. Frances, 'No More Amazons', p. 101
13. Quoted in ibid, p. 110
14. P. Poynton, 'The Development of the Assembly Line in Australia', *Arena,* no. 58, 1981, pp. 70–71
15. ibid, p. 74
16. C. Healy (ed.), *The Lifeblood of Footscray: Working Lives at Angliss Meatworks,* nd, pp. 3–13
17. L. Taksa, 'Oral History and the Literary Culture of the Workplace', paper delivered to the Australian–Canadian Labour History Conference, Sydney: 1988
18. *Rydge's,* 1 April 1940, p. 270
19. G. Reekie, ' "Humanising Industry" ', Paternalism, Welfarism and Labour Control in Sydney's Big Stores 1890–1930', *Labour History,* no. 53, November 1987
20. Report of the Royal Commission into the effect of the workings of the system known as the job and time card system introduced into the Tramway and Railway Workshops of the Railway Commissioners in the State of New South Wales, *NSW Parliamentary Papers,* 1918, vol. 6, p. 8
21. G. Patmore, 'Systematic Management and Bureaucracy. The NSW Railways prior to 1932', *Labour and Industry,* vol. 1, no. 2, June 1988, pp. 316–7
22. Frances, 'No More Amazons', p. 102
23. C. Niland, 'Scientific Management and the 44-Hour Week', *Labour History,* no. 53, November 1987
24. Quoted in Frances, 'No More Amazons', p. 104
25. ibid, pp. 103–4
26. Quoted in ibid, p. 106
27. Healy, op. cit., pp. 55–6
28. Poynton, op. cit.
29. J. Hagan, *The History of the A.C.T.U.,* 1981, p. 85
30. Quoted in ibid
31. ibid
32. My thanks to Raelene Frances for this point
33. Frances, 'No More Amazons', p. 111
34. Quoted in Reekie, 'Humanising Industry', p. 18
35. Taksa, op. cit.
36. J. Mathews, *Good and Mad Women. The Historical Construction of Femininity in Twentieth Century Australia,* 1984, pp. 34–7
37. B. Kingston, *My Wife, My Daughter and Poor Mary Ann,* pp. 8–9
38. C. Bacchi, 'The Nature–Nurture Debate in Australia 1900–1914', *Historical Studies,* vol. 19, no. 75, October 1980, pp. 136–40
39. ibid, passim. See also G. Davison, 'The City-bred Child and urban reform in Melbourne 1900–1940', in P. Williams (ed.), *Social Process and the City,* Sydney: Allen and Unwin, 1983

40 Lake, 'Identifying the Masculine Context'
41 D. Deacon, 'Taylorism in the Home: The Medical Profession, The Infant Welfare Movement and the Deskilling of Women', *Australian and New Zealand Journal of Sociology,* vol. 21, no. 2, July 1985, pp. 169–71
42 B. Gammage and P. Spearritt (eds), *Australians, 1938,* Sydney: Fairfax, Syme and Weldon, 1987, p. 144
43 E. Willis, *Medical Dominance,* pp. 115–6
44 N. Williamson, ' "She walked ... with great purpose": Mary Kilpatrick and the history of midwifery in New South Wales', in Bevege *et al., Worth Her Salt,* pp. 5 and 8
45 ibid, p. 8
46 Deacon, op. cit., p. 165
47 K. Reiger, *The disenchantment of the home: Modernising the Australian Family 1880–1940,* 1985, Chapter 6
48 Quoted in K. Reiger, 'Babies' in Gammage and Spearritt, op. cit., p. 150
49 J. Cook, 'Housework or Scientific Management : The Development of Domestic Sciences in Western Australian State Schools, 1900–1940', in L. Layman (ed.), *The Workplace—Time Remembered,* no. 5, 1982
50 Quoted in ibid, p. 91
51 Real Property Annual, 1921, p. 35
52 Letter to Dr Wallace, 31 October 1943, Wallace Collection, University of Melbourne Archives; R. Barton, 'Household Technology in Western Australia, 1900–1950', *Journal of the Oral History Association of Australia,* no. 7, 1985 p. 111
53 Barton, op. cit., pp. 120–1; Kingston, *My Wife, My Daughter and Poor Mary Ann,* pp. 21–4, 49

8 Unemployment and full employment

1 Royal Commission into National Insurance, *C.P.P.* 1926–1927–1928, vol. 4, Third Progress Report, p. 20
2 'Report on Unemployment and Business Stability', Development and Migration Commission in *C.P.P.,* 1926–1927–1928, pp. 12–14
3 C. Forster, 'Unemployment and the Australian Economic Recovery of the 1930s', Working Papers in Economic History, no. 45, Department of Economic History, RSSS, Australian National University, Canberra: 1985, Table 1
4 These figures were compiled from the 1933 Census and can be seen in greater detail in C. Fox, 'Unemployment and the Politics of the Unemployed: Victoria in the Great Depression 1930–1937', PhD Thesis, University of Melbourne, 1985
5 D. Clarke, 'Fools and Madmen', in J. Mackinolty, *The Wasted Years? Australia's Great Depression,* Sydney: George Allen and Unwin, 1981, p. 188
6 M. Heagney, *Are Women Taking Men's Jobs?,'* 1935
7 P. Spearritt, 'Depression Statistics', in Mackinolty, *The Wasted Years?,* p. 208
8 ibid. pp. 201–207
9 Fox, op. cit., p. 124

10 ibid. p. 131
11 E.R. Walker, *Unemployment Policy with Special Reference to Australia,* Sydney: Angus and Robertson 1936, p. 85
12 Victorian THC Minutes, 22 December 1932. See also C.R. Broomhill, 'Under-employment in Adelaide During the Depression', *Labour History,* no. 27, November 1974
13 *1933 Census,* vol. 1, pp. 232 and 234
14 Fox, op. cit., pp. 149–150
15 Quoted in ibid, p. 283
16 W. Lowenstein, *Weevils in the Flour: An oral record of the 1930s depression in Australia,* Melbourne: Hyland House, 1978
17 J. Chute, 'Reconciliation of the Female Role: Depression Women in Footscray in the 1920s and 1930s', BA Honours Thesis, University of Melbourne, 1983
18 F.A. Bland, 'Unemployment Relief in Australia', *International Labour Review,* vol. XXX, no. 1, July 1934
19 For single men see C.R. Broomhill, *Unemployed Workers: A Social History of the Great Depression in Adelaide,* 1978; and G.C. Bolton, *A Fine Country to Starve In,* Perth: University of Western Australia Press, 1972. For single girls see Fox, op. cit., pp. 256–8. For Aborigines see A. Haebich, *'For their own good . . .'* Chapter 9
20 In Victoria, for example, the proportion was under one-fifth. In April 1933, when the Census showed that there were 106 000 unemployed workers in Victoria, there were only 23 000 on sustenance. In June 1933, when the Census showed that there were 99 000 males unemployed, the Government Labour Exchange had only 38 000 unemployed men on its books. Fox, op. cit., p. 153 and 606
21 Macintyre, *Winners and Losers,* p. 75
22 Fox, op. cit., Chapter 4 passim
23 ibid
24 The following analysis comes mainly from Fox, Macintyre, Broomhill, Bolton and N. Wheatley, 'The Disinherited of the Earth', in Mackinolty, *The Wasted Years?;* B. Costar, 'Controlling the Victims: The Authorities and the Unemployed in Queensland during the Great Depression', *Labour History,* no. 54, 1989; G. Spencely, 'Assessing the Responses of the Unemployed to the Depression of the 1930s', *Journal of Australian Studies,* no. 24, May 1989; C. Fox, 'The Unemployed and the Labour Movement: The West Australian Relief and Sustenance Workers' Union 1933–1934', *Studies in Western Australian History,* 5 December 1982
25 M.A. Jones, *The Australian Welfare State: growth, crisis and change,* Sydney: George Allen and Unwin, 1983, p. 53
26 ibid, p. 222
27 ibid, p. 366
28 P. Hasluck, *The Government and the People 1942–1945: Australia in the War of 1939–1945,* 1970, pp. 235–6
29 S.J. Butlin and C.B. Schedvin, *The War Economy 1942–1945: Australia in the War of 1939–1945,* 1977, pp. 13 and 367–8
30 M. McKernan, *All In! Australia During the Second World War,* 1983, pp. 225–7

31 T. Sheridan, op. cit., p. 156
32 ibid
33 Butlin and Schedvin, op. cit., p. 349
34 T. Rowse and P. Ryan, 'Women, Arbitration and the Family', in A. Curthoys, S. Eade and P. Spearritt, *Women at Work,* 1975, p. 16
35 C. Pinto, 'Mobilizing and Demobilizing Bertha', An Analysis of Public Discourse on Women's Work, 1942–1946, BA Honours, University of Melbourne, 1988, p. 12
36 L. Davis, 'Minding Children or Minding Machines...Women's Labour and Childcare During World War II', *Labour History,* no. 53, November 1987, pp. 88–9
37 R. Kramar, 'Female Employment During the Second World War', in *Third Women and Labour Conference Papers, 1982,* The Conveners, Third Women and Labour Conference, Salisbury East, 1982
38 N. Kingston, 'My experiences in the AWAS during World War II', in Bevege *et al.,* 'Worth Her Salt'
39 Hasluck, 'The Government and the People, 1939–1941', p. 269
40 ibid, p. 407
41 J. Curlewis, 'Women Working in Heavy Industry in World War II', in Women and Labour Publications Committee, *All Her Labours,* Sydney: Hale and Iremonger, 1984
42 Sheridan, op. cit., p. 161
43 Butlin and Schedvin, op. cit., p. 369. Kramar, op. cit., p. 4
44 Butlin and Schedvin, op. cit., pp. 199–201
45 Kramar, op. cit., p. 7
46 L. Beaton, 'The importance of women and labour: women at work in World War II', in Bevege *et. al.,* 'Worth Her Salt'
47 C. Larmour, 'Women's Wages and the WEB', in Curthoys *et al.,* 'Women at Work'
48 McKernan, op. cit., p. 213
49 Davis, op. cit., p. 97
50 M. Lake, 'The War over Women's Work', in V. Burgmann and J. Lee, *A Most Valuable Acquisition: A People's History of Australia since 1788,* Melbourne: McPhee Gribble–Penguin, 1988, p. 208
51 Sheridan, op. cit., pp. 162–3
52 Quoted in Pinto, op. cit., p. 10
53 Ryan and Rowse, op. cit., p. 16
54 R. Kuhn, 'Labour Movement Economic Thought in the 1930s: Under consumptionism and Keynesian economics', *Australian Economic History Review,* vol. 28, no. 2, September 1988, p. 55
55 R. Watts, *The Foundation of the Australian Welfare State,* 1987, p. 111
56 Quoted in P. Hasluck, *The Government and the People 1942–1945,* p. 512
57 P. Love, *Labour and the Money Power: Australian Labour Populism 1890–1950,* Melbourne, MUP, 1984, p. 149
58 See, for example, R.R. Walker in Watts, op. cit., p. 119
59 L.F. Crisp, *Ben Chifley: a political biography,* London: Longmans, 1961, pp. 189–90
60 Watts, op. cit., pp. 80–91 and 100

ENDNOTES

61 W.J. Waters, 'Australian Labor's Full Employment Objective, 1942–5', in J. Roe (ed.), *Social Policy in Australia*, p. 242
62 S. Cornish, *Full Employment in Australia: The Genesis of a White Paper*, Canberra: Department of Economic History, The Faculties, Australian National University, 1981, p. 189
63 ibid, pp. 186–193
64 C. Allport, 'Left off the Agenda: Women, Reconstruction and New Order Housing', *Labour History*, no. 46, May 1984

9 The changing workforce 1945–1974

1 This account comes from J. Hagan, *The History of the A.C.T.U.*, pp. 209–13, and R. Maddock and F. Stilwell, 'Boom and Recession', in A. Curthoys *et al.* (eds), *Australians from 1939*, 1987, pp. 259–60
2 Hagan, op. cit.; J. Lees and J. Senyard, *The 1950s ... how Australia became a modern society and everyone got a home and a car*, 1987
3 A. Delgado, *The Enormous File: A Social History of the Office*, 1979, pp. 95–8. See also the photographs in *Rydges*, 1 June, 1934, p. 575
4 Quoted in G.S. Lowe, *Women in the Administrative Revolution*, Cambridge: Polity Press, 1987, p.125
5 ibid. See also *Rydges*, 1 August, 1939, p. 628
6 See the photo in *Modern Office*, November 1978
7 ibid
8 I. Reinecke, *Micro Invaders: How the New World of Technology Works*, 1982, p.164
9 The argument here is summarised in M. Bray and C. Littler, 'The Labour Process and Industrial Relations: Review of the Literature', *Labour and Industry*, vol. 1, no. 3, October 1988, p. 561
10 These figures come from K. Hargreaves, *Women At Work*, 1980, pp. 19–21; S. Eccles, 'Women in the Australian Labour Force', in Sydney, M.D. Broom (ed.), *Unfinished Business: Social Justice for Women in Australia*, 1984, passim; J. Mathews, *Good and Mad Women*; and C. O'Donnell and P. Hall, *Getting Equal: Labour Market Regulation and Women's Work*, 1988, Chapter 1
11 Hargreaves, op. cit., p. 23; and O'Donnell and Hall, op. cit., p. 20
12 Hargreaves, op. cit., p. 176
13 Lees and Senyard, op. cit., p. 66
14 M. Power, 'The Making of a Woman's Occupation', *Hecate*, vol. 1, no. 2, July 1975, pp. 26–8. See also Hargreaves, op. cit., pp. 25–6
15 S. Eccles, op. cit., p. 86 and R. Pringle, *Secretaries Talk: Sexuality, Power and Work*, Sydney: George Allen and Unwin, p. 167
16 S. Encel, N. MacKenzie and M. Tebbutt, *Women and Society: An Australian Study*, 1974, pp. 135–43
17 Fox and Lake, op. cit., pp. 160–1
18 R. Seymour, 'A Framework for Research of Office Work', Fourth Women and Labour Conference Papers, Brisbane, 1984
19 Quoted in Pringle, *Secretaries Talk*, p. 18
20 Lees and Senyard, op. cit., p. 77
21 Hargreaves, op. cit., p. 77
22 J. Collins, *Migrant Hands in a Distant Land*, 1988, pp. 20–33
23 ibid, p. 21

24 Quoted in Collins, op. cit., p. 10
25 B. Probert, *Working Life: Arguments about work in Australian society,* 1989, p. 113
26 Collins, op. cit., pp. 30–31
27 ibid, pp. 77–8
28 This is the gist of both Collins' and Lever-Tracy and Quinlan's arguments. See for instance Collins, op. cit., pp. 120–122 and C. Lever-Tracy and M. Quinlan, *A Divided Working Class: Ethnic Segmentation and Industrial Conflict in Australia,* 1988, Chapter 2
29 Centre for Urban Research and Action (CURA), *"But I wouldn't want my wife to work here"... A Study of Migrant Women in Melbourne Industry,* 1976, p. 2
30 D. Storer, 'Migrant Employment. Some dimensions', in Centre for Continuing Education, Sharing out the Work. Conference Papers and Reports, Canberra: ANU, July 1978, p. 78
31 G.W. Ford *et al.,* 'A Study of Human Resources and Industrial Relations at the Plant Level in Seven Selected Industries', in Policies for the Development of Manufacturing Industry, A Green Paper, vol. 4, Commissioned Studies, AGPS, 1976, p. 31
32 Centre for Urban Research and Action, op. cit., p. 35
33 ibid, p. 20
34 Probert, op. cit., p. 120
35 CURA, op. cit., p. 82
36 Ford, op. cit., p. 24
37 ibid, p. 29
38 B. Morris, 'From Under employment to Unemployment: The Changing Role of Aborigines in a Rural Economy', *Mankind,* vol. 13, no. 6, April 1983
39 Quoted in T. Rowse, 'Assimilation and After', in Curthoys *et al., Australians from 1939,* p. 135
40 ibid
41 R. Broome, *Aboriginal Australians: Black Responses to White Dominance 1788–1980,* Sydney: George Allen and Unwin, 1982, p. 137
42 Hodson, op. cit., pp. 82–3. See also M. Calley, 'Economic Life of Mixed-Blood Communities in Northern New South Wales', *Oceania,* no. 26, 1955/6
43 These three paragraphs are compiled from Hodson, op. cit.; Calley, op. cit.; P.E. Felton, 'Aboriginal Employment Problems in Victoria', in I.G. Sharp and C. Tatz (eds), *Aborigines in the Economy: Employment, Wages and Training,* 1966; J.H. Bell, 'The Economic Life of Mixed Blood Aborigines on the South Coast of New South Wales', *Oceania,* no. 26, 1955–6; R.G. Castle and J.S. Hagan, 'Dependence and Independence', in Curthoys *et al.,* 'Who are our Enemies?'
44 A. & R. Doobov, 'Queensland: Australia's Deep South', in F. Stevens (ed.), *Racism: The Australian Experience: A Study of Race Prejudice in Australia, vol. 2—Black Versus White,* Sydney: Australian and New Zealand Book Company, 1972, pp. 159–63. See also Rose, op. cit.
45 Quoted in B.E. Christopher and J. McGinness, 'The Queensland Aboriginal Wages System', in Stevens, 'Racism', p. 171
46 Calley, op. cit., p. 201

47 See for example Hodson, op. cit., Chapter 5
48 ibid, p. 118. See also Castle and Hagan, op. cit.; Morris, op. cit., pp. 511–3; and Bell, op. cit., pp. 188–9 for a similar but less well developed view from the 1950s
49 Morris, op. cit.
50 P. Marshall (ed.), *Rapa rapa. Kularr Martuwarra: Stories from the Fitzroy River Drovers,* 1988. P.M. Rogers, *The Industrialists and the Aborigines: A Study of Aboriginal Employment in the Australian Mining Industry,* 1973. But see particularly D. May, 'Aboriginal Labour in the North Queensland Cattle Industry 1897–1968', pp. 385–6
51 Hodson, op. cit., p. 92
52 Morris, op. cit., p. 514, shows that the rural labour force in New South Wales fell from 40 000 in 1939 to 18 000 in 1975
53 Aboriginal Social Indicators, 1984, Department of Aboriginal Affairs, Canberra: AGPS, 1984
54 George Dutton, quoted in K. Gilbert, *Living Black: Blacks talk to Kevin Gilbert,* 1977, pp. 132–3
55 Quoted in Hodson, op. cit., p. 132
56 T. Sheridan, 'Bosses and Workers', in A. Curthoys *et al., Australians Since 1939,* p. 292
57 Hargreaves, op. cit., p. 285
58 O'Donnell and Hall, op. cit., p. 12
59 Hargreaves, op. cit., p. 302
60 ibid, pp. 302–4
61 O'Donnell and Hall, op. cit., p. 12
62 Ryan and Conlon, op. cit., Chapter 6
63 A. Markus, 'Labour and Immigration 1946–9. The Displaced Persons Programme', *Labour History,* no. 47, November 1984, pp 85–90
64 ibid, p. 90
65 J. Martin, *The Migrant Presence: Australian Responses 1947–1977,* Sydney: 1978, pp. 187–8; and Markus, 'Labour and Immigration', p. 90
66 Quoted in Martin, op. cit., p. 202
67 CURA, 'But I wouldn't want my wife to work here', pp. 56–60. See also P. Georgiou, 'Migrants, Unionism and Society', *The Australian and New Zealand Journal of Sociology,* no. 9, 1973
68 Quoted in op. cit., p. 250
69 Lever-Tracy and Quinlan, op. cit., p. 250
70 Ford *et al.,* op. cit., p. 31
71 Martin, op. cit., pp. 201–2
72 This account comes from Lever-Tracy and Quinlan, op. cit., Chapter 5
73 A. Markus, 'Talka Longa Mouth: Aborigines and the Labour Movement 1890–1770', in A. Curthoys and A. Markus, *Who Are Our Enemies?,* pp. 145–51
74 M. Hess, 'The Pilbara Pastoral Workers' uprising of 1946', *Papers in Labour History,* no. 3, May 1989
75 Quoted in L. Davies, 'Protecting Natives?: The Law and the 1946 Aboriginal Pastoral Workers' Strike', *Papers in Labour History,* no. 1, January 1988, p. 35

76 ibid, p. 40
77 Markus, 'Talka Longa Mouth', pp. 154–5
78 Quoted in Marshall, op. cit., p. 208
79 Broome, op. cit., p. 141

10 Management, technology and the future

1 B. Jones, Evidence given to the Senate Standing Committee on Science, Technology and the Environment, Official Hansard Report, Minutes of Evidence, Commonwealth of Australia, Canberra, 1985, pp. 642–3
2 R. Eckersley, 'Australian attitudes to science and technology and the future', a Report for the Commission of the Future, Canberra: AGPS, 1988
3 L.W. Rogers, 'A History of the foundation and development of the Australian Institute of Management', no publisher or date but probably 1964
4 Enrolments in Economics and Commerce at University of Western Australia, for instance, increased from 13% of total enrolments in 1980 to 18.7% in 1989 while enrolments in Arts declined from 32% of the total to 25.6% in the same period. The University of Western Australia, Unistats 1989, p. 41
5 Perth Yellow Pages, 1990, pp. 1173–6
6 P. Cochrane, ' "Company time." Management, Ideology and the Labour Process', 1940–1960',
7 Quoted in ibid, pp. 57–8
8 Quoted in ibid, p. 64
9 ibid, p. 65
10 *Rydges,* 1 February 1941, p. 71
11 Quoted in H. Bourke, 'Industrial Unrest as Social Pathology. The Australian Writings of Elton Mayo', *Historical Studies,* vol. 20, no. 79, October 1982, p. 227
12 *Rydges,* 1 November 1972, pp. 71–6
13 *Rydges,* 1 September 1978, p. 26
14 *Rydges,* 1 April 1980, p. 101
15 For a discussion of the nature and use of quality control circles in two Australian factories see P. McGraw and R. Dunford, 'The Strategic Use of Quality Control Circles in Australian Industrial Relations', *Journal of Industrial Relations,* vol. 29, no. 2., June 1987
16 Quoted in T. Bramble, 'Award Restructuring in the Australian Trade Union Movement: A Critique', *Labour and Industry,* vol. 2, no. 3, October 1989, p. 377
17 A. Game and R. Pringle, *Gender at Work,* p. 66
18 J. Mathews, *Tools of change: New Technology and the Democratisation of Work,* 1989, p. 64
19 *Manufacturing and Management,* November 15 1955, p. 163
20 This information comes from *Australian Factory,* 2 February 1959, p. 27, and 1 February 1958; and *Manufacturing and Management,* vol. 15, no. 9, 1955, pp. 91–2
21 Mathews, 'Tools of Change', pp. 44–8
22 ibid, pp. 57–9

23 *Australian Technology Review*, 3, 1 February, 1989
24 See for example *Australian Factory*, 1 September 1962, pp. 64–5
25 The use of the automated plant's control room as a symbol of the benefits of technology is criticised by Braverman, op. cit., esp. p. 224
26 Submission by the Office of the Status of Women, Department of Prime Minister and Cabinet to the Senate Standing Committee on Science, Technology and the Environment, Minutes of Evidence, pp. 2135–6. See also A. Forward, 'Technological change and women's employment', in R.D. Lansbury and E.M. Davis (eds), *Technology, work and industrial relations,* Melbourne: Longman Cheshire, 1984
27 R.D. Lansbury and E.M. Davis, 'Technological change and industrial relations in Australia: an introduction', in ibid, p. 7
28 Quoted in C. Williams, *Blue, White and Pink Collar Workers in Australia: Technicians, bank employees and flight attendants,* 1988, p. 36
29 L. Palmer, 'Telephone exchange maintenance', in E. Willis, *Technology and the Labour Process: Australasian Case Studies*
30 See the evidence of John Mathews to the Senate Standing Committee on Science, Technology and the Environment, pp. 1238–9
31 ACTU/TDC Mission to Western Europe, 'Australia Reconstructed', Canberra: AGPS, 1987, p. 158
32 For the Government's attitude to new technology see the reply by the Minister Senator Gareth Evans to the report of the Senate Standing Committee on Science, Technology and the Environment, in Commonwealth Parliamentary Debates, 2 June 1988, pp. 3403–7
33 For a recent statement of the Hawke Government's position see P. Morris, The Minister for Industrial Relations, 'Looking Forward: A New Industrial Relations for Australia', *Labour and Industry,* vol. 2, no. 3, October 1989
34 This information comes from discussion with officials of the two unions
35 T. Bramble, 'Political Economy and Management Strategy in the Metal and Engineering Industry', *Journal of Industrial Relations,* vol. 31, no. 1, 1989, p. 36
36 Morris, 'A New Industrial Relations for Australia', p. 368
37 A. Gorz, *Paths to Paradise: On the Liberation from Work,* London: Pluto Press, 1985; B. Jones, *Sleepers Wake! Technology and the Future of Work,* 1982
38 B. Jones, 'Managing Today for Tomorrow', from an address quoted in *Newsletter of the Australian Robotics Association,* 19 October 1988
39 Gorz, op. cit.
40 Quoted in Probert, 'Working Life', p. 165
41 B. Probert and J. Wajcman, 'Technological Change and the Future of Work', *Journal of Industrial Relations,* vol. 30, no. 3, September 1988
42 Mathews, *Tools of Change,* esp. part 4
43 Probert and Wajcman, op. cit.
44 See the report in *The West Australian,* 24 February 1990, p. 28

Bibliography

Abbreviations used in bibliography

ANU	Australian National University
AWM	Australian War Memorial
CUP	Cambridge University Press
MUP	Melbourne University Press
OUP	Oxford University Press
RSSS	Research School of Social Sciences, ANU
SUP	Sydney University Press
UNSWP	University of New South Wales Press
UQP	University of Queensland Press
UWA	University of Western Australia

Manuscript sources

Government inquiries

Report of the Board Appointed to Enquire into the Management of the Williamstown Workshops, *Victorian Parliamentary Papers,* vol. 4, 1869

Select Committee on the Employment of Children, *New South Wales Legislation Assembly, Votes and Proceedings,* 1875-6

Report of the Chief Inspector of Factories on the Sweating System, *Victorian Parliamentary Papers,* vol. 3, 1890

Royal Commission on Technical Education, *Victorian Parliament, Legislative Assembly Votes and Proceedings,* vol. 3, 1901

Royal Commission into the Decline of Apprenticeships of Boys to Skilled Trades, *New South Wales Joint Volume of Papers,* vol. 2, 1911-12

Royal Commission of Inquiry into the effects of the working of the system known as the job and time card system introduced into the Tramway and Railway Workshops of the Railway Commissioners in the State of New South Wales, *New South Wales, Parliamentary Papers,* vol. 6, 1918

Royal Commission into National Insurance, *Commonwealth Parliamentary Papers,* 1926-7-8, Third Progress Report

Development and Migration Commission, in *Commonwealth Parliamentary Papers,* 1926-7-8

Royal Commission on youth unemployment and the apprenticeship system. *Western Australia Parliamentary Papers,* vol. 1, 1938

Report of the Victorian Housing Investigation and Slum Abolition Board, Victorian Government Printer, 1937

Policies for the Development of Manufacturing Industry: A Green Paper. AGPS, 1976

Senate Standing Committee on Science, Technology and the Environment. Official Hansard Report, Minutes of Evidence, Commonwealth of Australia 1987. (The official report was published as *Technology Assessment in Australia*, 1987.)

Other government publications
Aboriginal Social Indicators 1984, Department of Aboriginal Affairs, AGPS, 1984. Commonwealth Arbitration Reports

Other manuscript sources
Victorian Trades Hall Council Minutes
Australian Bank Employees Union Records. Canberra: ANU, ABL
Wallace Collection, Melbourne University Archives
George Gray letters, Manuscript Collection. Melbourne: La Trobe Library
Foy and Gibson Collection, Melbourne University Archives

Journals
Australian Leather Journal and Boot and Shoe Record
Australian Factory
Australian Manufacturer
Manufacturing and Management
Modern Office
Newsletter of the Australian Robotics Association
Real Property Annual
Rydges
The Chemist and Druggist of Australia
The Coach and Motor Body Builder for Australia and New Zealand
The Tocsin
Weekly Times, Melbourne

Books and articles

Alford, K. *Production or Reproduction: An Economic History of Women in Australia 1788–1850*, Melbourne: OUP, 1984

Anderson, C. 'Aborigines and Tin Mining in Northern Queensland: A study in the anthropology of contact history', *Mankind,* vol. 13, no. 6, 1983

Atkinson, A. 'Four Patterns of Convict Protest', *Labour History,* no. 37, November 1979

Aveling, M. and Atkinson, A. (eds) *Australians 1838,* Sydney: Fairfax, Syme and Weldon, 1987

Barbalet, M. *Far From a Low Gutter Girl: The forgotten world of state wards: South Australia 1887–1940,* Melbourne: OUP, 1983

Bacchi, C. 'The nature-nuture debate in Australia, 1900–1914', *Historical Studies,* vol. 19, no. 75, October 1980

Bennett, J.M. *A History of Solicitors in New South Wales,* Sydney: Legal Books, 1984

Blainey, G. *The Rush That Never Ended: A History of Australian Mining*, Melbourne: MUP, 1974
—— *Triumph of the Nomads: A History of Ancient Australia*, Melbourne: Sun Books, 1978
Bourke, M. 'Industrial Unrest as Social Pathology: The Australian Writings of Elton Mayo', *Historical Studies*, vol. 20, no. 79, October 1982
Bramble, T. 'Award Restructuring and the Australian Trade Union Movement: A Critique', *Labour and Industry*, vol. 2, no. 3, 1989
Bray, M. and Rimmer, M. *Delivering the Goods: A History of the New South Wales Transport Workers Union 1888–1986*, Sydney: George Allen and Unwin, 1987
Braverman, H. *Labour and Monopoly Capital: The Degradation of Work in the Twentieth Century*, New York: Monthly Review Press, 1974
Brooks, A. 'A Man is as God as his Master', in Burgmann, V. and Lee, J. *Making A Life: A People's History of Australia since 1788*, Melbourne: McPhee-Gribble, 1988
Broome, R. *Aboriginal Australians: Black Responses to White Dominance, 1788–1980*, Sydney: George Allen and Unwin, 1982
—— *The Victorians: Arriving*, Sydney: Fairfax, Syme and Weldon, 1984
Broomehill, R. *Unemployed Workers: A Social History of the Great Depression in Adelaide*, St Lucia: UQP, 1978
Buckley, K. *The Amalgamated Engineers in Australia, 1852–1920*, Canberra: ANU Press, 1970
Buckley, K. and Wheelright, T. *No Paradise for Workers: Capitalism and the Common People 1788–1914*, Melbourne: OUP, 1988
Burgmann, V. and Lee, J. (eds) *Making a Life: A People's History of Australia since 1788*, Melbourne: McPhee-Gribble/Penguin Books, 1988
Butlin, N.G. *Investment in Australian Economic Development 1861–1900*, Canberra: Department of Economic History, RSSS, ANU, 1972
Butlin, S.J. *War Economy 1939–1942: Australia in the War of 1939–1945*, Canberra: AWM, 1955
Butlin, S.J. and Schedvin, C.B. *The War Economy 1942–1945: Australia in the War of 1939–1945*, Canberra: AWM, 1977
Buxton, G.L. *The Riverina 1861–1891: An Australian Regional Study*, Melbourne: MUP, 1967
Cannon, M. *Life in the Country: Australia in the Victorian Age, 2*, Melbourne: Thomas Nelson, 1973
—— *Life in the Cities: Australia in the Victorian Age, 3*, Melbourne: Thomas Nelson, 1975
Centre for Urban Research and Action, *But I wouldn't want my wife to work here—A Study of migrant women in Melbourne industry*, Fitzroy: CURA, 1976
Choi, C.Y. *Chinese Migration and Settlement in Australia*, Sydney, SUP, 1975
Cochrane, P. ' "Company Time": Management Ideology and the Labour Process 1940–1960', *Labour History*, no. 48, May 1985
Coghlan, T.A. *Labour and Industry in Australia: From the First Settlement in 1788 to the Establishment of the Commonwealth in 1901*, in 4 volumes, Melbourne, Macmillan, 1969
Collins, J. *Migrant Hands in a Distant Land*, Sydney: Pluto Press, 1988

Connell, R.W. and Irving, T.M. *Class Structure in Australian History,* Melbourne: Longman Cheshire, 1980

Cook, J. 'Housework as Scientific management: The Development of Domestic Science in WA State Schools', in Layman, L. (ed.) *The Workplace: Time Remembered,* no. 5, 1982

Corris, P. *Passage, Port and Plantation: A History of Solomons Islands Labour Migration 1870–1914,* Melbourne: MUP, 1973

Curthoys, A. 'The Sexual Division of Labour: Theoretical Arguments', in Grieve, N. and Burns, A. (eds) *Australian Women: New Feminist Perspectives,* Melbourne: OUP, 1986

Curthoys, A., Eade, S. and Spearritt, P. (eds) *Women at Work,* Canberra: Australian Society for the Study of Labour History, 1975

Curthoys, A. and Markus, A. *Who Are Our Enemies?: Racism and the Working Class in Australia,* Sydney: Hale and Iremonger, 1978

Curthoys, A., Martin, A.W. and Rowse, T. (eds) *Australians from 1939,* Sydney: Fairfax, Syme and Weldon, 1987

Davison, G. *The Rise and Fall of Marvellous Melbourne,* Melbourne: MUP, 1979

Davison, G., McCarty, J.W. and McLeary, A. (eds) *Australians 1888,* Sydney: Fairfax, Syme and Weldon Associates, 1987

Deacon, D. 'Taylorism in the Home: The Medical Profession, the Infant Welfare Movement and the De-skilling of Women', *Australia and New Zealand Journal of Sociology,* vol. 21, no. 2, July 1985

Delgado, A. *The Enormous File: A Social History of the Office,* London: John Murray, 1979

Dingle, T. *The Victorians: Settling,* Sydney: Fairfax, Syme and Weldon, 1984

—— *Aboriginal Economy: Patterns of Experience,* Melbourne: McPhee Gribble-Penguin Books, 1988

Dunsford, R. 'Scientific Management in Australia: A Discussion Paper', *Labour and Industry,* vol. 1, no. 3, October 1988

Eccles, S. 'Women in the Australian Labour Force', in Broom, D. (ed.) *Unfinished Business: Social Justice for Women in Australia,* Sydney: George Allen and Unwin, 1984

Ellem, B. *In Women's Hands? A History of Clothing Trades Unions in Australia,* Sydney: NSWU Press, 1989

Elkin, A.P. *The Australian Aborigine,* Sydney: Angus and Robertson, 1968

Encel, S., MacKenzie, W. and Tebbutt, M. *Women and Society: An Australian Study,* Melbourne: Cheshire, 1984

Evans, W. (ed.) *Diary of a Welsh Swagman, 1869–1894,* Melbourne: Sun Books, 1977

Fisher, S. 'Sydney women and the workforce 1870–1890', in Kelly, M. (ed.) *Nineteenth Century Sydney: Essays in Urban History,* Sydney: SUP in association with the Sydney History Group, 1978

Fisk, E.K. *The Aboriginal Economy in Town and Country,* Sydney: George Allen and Unwin, 1985

Fitzgerald, S. *Rising Damp: Sydney 1870–90,* Melbourne: OUP, 1987

Flood, J. *Archaeology of the Dreamtime: The Story of Prehistoric Australia and its People,* Sydney: Collins Publishers, 1989

Fox, C.J. Unemployment and the Politics of the Unemployed: Victoria in

the Great Depression 1930–1937, PhD, University of Melbourne, 1985
Fox, C. and Lake, M. (eds) *Australians at Work: commentaries and sources,* Melbourne: McPhee Gribble–Penguin, 1990
Frances, R. 'No More Amazons: Gender and Work Process in the Victorian Clothing Trades 1890–1939', *Labour History,* no. 50, November 1986
—— 'The clothing and boot industries 1880–1939', in Willis, E. (ed.) *Technology and the Labour Process,* Sydney: George Allen and Unwin, 1988
—— 'Never done but always done down', in Burgmann, V. and Lee, J. *Making a Life*
Freeland, J.M. *The Making of a Profession: A History of the Growth and Work of the Architectural Institute of Australia,* Sydney: Angus and Robertson, 1971
Frost, A. 'New South Wales as *terra nullius:* the British denial of Aboriginal Land Rights', *Historical Studies,* vol. 19, no. 77, October 1981
Game, A. and Pringle, R. *Gender at Work,* Sydney: George Allen and Unwin, 1983
Gilbert, K. *Living Black. Blacks talk to Kevin Gilbert,* Melbourne, Allen Lane, 1977
Gollan, R. *The Coalminers of New South Wales: A History of the Union 1860–1960,* Melbourne, MUP, 1963
—— *Radical and Working Class Politics: A Study of Eastern Australia 1850–1910,* Melbourne, MUP, 1976
Gordon, D.M., Edwards, R. and Reich, M. *Segmented work, divided workers: The historical transformation of labor in the United States,* New York: CUP, 1982
Gothard, J. ' "Radically unsound and mischievous": female migration to Tasmania 1856–1863', *Historical Studies,* vol. 23, no. 93, October 1989
Griffin, G. *White Collar Militancy: The Australian Banking and Insurance Unions,* Sydney: Croom Helm, 1985
Grimshaw, P., McConville, C. and McEwen, E. *Families in Colonial Australia,* Sydney: George Allen and Unwin, 1985
Hagan, J. *The History of the ACTU,* Melbourne: Longman Cheshire, 1981
Hargreaves, K. *Women at Work,* Ringwood: Penguin, 1980
Hasluck, P. *The Government and the People 1939–1941: Australia in the War of 1939–1945,* Canberra: AWM, 1953
—— *The Government and the People 1942–1945: Australia in the War of 1939–1945,* Canberra: AWM, 1970
Heagney, M. *Are Women Taking Men's Jobs?,* Melbourne: Hilton and Vietch, 1935
Healy, C. (ed.) *The Lifeblood of Footscray: Working lives at the Anglis Meatworks,* Melbourne: Melbourne Living Museum of the West, n.d.
Hearn, J. 'Migrant Participation in Trade Union Leadership', *Journal of Industrial Relations,* vol. 18, no. 2, 1976
Hill, J. *From Subservience to Strike: Industrial Relations in the Banking Industry,* St Lucia: UQP, 1982
Hirst, J. *Convict Society and its Enemies,* Sydney: George Allen and Unwin, 1983

Hughes, R. *The Fatal Shore: A History of the Transportation of Convicts to Australia 1787–1868*, London: Pan Books, 1987
Hume, L. 'Working Class Movements in Sydney and Melbourne before the Gold Rushes', *Historical Studies*, vol. 9, no. 35, 1960
Johnston, R. *History of the Queensland Bar*, Brisbane Bar Association of Queensland, 1978
Jones, B. *Sleepers Wake: Technology and the future of work*, Melbourne: OUP, 1982
Joyce, P. (ed.) *The historical meanings of work*, Cambridge: CUP, 1987
Kiddle, K. *Men of Yesterday: A social history of the Western District of Victoria 1824–1890*, Melbourne: MUP, 1967
Kingston, B. *My Wife, My Daughter and Poor Mary Ann: Women and Work in Australia*, West Melbourne: Thomas Nelson, 1977
—— *The Oxford University History of Australia Vol. 3: Glad Confident Morning*, Melbourne: OUP, 1988
Kitay, J. and Littler, C. 'The State and the Labour Process in Australia', paper delivered to the Australian–Canadian Labour History Conference, Sydney University, December 1988
Knight, K. 'Patronage and the 1894 Royal Commission of Inquiry into the New South Wales Public Service', *Australian Journal of Politics and History*, no. 7, 1961
Lansbury, R.D. and Davis, E.M. *Technology, Work and Industrial Relations*, Melbourne: Longman, Cheshire, 1984
Layman, L. and Goddard, J. *Organise! Labour. A visual record of the labour movement in Western Australia*, Perth: Trades and Labour Council, 1988
Lee, J. 'A Re-division of Labour. Victoria's Wages Boards in Action, 1896–1903', *Historical Studies*, vol. 22, no. 88, April 1987
Lee, J. and Fahey, C. 'A Boom for Whom? Some Developments in the Australian Labour Market 1870–1891', *Labour History*, no. 50, May 1986
Lees, S. and Senyard, J. *The 1950s ... how Australia became a modern society and everyone got a home and a car*, Melbourne: Hyland House, 1987
Lever-Tracy C. and Quinlan, M. *A divided working class: Ethnic segmentation and industrial conflict in Australia*, London: Routledge and Kegan Paul, 1988
Lowenstein, W. and Hills, T. *Under the Hook: Melbourne Waterside Workers Remember 1900–1980*, Melbourne: Melbourne Bookworkers in Association with the Australian Society for the Study of Labour History, 1982
Lynzaat, A.M. 'Respectability and the Outworker: Victorian Factory Acts, 1885–1903', in MacKinolty, J. and Radi, H. (eds) *In Pursuit of Justice: Australian Women and the Law 1789–1979*, Sydney: Hale and Iremonger, 1979
Macintyre, S. *Winners and Losers: The Pursuit of Social Justice in Australian History*, Sydney: George Allen and Unwin, 1985
—— *The Oxford History of Australia, Vol. 4, 1901–1942, The Succeeding Age*, Melbourne: OUP, 1986

—— *The Labour Experiment,* Melbourne: McPhee Gribble Publishers, 1989
Maddock, K. *The Australian Aborigines: A Portrait of their Society,* Ringwood, Penguin Books, 1982
Mulvaney, J. and White, J.P. *Australians to 1788,* Sydney: Fairfax, Syme and Welden, 1987
Markus, A. *Fear and Hatred. Purifying Australia and California 1850–1901,* Sydney: Hale and Iremonger, 1979
—— 'Labour and Immigration, 1946–9: The Displaced Persons Programme', *Labour History,* no. 47, November 1984
Markey, R. 'The Aristocracy of Labour and Productive Re-organisation in New South Wales c. 1880–1900', *Australian Economic History Review,* vol. 8, no. 28, March 1985
Marshall, N.J. *A Jubilee History, 1928–1978. The Institute of Chartered Accountants in Australia, Victorian Branch,* Melbourne, 1978
Marshall, P. *Rapa rapa. Kularr Martuwarra. All right, now we go side the river along that sundown way: Stories from the Fitzroy River Drovers,* Broome: Magabala Books, 1989
Martin, J. *The Migrant Presence: Australian Responses 1947–1971,* Sydney: George Allen and Unwin, 1978
Mathews, Jill. *Good and Mad Women: The Historical Construction of Femininity in Twentieth Century Australia,* Sydney: George Allen and Unwin, 1984
Mathews, John. *Tools of Change. New technology and the democratization of work,* Sydney: Pluto Press, 1989
McCarthy P. 'Labour and the Living Wage, 1890–1910', *Australian Journal of Politics and History,* no. 13, 1967
McGrath, A. *'Born in the Cattle': Aborigines in the Cattle Country,* Sydney: George Allen and Unwin, 1987
McGraw, P. and Dunford, R. 'The Strategic Use of Quality Control Circles in Australian Industrial Relations', *Journal of Industrial Relations,* vol. 29, no. 2, June 1987
McKernan, M. *All In! Australia During the Second World War,* Melbourne: Nelson, 1983
Mercer, J. *The Other Half: Women in Australian Society,* Ringwood, Penguin, 1985
Merritt, J. *The making of the A.W.U.,* Melbourne: OUP, 1987
Moore, C. *Kanakas! A History of Melanesian Mackay,* Boroka, University of Port Moresby Press, 1985
Morris, B. 'From Underemployment to Unemployment: The Changing Role of Aborigines in a Rural Economy', *Mankind,* vol. 13, no. 6, April 1983
Nicholas, S. (ed.) *Convict Workers: Reinterpreting Australian Past,* Melbourne: CUP, 1988
O'Brien, A. *Poverty's Prison: The Poor in New South Wales 1880–1918,* Melbourne: MUP, 1988
O'Donnell, E. and Hall, P. *Getting Equal: Labour Market Regulation and Women's Work,* Sydney: George Allen and Unwin, 1988
Pensabene, T.S. *The rise of the medical practitioner in Victoria,* ANU

Health Research Project, Research Monograph 2. Canberra: ANU Press, 1980

Power, M. 'The Making of a Woman's Occupation', *Hecate,* vol. 1, no. 2, July 1975

—— 'A Woman's Work is Never Done—by Men', *Journal of Industrial Relations,* vol. 17, no. 3, September 1975

Poynton, P. 'The Development of the Assembly Line in Australia', *Arena,* no. 58, 1981

Probert, B. *Working Life: Arguments about work in Australian Society,* Melbourne: McPhee Gribble, 1989

Quinlan, M. 'Early Trade Union Organisations in Australia: Three Australian Colonies, 1829–1850', *Labour and Industry,* no. 1, October 1987

Reekie, G. 'Female Office Workers in Western Australia 1895–1920: The Process of Feminisation and Patterns of Consciousness', in Layman, L. (ed.) *The Workplace, Time Remembered,* no. 5, 1982

—— ' "Humanizing Industry": Paternalism, Welfarism and Labour Control in Sydney's Big Stores, 1890–1930', *Labour History,* no. 53, November 1987

Reeves, A. and Stephen, A. *Badges of Labour, Banners of Pride. Aspects of Working Class Celebration,* Melbourne: Museum of Applied Arts and Science (Melbourne), n.d.

Reiger, K. *The Disenchantment of the Home: Modernizing the Australian Family, 1880–1940,* Melbourne: UQP, 1985

—— 'At home with technology', *Arena,* no. 75, 1986

Reinecke, I. *Micro-Invaders: How the new world of technology works,* Ringwood: Penguin, 1982

Robinson, P. *The Hatch and Brood of Time: A study of the first generations of native born white Australians, 1788–1828,* Melbourne: OUP, 1985

Rogers, P.H. *The Industrialists and the Aborigines: A Study of Aboriginal Employment in the Australian Mining Industry,* Sydney: Angus and Robertson, 1973

Rose, F.G.G. *The Traditional Mode of Production of the Australian Aborigine,* Sydney: Angus and Robertson, 1987

Rotella, E.J. *From Home to Office: United States Women at Work 1870–1930,* Ann Arbor: UMI Research Press, 1981

Ryan, E. *Two Thirds of a Man: Women and Arbitration in New South Wales,* Sydney: George Allen & Unwin, 1984

Ryan, E. and Conlon, A. *Gentle Invaders: Australian Women at Work, 1788–1974,* Sydney: Nelson, 1975

Ryan, P. and Rowse, T. 'Women, Arbitration and the Family', in Curthoys, A. *et al.* (eds) 'Women at Work'

Sahlins, M. *Stone Age Economics,* New York, Aldino de Gruyter, 1972

Sharp, I.G. and Tatz, C.M. *Aborigines and the Economy. Employment, Wages and Training,* Melbourne: Jacaranda Press, 1966

Sheridan, T. *Mindful Militants: The Amalgamated Engineering Union in Australia 1920–1972,* Melbourne: CUP, 1975

Sinclair, W.S. 'Women and Economic Change in Melbourne 1870–1921', *Historical Studies,* vol. 20, no. 79, October 1982

Spence, W.G. *Australia's Awakening,* Sydney: Worker's Trustees, 1909

Spencely, G.S. 'Assessing the Response of the Unemployed to the Depression of the 1930s', *Journal of Australian Studies,* no. 24, May 1989

Stevens, F. *Aborigines in the Northern Territory Cattle Industry,* Canberra: ANU Press, 1974

Sullivan, M. *Men and Women of Port Phillip,* Sydney: Hale and Iremonger, 1985

Svensen, S. *The Shearers' War: The Story of the 1891 Shearers' Strike,* St Lucia: UQP, 1989

Taksa, L. Oral History and the Literary Culture of the Workplace, paper delivered to the Australian–Canadian Labour History Conference: Sydney, 1988

Thompson, P. *The Nature of Work: An Introduction to Debates on the Labour Process,* London: MacMillan, 1983

Twopeny, R. *Town Life in Australia,* Ringwood: Penguin Colonial Facsimiles, 1977

Vamplew, R.W. (ed.) *Australians: Historical Statistics,* Sydney: Fairfax, Syme and Weldon, 1987

Walker, J. *Jondaryan Station: The Relationship between Pastoral Capital and Pastoral Labour 1840–1890,* St Lucia: UQP, 1988

Walsh, G.P. 'Factories and Factory Workers in New South Wales 1788–1900', *Labour History,* no. 21, November 1971

Ward, R. *The Australian Legend,* Melbourne: OUP, 1977

Waters, F. *Postal Unions and Politics: A History of the Amalgamated Postal Workers' Union of Australia,* St Lucia: UQP Press, 1978

Waters, W.J. 'Australian Labor's Full Employment Objective, 1942–5', in Roe, J. (ed.) *Social Policy in Australia: Some Perspectives 1901–1975,* Stanmore: Cassell, 1976

Waterson, D.B. *Squatter, Selector and Storekeeper: A History of the Darling Downs 1859–93,* Sydney: SUP, 1968

Watts, R. *The Foundation of the Australian Welfare State,* Sydney: Allen and Unwin, 1987

Williams, C. *Open Cut: The Working Class in an Australian Mining Town,* Sydney: George Allen and Unwin, 1981

—— *Blue, White and Pink Collar Workers in Australia: Technicians, Bank Employees and Flight Attendants,* Sydney: Allen and Unwin, 1988

Willis, E. *Medical Dominance: The division of labour in Australian health care,* Sydney: George Allen and Unwin, 1983

—— (ed.) *Technology and the Labour Process: Australasian Case Studies,* Sydney: Allen and Unwin, 1988

Wright, C. 'The Formative Years of Management Control at the Newcastle Steelworks, 1913–1924', *Labour History,* no. 55, November 1988

Yarwood, A.T. and Knowling, M.J. *Race Relations in Australia: A History,* North Ryde: Methuen, Australia, 1982

Index

abattoir workers, 65, 115, 117–18
Aborigines, aged division of labour, 4–5; agriculture, 7, 155; country work, 14–15, 44–7, 154–8; christianity 15–16, 46–7, 98; closer settlement, 46, 155; early settlers, 12–16; exchange, 8–9; kinship, 2–3, 156–7; land, 2–3; manufacture, 6–7; men's work, 3–5; mining, 45; missions, 46–7; pastoral frontier, 44–6, 98–9, 155; pearling, 45; protection, 16, 98–9; religion, 9–11, 46–7; seasonality of work, 5–6, 155; standard of living, 11–12; trade unions, 162–4; *terra nullius*, 12–13; unemployment, 130, 154, 157, 164; wages, 156; women's work, 3–5; World War Two, 155
absenteeism, 137, 153
accountants, 76, 77
administrative secretaries, 148
Afghans, 48
Alderson, W.M., 58
Amalgamated Engineering Union, 134, 137
Angliss Meatworks, 117–18
apprentices, 61, 62, 63, 104, 134, 173
Arabana tribe, 8, 9
architects, 76, 77, 78, 153
arbitration, 85, 96, 102–5, 107–9, 116, 156, 160, 169
assembly line, 114–5, 149–50
Atkinson, A., 24
Australia Reconstructed, 174
Australian Agricultural Company, 18
Australian Bank Officers' Union, 81
Australian Council of Trade Unions, 118, 137, 159, 160, 163, 173
Australian Council of Salaried and Professional Associations, 159

Australian Manufacturer, 113
Australian Methods Engineer's Association, 167
Australian Paper Mills, 115
Australian Telecommuications Employees' Association, 173
Australian Workers' Union, 111
automation, *see* technological change.

Babbage, C., 56
Baker, David, 111
Ball and Welch, 60
bank tellers/clerks, 80, 81, 84–5, 134
Barbalet, M., 68
Barton, R., 124
Bean, C.E.W., 36
Beveridge, P., 4
Boans (Perth), 116
bonus payments, 114, 167
bootmakers, 62, 70, 153
boundary riders, 35
Boyce, Benjamin, 29
Braverman, H., 61
brewery workers, 60
Broken Hill Proprietary, 111, 115
Broome, R., 164
British Tobacco Company, 115
building workers, 63, 64–5
Burns Philp, 48
biscuit factories, 153
Buxton, G. L., 41

Calwell, A., 151–60
Campbell, R., 17
carters and drivers, 60, 64
Central Unemployed Committee, 131
chemists, 79
Chifley, B., 125, 138–9, 140, 160
childbirth, 121–2
childcare, 138, 141, 146, 148–9, 160
children, 46, 57–8, 59, 61, 66, 70,

215

81, 97–8, 100, 101, 114, 130, 156
child protection acts, 97–8
Chinese, 47, 48, 49, 51–3, 94, 95
Chisolm, C., 30
Cinghalese, 48
civil service, 81, 82–3, 85, 147
civil service acts, 109
civil service boards, 83, 109
Clarke, 'Big', 58
Clarke, C.M.H., 27
clerks, 79–83, 109, 134, 144–5, 147–8
clothing factories, 69–70, 106–7, 114, 119
clothing workers, 62, 65, 69–72, 105–7, 108, 116, 119, 152
Clyde Company, 18
coach builders, 114
coach builders' unions, 114
Colonial Sugar Refinery, 48, 50, 65
commercial colleges, 85, 86
Commonwealth Bank, 115
Commonwealth Employment Service, 140
Communist Party of Australia, 131
compulsory education, 90, 97
Cook, James, 11, 13
coolie labour, 26, 47
Coombs, H.C., 139
computerisation, 145, 171–2
confectionery workers, 60
convict workers, 18–24 *passim*; assignment, 20, 22–4; convict rights, 23–4; discipline, 23; female factories, 21–2; government gangs, 21; marriage, 22; punishment gangs, 21; resistance, 24; task work, 21; wages, 23
Copland, D., 141
copy clerks, 84
Council of Australian Government Employee Organisations, 159
council workers, 129
Cruikshank, Rose, 136, 137
Cunningham, P., 13, 18
Currie, Kate, 42
Currie, Tom, 42
Curtin, John, 137, 138
Curthoys, Ann, 147

Dawn, The, 68
Dawson, James, 8
David Jones, 119
Davies, Rose, 136
Deakin, Alfred, 103, 107
dentists, 76, 77, 153
depressions, 1890s, 57, 126, 139; 1930s, 126–33, 139
Derham, E. T., 82
de-skilling, 61, 62–3, 70, 82, 114, 115
displaced persons, 151, 152
Diyari tribe, 8
Dobeson, Thomas, 65
Dole and Relief Workers' Council, 131
domestic servants, 20, 65–9, 87–8, 106, 123–4, 130, 136, 155, 157
Dooley Bin Bin, 163
Duflot, Paul, 73

early closing of shops, 101–2
education, 73–4, 81, 89, 94, 97, 100
eight-hour day, 93–4
Elkin, A.P., 2, 5
engineering profession, 76, 77, 79
equal pay, *see* wages.
eugenics, 120
Evans, R., 44
experts, 121
Eyre, Edward, 15

factories, *see* manufacturing
factory acts, 100–1
factory workers, 29–30, 57–60, 63, 69–71
families, 2–3, 40–3, 66
farm labourers, 36–7, 134, 155–6
Federal Council for the Advancement of Aborigines, 163
Federated Seaman's Union, 95
Fels, Marie, 15
firestick farming, 7
Fordism, 114–5
Ford, Henry, 106, 114
Ford Motor Company (Australia), 153, 162, 172
Ford, William, 154
Frances, Raelene, 117
fruit picking, 155
full employment, 139, 141, 178

Galloway, James, 93
Gas Light Company (Sydney), 29
General Motors Holden, 162
Gipps, Governor, 22

INDEX

Gnowangerup, 157
gold mining, 33–5, 39, 51–3
Gollan, R., 102
Gorz, A., 178–9
governesses, 90
Gray, George, 58
Guest, T.B., 59

Hagan, Jim, 119
harvesters, 29
Hasluck, Paul, 154
Hawke, R.J., 177
Heagney, M., 127
Herbig family, 42
Higgins, H.B., 103–4, 107–8
Hirst, John, 23
Holdens, 114–8
homeopathy, 78
housework, 30, 68–9, 123–4, 180
Howe, G., 19
human relations management techniques, 167–8
Hughes, Robert, 20
Hunter, Governor, 17

immigration, *see* migrant workers and migration.
Immigration Restriction Acts, 53, 99–100, 102
incentive payments, 118, *see also* bonus payments.
indentured labour, 25, 26, 47–9
Indians, 47, 48, 49
industrial psychologists, 167
infant mortality, 122
Infant Welfare Movement, 122
intermittency, 29, 63–5, 126

jam and pickle workers, 65
Japanese, 48, 49
Javanese, 48, 99–100
Jenkins, Joseph, 36–7
Jigalong Aboriginal community, 163
job enrichment, 169
Jondaryan Station, 35
Jones, Barry, 178–9

Kable, H., 17
Karadjeri Tribe, 5, 6
Kernot, Professor, W.M., 76
Keynes, J.M., 139, 140
Kiddle, M., 34
King, Governor, 19
Krause, Emily, 42

Kuhn, R., 138

labour saving devises, *see* technological change.
Labour and National Service, Department of, 139
labourers, 149–50
Lang, Jack, 127
Lane, William, 37, 39, 107
Latrobe, Lieutenant Governor, 34
Lawson, Henry, 43
Law, James, 114
lawyers, 76, 78
Lever-Tracy, C., 162
Lithgow Small Arms Factory, 113
living wage, *see* wages
Lord, Simeon, 17, 29
Love, Peter, 140
lumpers, 64
Lutherans, 41

Macarthur, Elizabeth, 18
Macarthur family, 26
Macassans, 7, 11
MacKay, H.V., 59, 103–4
Macquarie, Governor, 14, 19–20, 21
'Malays', 48, 99–100
management, 153, 166–9
management consultants, 166–7
'Manillamen', 48
Manpower Directorate, 134, 135, 137, 155
manufacturing, 29–30, 54–60 *passim*, 62–3, 65, 69–71, 110–9 *passim*, 127, 133–4, 143, 146, 165
Markey, Ray, 60
Master and Servants Acts, 26–8, 93, 98
maternity benefits, 140
Mathews, John, 172, 179
Mayo, Elton, 168
McKenna, Clancy, 163
McLeod, Don, 163
meatworkers, 115, 117–18
meatworkers' unions, 118
mechanisation, 36–7, 42, 56, *see also* technological change.
medical profession, 74–5, 76–7, 78, 79, 121–3
men, Andrew Ure, 56; Aborigines, 4–5, 14, 156; colonial sexual division of labour, 25, 26; convict labour, 19, 20–1; Charles

Babbage, 56; clerks, 80–4; domestic economy, 40–2; ethnic division of labour, 152; factory acts, 101–2, family wage, 95–6, 103; feminisation of work, 62; full employment, 141; geographical mobility, 33–8; independence, 37–9, 43; 'ideal bourgeois family', 86–7; masculinity, 37–8; professions, 74; seasonal work, 28; selection, 40–3; skill, 61; 'strong masculine labour', 33; trade unions, 92–6, 159; unemployment, 126–8; unemployment relief, 130; World War One, 85; World War Two, 137–8; yeoman farmer, 40–1; housework, 179
Men and How to Manage Them, 67
Merritt, John, 36
metal trades, 136
midwives, 121
migrant workers, Asian, 152; British, 151–2; Afghans, 48–9; Chinese, 47, 48, 51–3; Cinghalese, 48, displaced persons, 151; Indian, 48; Japanese, 48, 49, 100; 'Manillamen', 48; 'Malays', 48, 49, 99; Pacific Islanders, 49–51, 99; post-war migrations, 151–5; Northern European, 152, trade unions, 160–2; Southern European, 152–4; Western European, 152
migrant workers' conferences, 162
migration, 26, 39, 47–53 *passim*, 89, 93, 94, 96, 99–100, 151–4
Mitchell, Thomas, 7
Moore, Clive, 51
Morris, Barry, 154
Mort, T.S., 59
Mount Sturgeon Station, 35
Mudie, James, 23
multi-skilling, 169
munitions workers, 134, 136
Muscio, Bernard, 113
Myer's Report, 174

native police, 15
'new protection', 103–4
'new unions', 94–5
new technology, *see* technological change
Nightingale, Florence, 90, 135

Norfolk Island, 21, 23
North Australian Workers' Union, 163
numerical control, 171
nursing, 89–90, 109, 121, 122, 135
'Nyungar time', 157

office landscaping, 145
office work, 79–86, 143, 144–6
Olympic Tyres, 167
'old unions', 94
One Big Union of Unemployed, 131
Osborne, Lucy, 90
outwork, 71, 101, 106–7, 179

Pacific Islanders, 47–8, 49–51, 99
paternalism, 58
patronage, 82–3
part-time work, 128, 146
pastoral workers, 14, 34–5, 154, 155, 156, 163–4
pastoralists, 14–15, 30, 44–5, 163–4
pearling, 45, 99–100
Pelaco, 114, 119
personnel officers, 167
philanthropy, 89
Philips Australia, 168
Phillip, Governor, 21
Pilbara Aboriginal workers' strike, 163
Port Arthur, 21
Port Macquarie, 21
postmistresses, 109
Postmaster General's Department, 115
Price, Charles, 53
printers, 19, 62, 107
professions, 73–9, 148; classical education, 74, 75, 78; ethics, 75; knowledge, 75–7, 79; Parliamentary leglisation, 78–9; professional associations, 75, 77; royal charters, 75; science, 79; sexual division, 74
protective legislation, Aborigines 98–9; children 97–8; Factory Acts, 100–1; Pacific Islanders, 99; 'Malays', 99–100; women, 97–8

quality control circles, 169, 175
Quinlan, Michael, 162

railway workers, 64, 116, 119
Real Property Annual, 123

INDEX

Re-establishment and Employment Bill, 141
Relief and Sustenance Workers' Union, 131
Reiger, Kereen, 121
religion, 9–11
repetitive strain injury, 173
responsible autonomy, 146, 168
Rexona, 168
Riley, Fred, 65
Roberts, T., 33, 37
Rogers, Elizabeth, 71
rural work, 14, 30–1, chapter 3 *passim*
Rural Workers' Union, 108
Ryan, Edna, 105
Rydge's, 113, 167, 168

Sahlins, M., 9
Saint Monday, 58
sawyers, 29
scientific management, chapter 7 *passim*, 167–8, 176
seamen, 29
secretaries, 144, 147–8
Secretaries Forum, 148
seasonal work, 5–6, 35–7, 43, 126–7, 153, 155–6
Selby, Penelope, 31
selection, 38–43
shearers, 29, 36
shearers' unions, 95
Sheet Metal Workers' Union, 163
shift work, 150
shipwrights, 62
shop assistants, 91, 101, 119, 176
Sidchrome, 168
skill, 61
skilled workers, convicts, 19; early New South Wales, 28; Broken Hill Proprietary, 111–2, assembly lines, 115, 117–8; Charles Babbage, 56, Andrew Ure, 56; de-skilling, 61, 62–3, 70, 82, 114, 176; eight-hour day, 94; independence, 58; Master and Servants Acts, 93; migration, 93; multi-skilling, 173–5; Taylorism, 112–4; trade unions, 92–5; the unskilled, 61–2, 65; World War Two, 133
Smith, Adam, 55
Spence, W.G., 37, 39
stenographers, 147

stevedores, 64
stockmen, 44
stonemasons, 62, 94
Strehlow, T.G.H., 10
sugar industry, 50–1
Sunshine Harvesters, 103
supermarket work, 169
Syme, Muir and Co., 48
Sydney Benevolent Society, 66

Tait and Co., 48
Taksa, Lucy, 119
Tasmanian Society of Friends, 89
Taylor, Frederick Winslow, 112, 166, 167
Taylor, M., 122
Taylorism, 112–9, 123, 144–5, 166–7
tailoresses, 105–6
Tailoresses' Union, 105–6
teachers, 89, 90–1, 109
technological change, 83–5, 109, 116, 157, 169–75 *passim*, 178–9
Telecom, 173
telegraphists, 109
telephonists, 109
Termination, Change and Redundancy Award, 174
terra nullius, 12, 13
Terry, S., 17
textile workers, 70, 153
Theodore, Ted, 139
Thompson, E.P., 57
Tirora, Tribe, 8
time and motion studies, 114, 117, 144, 167
tin mining, 45
Toffler, A., 178–9
trade unions, 93–6, 105–9, 158–64, 176–7; Aborigines, 162–4; de-skilling, 116–9; eight-hour day, 94; family wage, 95–6; incentive payments, 118–9; migration, 160–2; migrant workers, 160–2; outwork, 107; new technology, 173–5; The Accord, 177; women, 105–7, 159–60
Trades Hall Council (Melbourne), 95
Trades and Labour Councils (Sydney and Brisbane), 95
trapping, 155
Trollope, A., 35
Truby King, Dr F., 122

Twopeny, R., 88
typists, 84, 109, 147
typewriters, 84

underconsumptionism, 138
Underwood, J., 17
unemployed politics, 131–3
Unemployed Workers' Movement, 131
unemployment, Aborigines, 154–5, 157; Great Depression, 126–33, 128–9; location, 128; new technology, 172–3; men, 127; post World War Two, 141, 142; World War Two, 133; women, 27; nineteen nineties, 178–9
unemployment relief, 37, 130, 140
United Fronts of Employed and Unemployed, 131
unskilled workers, 20, 56, 63–6, 149–58 *passim*; trades unions, 94–5; migration, 149–54; wages, 150
Ure, Andrew, 56

Van Dieman's Land Company, 18
vehicle builders, 115
Victorian Clothing Trades Union, 116–7

wages, convicts, 23; domestic servants, 67–8; early free workers, 25; equal pay, 108, 109, 160; fruit packers and pickers, 108; family wage, 95–6, 103–4, 107–8; Harvester Judgement, 103–4; multi-skilling, 169, Women's Employment Board, 136–7; World War Two, 134–5
wages boards, 102
Wallis, Alf, 117
Walker, E.R., 128
Ward, Russell, 28
Waterside Workers' Federation, 173
Watson, John, 164
welfarism, 115
whalers, 29
White Australia Policy, 99, 102
Whitlam, E.G., 149
Williamstown Railway Workshops, 59–60

Wik Monkan Tribe, 6
Wilcannia, 158
women, Aborigines, 3–4, 5, 14, 156; arbitration, 107–9; Babbage, Charles, 56; banks, 84–5; charities, 66, 89, 121; childbirth, 121–2; childcare, 138, 141, 146, 148–9, 160; child rearing 41–2; convicts, 20, 21–3, 24; civil service, 85, 109, 148–9; domestic service, 20, 22, 23, 30, 50, 67, 68–9, 87–8, 123, 124, 136; Factory Acts, 101–2; factory work, 69–72, 116–7, 119, 136, 146, 152–4; family wage, 107–8; feminisation of work, 62; full employment, 141–2; housework, 30, 68–9, 123–4, 180; 'ideal bourgeois family', 86–7, 121, 142; marriage, 22, 30; 'men's jobs', 107; middle class status, 87, 89–90; migration, 89, 151–4; nursing, 90; out work, 71–2, 101, 106–7; office work, 84–6, 146–9; professions, 74; selection, 40–3; servant problem, 88–9; skilled work, 61; teaching, 91; trades unions, 105–10, 116–7, 119, 159–60; Ure, Andrew, 56; World War One, 84–5; World War Two, 135–8; unemployment, 127
Women's Action Committee, 159
Women's Employment Board, 137
Women's Land Army, 136
Women's Trade Union Commission, 159
word processors, 145, 173
work group, 175
workers' participation, 168
Working Women's Centre, 159
Working Women's Charter, 159
World War One, 84–5
World War Two, 133–8
Wrixon, H.J., 39

Yandegarra Aboriginal Community, 163
yeoman farmers, 38–40

Zangalis, George, 161